MINISTRY
AND
IMAGINATION

MINISTRY
AND
IMAGINATION

URBAN T. HOLMES, III

A CROSSROAD BOOK

THE SEABURY PRESS / NEW YORK

The Seabury Press
815 Second Avenue
New York, N.Y. 10017

Printed in the United States of America

Library of Congress Cataloging in Publication Data

Holmes, Urban Tigner, 1930–   Ministry and imagination.
"A Crossroad book."
1.Pastoral theology. 2.Experience (Religion) I.Title.
BV4011.H583   253   76–1851   ISBN 0–8164–0292–2

FOR BOB, ERNEST, AND JOE

. . . priests of the imagination

CONTENTS

INTRODUCTION

When *The Future Shape of Ministry* was published in 1971, I was not allowed to rest with what I had said there. It was gratifying to discover that this book, which was largely the result of four or five years of teaching pastoral theology at Nashotah House, an Episcopal seminary in exurbia Milwaukee, was well received. It was rather surprising to discover, however, that I had only laid a foundation upon which I was expected to continue to build. I found myself speaking in all kinds of places on the subject of the future of ministry to people who both received me most graciously and yet found the book incomplete.

This work is the result, therefore, of four years of following where the *The Future Shape of Ministry* might lead. In that sense it is a sequel to the previous book, although it stands on its own as a study in pastoral theology. There is very little in *The Future Shape of Ministry* I would change radically. There are some emphases that I think need adjustment, some points which need clarification. In this study I attempt to do this. Yet the two books are quite different. The first study follows a chronological outline; this one is more analytical. *The Future Shape of Ministry* sought to be general and comprehensive. My intention here is to pursue a particular dimension of ministry which lies at the heart of all ministry.

This I seek to do by developing *one* aspect of ministry which, while closely related to questions of pastoral care, church, society, and theological reflection, is more directly involved with the awareness of God's presence in the ministering community. Some will call this aspect an altered state of consciousness, openness to the word of God, ecstasy, or transcendental experience; but I am concerned for the experience of God in the present. My belief is that if we can recover a plausible piety—a word whose good reputation I would reinstate—

1

in our time, this will go a long way to vivifying all other aspects of ministry inasmuch as they are the expressions of the salvific work of the body of Christ.

It is my contention that for a long time the church's ministry has been wandering away from its appointed purpose, not as the result of any concerted plan but more or less by circumstance of the times. For a generation now it has been common to speak of the "crisis of ministry," but the solutions to this crisis have been less than impressive because they have not gone deep enough in diagnosing the problem. As I see it, there are at least four root causes, all interrelated, for the crisis in ministry.

The first that we need to recognize goes back to the sixteenth century. Any solutions must take these into account. This has nothing to do with the Reformation *per se* and Protestants *versus* Catholics—two terms which are, in my mind, false dichotomies—but with a spirit of the time which pervaded all of Christendom. This was the overweening concern for the logical reduction of experience and the control that came from possessing information that could be organized in a syllogistic manner. It was a point of view that arose naturally from the Renaissance and humanism, which encouraged us to think that truth and the solution to life's problems lie in the capacity of man's reason. The power of ambiguity, a sensibility to life, and the relation between beauty and goodness came to be lost to the God at the end of a syllogism.

The effect of this was to place a great deal of emphasis in the church on the sermon and the catechism. An educated clergy became essential. A friend of mine has said of the Puritans that they seemed to believe it was better in the eyes of God to read a three-page commentary on a prayer than to pray the prayer itself. The whole theological movement, which was rooted in the analytical issues of the Reformation, gave rise to both a Protestant and a Roman Catholic scholasticism that claimed to have reduced the mysteries of God to propositional formulae.

The result was the "deposition" of all but a few Christians from the active ministry. We separated the educated clergy, who had experienced seminary or university, from the ill-informed laity. The more we taught the "priesthood of all believers" the less we believed and practiced it. The parson, because of his superior wisdom and information, became the delivery system for the answers of God to all our problems. Ministry became narrowed to less than one percent of the baptized membership of the church, and we were divided between the "do-ers" and the "do-ees."

The full import of this shift was long in coming, but come it did. For as the church took unto itself more and more responsibilities in recent years, it became the task of the single minister, the parish priest or pastor, to carry out the entire work of the ministry. When this work had been primarily and almost exclusively the preaching of a Sunday sermon, the task was manageable. When, however, the person had to be an expert in a great number of things, it became impossible. So we experienced the breakdown of the pastor and the loss of confidence in a vocation in which persons were expected to do all things well.

The problem was compounded by a second cause for the crisis in ministry. This was the dissolution, as a result of the industrial revolution, of the natural communities in which ministry was rooted and through which it was done. If one visits the country churches of England one is impressed generally by several things. Their size, for instance; they are small, and there is the temptation to wonder how many services they have on Sunday. The answer is, of course, one. That is all they need. Secondly, there are a great many churches within walking distance of one another, just as in New York City. Of course, that was the point; people had only one way of getting there—"shank's mare." Thirdly, one could observe that these country churches were surrounded, not by parish houses and educational buildings but by cemeteries where generation after generation of families lay side by side in the soil from which they sprung. There we have a vivid reminder of our end and of the communion of saints.

Ministry was built upon these stable parish churches; they required no external bureaucracy for their existence but existed because of the internal bonds that fed the community. When the agrarian system failed and people moved into the cities—the people to whom John Wesley and his associates preached—the whole community system for ministry collapsed. It was then that the modern city parish was born—although it developed slowly—depending on the program and on the great numbers who responded to the program. The parish house, the financial campaigns, the large church building with multiple services, the guilds and their programs, all grew up as a part of the effort to remake church life in accordance with the industrial age.

There is no doubt that the parish took on a new life and purpose in coming to this point, but there is also little doubt that much was lost. It is the contention of this study that a congregation that is doing its job must be one which is responsive to the presence of God in our midst *now*. This requires a kind of freedom and spontaneity that the structures of the bureaucratic parish can and frequently do stifle. The sacrifice to organization is a very high price, perhaps too high, for ministry to pay.

The development of the modern parish is a correlate of the third root cause in the crisis of ministry. This is the disestablishment of the church, or, as some put it, the decline of the Constantinian church. The seventeenth-century English parson knew what society expected of him. In the morning he taught the children of the wealthy (there was no middle class to speak of) the four R's: reading, 'riting, 'rithmetic, and religion. He worked on his sermon for Sunday as well. In the afternoon he walked his parish, preaching short homilies to prepare his people for death, and practicing a kind of folk medicine which probably hastened their end. In the evenings he went to bed. Every day he read the office, but on the Lord's Day Matins was followed by the Litany and Holy Communion, and the sermon he had prepared the previous week. He baptized the babies, married the young, and buried the dead—all events which he recorded in the parish register. He had no crisis of identity. The expectations were clear.

The turning point was the loss of his symbolic function in the eyes of the state as the person who presided over the notable events in the lives of the people in his parish. In 1793 in France, in 1837 in England, and at varying times in this country in the states along the eastern seaboard, there occurred the *secularization of the registers.* Now the clerk of court or his equivalent records the birth, marriage, and death of the nation's citizens, and the pastor is pushed out of the center of the civil life of the people. It sounds trivial, but it was and is not so unimportant an event.

For what happened more and more, as the church awoke to its lessening role in the life of the state, was that the clergy went hunting for their job description. It is interesting, as I have pointed out in *The Future Shape of Ministry,* that the importance of earning one's living by being a parish priest (without that time-honored clerical practice of "moonlighting") and being attired in a distinctive dress, rather than merely a more somber one, came about the time that the average pastor was losing a clear role-definition in the society as a whole. It is almost as if he were saying, "Look at me. I'm different and you need to support me as your resident 'difference.' " Whether we have recognized it or not, the last hundred years or more has been a struggle carried on in terms of the disestablishment of the church. Sunday schools, parish houses, seminaries in the Anglican Communion, are all reactions to the post-Constantinian era.

The effect of this has been to sharpen the need to describe *what* it is a priest or pastor does. The tendency is to do this in terms of the society in which we live, which has lead the church into the fourth cause of the crisis in ministry —which is the disenchantment of our culture. This is a particularly important development for this study and I will be discussing it at length. For the moment, we need to see the problem of a ministry whose task is to communicate what a society does not think communicable.

For the ministry of the church is the expression of an incarnational theology. Its principal *raison d'etre* is the belief that God does act now in history through its instrumentality—or so it would seem. If we accept the available paradigms for ministry from a disenchanted world, then, by very definition, the heart of that ministry is torn from the body of the church before we ever start. There can be no plausible transcendent vocation around which all other purposes cluster.

I am convinced, then, that if we are to understand the crisis in ministry over the last generation, we have to take into account these four elements: the narrowing of ministry to be carried out only by an educated cadre, the loss of the natural community, the disestablishment of the clerical role, and the disenchantment of our culture. It is not sufficient, however, to leave the matter here. For the church has responded to this crisis in at least four ways, which responses have compounded the problem. By compounding the problem I mean it has deepened the loss of the central purpose of the Christian ministry: the mediation of transcendence.

First, there has been the response of "business as usual." This appears most prominently in the conversative congregations, who would like to pretend that we are still living in seventeenth-century England or on the nineteenth-century American frontier. Here the Latin Mass and the Crusade for Christ find themselves as strange bedfellows. They both go on as if the last two hundred years were but a surface ripple in human consciousness.

In the Episcopal Church, which I know best, "business as usual" assumes the style of a priestly ministry in which a rector becomes ensconced in a parish for twenty or thirty years, maintaining himself by meeting the expectations of the congregation. All his needs for dominance—a character trait which research shows is uniformly high in Episcopal priests—are met because there are sufficient passive-dependents among his parishioners whose needs are met by meeting his. Usually there is growth of a kind in such a parish. There is an ample supply of passive-dependents in any society. The memorials accumulate, the church is redecorated (an excessive need for dominance seems to correlate to a kind of baroque good taste), and there is a great bustle of activity in the altar guild, acolyte organization, and boys' choir.

I once made the half-joking comment while speaking in a certain parish hall that priests in such parishes have their portrait painted on their twentieth anniversary in one of two poses. The first pose is in a worn cassock—growing slightly green under the armpits—standing in a field of daisies with little children hanging on their cincture. It is reminiscent of nineteenth-century paintings of Jesus. The other pose is in an ornate cope, standing by the altar, with one hand clutching the *People's Anglican Missal* and the other resting on the fair linen. Light filters through a stained-glass window behind the left shoulder. As I offered this second description, the audience suddenly appeared both shocked and delighted as they broke out in laughter. I had failed to note the portrait of the present incumbent behind me, which I had inadvertently described in detail.

I do not have much sympathy with this response of "business as usual" to the crisis in ministry. I think it only reinforces our pathology. A second response, quite different from the first and for which I have more respect, is that of the "ministry of the gaps." This is sometimes called a "brokerage" ministry. As I suggested in *The Future Shape of Ministry*, the parish-house movement was largely an attempt to meet a need that no one else was meeting: the care for the people coming to the growing cities either from abroad or from the country. The social gospel of which the parish-house movement was a part, was a response to the suffering of the laboring class in late nineteenth-century America. The identification of unmet needs and the satisfaction of those needs, or the connecting of them with persons and/or agencies capable of meeting them, is what I mean by a "gap" or "brokerage" ministry.

Clearly this kind of ministry emphasizes service. The church is a knowledgable friend. One of the early pioneers in the parish-house movement was Christ Church, Cincinnati. I was visiting there recently, and I was impressed just by the signs outside the parish hall advertising such programs as Planned Parenthood, the milk fund, Alcoholics Anonymous, and Recovery. St. Luke's Church in Atlanta, another example, has a noon "soup kitchen" and a "street school." Its television programs are geared to attract people who feel unwelcome in the churches and are looking for more to their lives. The clergy of the parish are able to put them in touch with persons who can help them if they themselves do not have the requisite skills or resources.

This is a good response, but if it were the only one, it would be inadequate. For essentially it focuses on the inability to cope. It does not engage the society where it is coping very well but without judgment. It is a "rear guard" action much of the time, which is commendable if at the same time we are working on the horizons of man's quest for meaning. It tends to be very much oriented toward problem-solving, and therefore can allow itself to be aware of only the dimensions of life for which solutions are likely. The effect here is to become caught in the presuppositions of the technocratic society, which allows very little room for mystery and transcendence.

The response of the "ministry of the gaps" is also found objectionable by some—quite inappropriately so—because it takes Jesus seriously. It is anxious to clothe the naked, heal the sick, feed the hungry, and visit the prisoners (Matt. 25:31–46). It becomes involved with the outcasts of this world, which is very threatening. Outcasts sometimes have different ideas and strange styles of life. Historically, the rejection of the social gospel in the second decade of this century—called the "great reversal"—was a result of a sudden fear of "bolshevism," the radical politics of the working classes. The "great reversal" turned the church inward and it became concerned for its own well-being.

This leads to the third response to the crisis of ministry, which I call the "I-can-do-anything-you-can-do-better" ministry. It is typified for me by an incident early in my ministry. At a laymen's supper in a certain parish, I was listening to a talk by the football coach of the local high school. He was showing films of the previous Friday night game, which was lost, and explaining what had happened. In due course the man sitting next to me grumbled, "He had a different excuse at Kiwanis Tuesday." I said, "Hey, wait a minute. He gave the same talk at Kiwanis? Half these guys here are members of Kiwanis, and we are hearing the same talk?" His reply was, "Well, Father, it's just always better when the church sponsors it."

For more than forty years, since World War I, the parishes of the land have pursued busy-ness for its own sake. This culminated in the fifties with the "edifice complex," when, some of us suspect, we pursued building purely for its own sake. Recently a priest commented to me that he had just completed a million dollar renovation of the parish hall, and now he and his curate needed to find ways to fill up the new building. Did I have any ideas, he asked? The symbol of the priesthood in this response is no longer the altar or even the pulpit, but the desk. He is Richard Niebuhr's "parish director."[1]

The church is not necessarily serving its vocation in this way. What virtue is there in running a parallel track of activities to the "Y," the city department of recreation, the service organizations, the Scouts, the mental health center, the department of public welfare, and the Junior League? Is it better because we have "baptized" it? There is in this an almost indiscriminate lending of the church's name to popular activities, even though it is sometimes difficult to see in just what way they are related to the Gospel. It certainly is *safe* to do these things because they are acceptable. They possess no threat to the *status quo,* from which in fact they emerged. The values revealed in such activities are much the same as the values of the secular society: "bread and circuses," a preoccupation with "doing" for its own sake, and a kind of "Band-aid" approach to social ills.

I think much of the unhappiness among the clergy in the sixties is the result of a rejection of the image of the pastor in which they were trained in the fifties. I have talked to many priests who complained bitterly about the lack of significant work for them, the "Mickey Mouse" nature of what they were required to do, the inadequacy of most parish life, and the simple fact that they felt guilty about having time on their hands. Their response, unless they simply choose to opt out, was—and still is—to seek a form of continuing education that better equips them in a *professional* set of skills. Professionalism is, then, the fourth response to the ministerial crisis.

I have written on professionalism at considerable length in *The Future Shape of Ministry*. My discomfort with the paradigm grows. This is largely because it is a model of interaction which comes out of the technological world, where control and prediction are highly valued. The effect is to reduce the kinds of behavior and values which effectively serve to open ourselves and others to transcendence.

The truth is that the four responses to the crisis in ministry never really get at the heart of the matter. They never deal with the issue of a ministry that exists to confront the world with the transcendent judgment of God and to mediate his absolute presence within a relative world. The question is one of revelation: How can you and I know God as he speaks to our world today? It is the task of ministry at its very core to awaken us to this reality. None of these four responses do that because they lean too heavily upon the past, upon the failure to cope, upon the gods of this world, or upon the values of the technological culture.

The fundamental issue in ministry today is the recovery of a sense of enchantment and the ability to be enchanting. I do not mean by this to reinforce the resurgence of "conservative" religion. I do not think the pietistic revival —neo-Pentecostalism, neo-patriarchalism, the Jesus movement, or Faith Alive —as good as it may be in some ways, has grasped the real issue of why God appears absent to so many people today. It is too typically an American middle-class religious phenomenon. I do think that the ministry of the church needs to experience a kind of long-term conversion much like that to which Carlos Castaneda witnessed in his personal history with a Yaqui Indian *shaman,* whom he calls Don Juan. Don Juan tells Castaneda at one time, "I'm going to utter perhaps the greatest piece of knowledge anyone can voice. . . . Do you know that at this very moment you are surrounded by eternity? And do you know that you can use that eternity, if you so desire?"[2] The real issue is eternity, whether in our ministry we see it and use it!

This book is devoted to this subject. As a sequel to *The Future Shape of Ministry,* the hope might be that I will tie up the loose ends from the previous book. It should not come as any surprise, however, if we understand the subject, that for every trail coming out of the first study there is a multiplication of paths to follow which I can only touch on here.

The book is an account of my own continuing pilgrimage, but not one carried on alone. There is no way for me to enumerate the countless companions, across the country and from Canada to the deep South—not to mention my colleagues at Nashotah House and now at the University of the South— who have joined their quest to mine from time to time. The chapters that follow will, I am sure, reveal my indebtedness to so very many wonderful people. At this point, I can only express profound thanks for those who have listened patiently to my thoughts and have shared enthusiastically their ideas over the last four years of lectures, seminars, conversations, and moments of shared silence and prayer.

Of course, as we all know, theology for better or worse is a collaborative venture. This is true even though I have not submitted this whole manuscript for anyone to read and criticize—although some individuals have commented on parts of it. I am not sure why I have changed my usual practice in this regard, except to say that this study is something very personal to me. As the dedication witnesses, however, it is a book born of those intimate relationships with persons where the gift of themselves has left me profoundly grateful.

There are a few names I ought to mention of persons who had a specific role in making this book possible. First of all, I must express my thanks to Harry H. Pritchett, Jr., who shares many of the views set forth in this book, and who, over the past two years, has greatly assisted me in sharpening my own ideas. Bill Harkins, the head librarian of the University of the South, gave me a place to write it away from the seminary I serve. Ed Camp, librarian of St. Luke's, found all the obscure bibliographical references I laid on him. Bob Gilday, my editor at Seabury Press, encouraged me and waited patiently for the manuscript. Barbara Hart typed the final draft from a much revised original. Lizabeth Anderson lent her skills to the drawing of the four diagrams. Then, as always, my wife Jane understood when weekends and nights were occupied with this book that became an obsession.

Urban T. Holmes

St. Joseph of Arimathea, 1975

PART ONE

THE CONTEXT OF MINISTRY

1
THE CITY

In an age of nuclear threat and ecological collapse, we know that the behavior of one individual can have consequences for all mankind. In the discoveries of the human sciences and the reflections of much current philosophy, we perceive that all life is a shared existence. In contemporary theology, we believe once again the ancient truth that "no man is an island," but that every person is his collective world of relationships in some profound ontological sense. He *is* his city.

From the very first moment of conception, the human organism within the body of its mother carries the history of evolution. The Silurian ponds, the flowering uplands of the cretaceous epoch, and the African savannahs of the Pliocene have all left their imprint clinging to the uterine wall. Nurtured like the crossopterygian—the first creature we know to have emerged from the oceans—in the placental fluid of the womb, the human must burst forth from the waters on to "dry land." Man is a product of his environment. Only the gift of grasses and fruits, with their high energy content, has made it possible that this tiny infant can grow into the body of a person over five feet, and maybe even seven feet, tall. Those distinguishing human characteristics of the truly opposable thumb, complete bipedalism, and the large brain in proportion to the body, seem somehow to be a function of the grasslands which the early anthropoids inhabited maybe five million years ago. The man who rules the earth today is the consummation of the community of life that has preceded him for hundreds of millions of years, which we call the genotype.

Yet as Thomas Luckmann, the German sociologist, has reminded us, it is only as the genotype seeks to transcend its biology that man finds his true self. The process of socialization, of becoming a self in terms of the external collectivity or social reality into which a person is born, is the fulfillment of man's religious nature.[1] Our identification with our parents and siblings, our neighborhood, and ultimately our culture are the means of rising above our chromosomes. That supreme gift of social existence, language, is itself a human phenomenon that lifts man above instinctual, coded behavior to the fruit of the good life amid his fellow man. The genotype becomes more, he becomes the phenotype: the reflection of that self that he discerns within the reciprocal relationships into which he was thrust by the accident of birth. Thus, as Aristotle astutely observed, man is *politike zoe*—a living being who inhabits the *polis* or city. Man is by nature, then, political or communal. He is a city creature.

It follows from this that those images of our personhood inherited from nineteenth-century Western culture, which imply that the essential nature of the self is singular, come under attack. Surely the attitudes resulting from such conceptions are still with us—particularly in the area of moral responsibility —but the theoretical undergirding of radical individualism itself has been lost in our profound awareness that man is far more than the individual in the integrity of his lonely consciousness. Yet it is also true that every individual is responsible for all that constitutes his person: his past, that is carried within his body and the memory of his community, and his present interdependence within the social and natural environment. To be human is to be a genotype and a phenotype who is also free, and therefore accountable for his exercise of this responsibility. Not only is man responsible to his past and present communities, but also for holding before himself the future of man in relationship.

I have begun in this manner because I want there to be no question from the start as to my understanding of the nature of man—his being or ontology —and that this has unquestionable and central implications for ministry. Ministry, as I have said elsewhere, is what the church does to make Christ a living reality in the lives of men. It is the communal nature of man that is to find wholeness by the power of Christ's Gospel. The perfected social reality —by which I mean more a coming to fullness of its possible being rather than its moral implications—is the *goal* of ministry. At the same time, the world of reciprocal relationships is the *means* of such perfection or wholeness. The function of man's becoming in the future is the interdependence of his past and present.

This means that the church as the idealization of the human city is neither incidental to ministry nor merely convenient. The church is the "communion

14

of saints," the family of those persons whose wholeness in Christ may be seen either as in process or achieved. There is no notion of the isolated individual standing alone before his Lord. A much more accurate image is that of St. John the Divine, who saw the company of the blessed as a great throng worshiping together, gathered as one about the throne of the Lamb (Rev. 4:1–5:14). There is no idea of one man as the *active* mediator of God to a *passive* assembly of submissive recipients. It is the royal priesthood, which is the rightful possession of us all by virtue of Baptism, and is the mediating power through which that creation God envisions comes to be (1 Pet. 2:9–10).

The purpose then of this initial chapter is to begin the discussion of ministry at its appropriate fundament: the church. I am personally convinced that one of the repeated errors of much discussion of ministry, such as the recent "Canterbury Statement" of the International Anglican-Roman Catholic Commission, has been the failure to precede the talk of ministry with a careful analysis of the ecclesial reality of which ministry is the active expression in nurture and witness. Any such discussion of the church as that which ministers must involve us in that body as both end and means.

The outline of this chapter is threefold, moving in three stages from church as goal to church as means. First, I will expand further on the relationship of the end of the Gospel to man as city. Second, I will speak of the nature of the social reality itself, pointing out that there are a number of modes in which the city of man functions, and that the Christian city needs to possess all such dimensions of the social reality if it is to be true to the nature and destiny of man. Finally, in what is perhaps the heart of this chapter, I will build upon this understanding of the multimodal nature of social reality to develop a notion of four essential vectors within the political life that are necessary for the promotion of the true end of man.

ON BECOMING HUMAN

There are a number of various images of man's final end in the Bible. They all relate to what we believe to be the true nature of man, in terms of which the effort is made to resolve the theodicy issue—the justification of present suffering—and the problem of death. This is to say that the goal of the religious life in the Scriptures is to achieve that state of being for which God created us, or to become more human. This process is called by some contemporary theologians (Karl Rahner, Teilhard de Chardin) "hominisation."

The image which undoubtedly dominates our thinking and perhaps that of

15

the New Testament is "salvation." With the emphasis upon the cross found in Western theology, particularly since Augustine of Hippo (354–430), there is for us a high saliency to the thought of our "being saved" and of Jesus as the Savior. The very name, Joshua or Jeshua or Jesus, means "savior" (Matt. 1:21). The image has some very great strengths. It is concrete and appropriate to our experience. We know what it feels like to be saved from something undesirable or threatening. All of us have experienced salvation, whether we were saved from drowning, an unpleasant social encounter, or anything in between.

The Greek word in the New Testament for "save" *(sōzō)* does not have quite the same nuance as its English translation. More often than not it means what we might expect, to save *from* great peril or threat. In the New Testament we are saved *from* sin (Matt. 1:21; 1 Tim. 1:15), disease (Luke 7:50; James 5:15), or death (Matt. 27:42; John 12:27; James 5:29). The word also has a different sense, however, not so easily conveyed in the English, meaning to "prosper" or "thrive." The New English Bible translates, for example, the familiar saying of Jesus in Luke 9:24 as follows: "Whoever cares for his own safety is lost; but if a man will let himself be lost for my sake, that man is safe." The emphasis here is not so much on being saved from something, but on *what* is saved or healthy or whole.

The Greek in this verse is literally "to save his soul [*psychēn*]." It is very easy to make a transition from the notion of saving a life, which is probably what "soul" means here, to the Orphic-Pythagorean notion of "soul" which so strongly influenced the Platonic tradition and the early Church Fathers. In this latter meaning the soul takes on a discrete ontological or metaphysical integrity, which is the essence of man. This entity is a naturally immortal substance, existing in its entirety apart from community and body and all their emotional implications.

Sometimes in the process, the word for this ontological entity is itself changed to "spirit" *(pneuma),* and the "soul" remains a kind of life force. Frequently, either the soul or the spirit is related to the power of reason, or the mind *(nous),* which becomes the principal expression of man's immortal soul or spirit. Behind this was the notion that man in essence is a nonmaterial, rational consciousness, possessing a necessary immortality. The body, if allowed as part of the human nature, ranks at the bottom of the tripartite nature of man: spirit, soul, and body. It is noteworthy that some manuals of theology define man in this tripartite sense, as if it were revealed truth and not the product of Greek speculation based upon the particular experience of that

16

people.[2] In all of this the community is often not even mentioned, perhaps because the body is a necessary "go-between" for consciousness and community. For example, language is a necessary instrument of consciousness, yet it is a cultural phenomenon requiring the body.

The notion of the substantial, immortal soul raises a question with which Christian speculation has played over the centuries. Where does the soul go at the moment of death? The map of the afterlife, for which we are indebted to Dante's (1265–1321) *Divine Comedy,* seeks to answer that question. Undoubtedly this great Italian poet employed the popular piety of a Christian society, particularly in regard to the horrors of hell. He lived in a time in which there was a growing sense of the demonic, fed by a certain Germanic morbidity. The biblical images of the place of eternal fire—named for the dump outside Jerusalem—to which the condemned were sent (Matt. 5:22; 10:28; Mark 9:47), joined with allusions to Satan, had generated centuries of speculation, culminating in Dante's work. He is perhaps the pivotal figure in a kind of literary genre, in which this life is seen as a process of decision between the yawning pits of hell ruled by Satan, who has become a far more substantial personality than he ever was in the New Testament (Mark 4:15; Acts 5:3; 1 Cor. 7:5, where Satan is the "adversary"), and the much less specific delights of heaven. The anguish of the late Middle Ages, fed by unceasing war and devastating plagues, made a fertile field for such speculation.

What made purgatory, heaven, and hell necessities, and what begot this geography of salvation, was the elaboration of the nature of man as an immortal, metaphysical substance called soul or spirit. Hell becomes the "city of the damned" and heaven the "city of the blessed." The task of ministry becomes the "cure (or caring for) of souls," saving them *from* hell and *for* heaven. Hell is something we anticipate far more vividly, however, than heaven.

There is, of course, always a sense in which the goal of religion must be related to man's inevitable longing for eternal life. The psychoanalyst, Robert Lifton, has suggested that such a desire may even be a part of man's genetic makeup.[3] What we picture inevitably is not just *from* what we have survived, but *what* has survived: the essence of man. This is why the goal of religion has to deal with humanity in itself, and why the Greek tradition of the immortal soul, possessing a natural capacity of survival for better or worse after death, was an important option that came to have such a dominant role in Christian thought.

The ancient Jew had the same longing as his Greek contemporary, but his notion of what constituted the essence of man, and therefore the process of hominisation, was seen as different. It is easy to exaggerate the difference between Jewish and Hellenistic concepts of life after death, for there was contact between the cultures. Yet in Jewish thought there is not the history of revulsion against the emotions that we find in the Greek experience, and perhaps there was a stronger sense of being a people. Therefore, man was not reduced in essence to his rational consciousness, even though there was this same desire for personal survival. Consequently there developed among some of the Jews from the second century before Christ a belief in the literal resurrection of the body. This belief began metaphorically, but developed into a conviction, a physical event, which was a resurrection to either an earthly or a heavenly kingdom, of either individuals or the people, and of either the Jews alone or the just alone or all people (Dan. 12:1–3; 2 Macc. 7:9,14,22–23, 29; cf. the earlier metaphors of Isa. 25–26; Ezek. 37:1–14). The origins of the resurrection image probably lie in Persian religion, and before that in primitive cults.

The doctrine of the resurrection of the bodies of the dead denotes a belief that man has no eternal life by natural right; but should everlasting life be given him by God, it must be in terms of the whole, integral man, body and soul. Prior to the resurrection, man lay in the grave, unlike in Dante's *Divine Comedy.*

This Jewish understanding of man is conveyed in a rabbinic parable. Antonius comes to the rabbi and asks him what is the relation of the soul to the body. The rabbi answers that it is like a king who once assigned a blind man and a cripple to guard his orchard. The cripple said to the blind man, "What lovely fruit. If only I could have some." The blind man said, "I cannot find it, but if you will get on my back and lead me, we can both share in the fruit." The king returned and saw his fruit gone. "Where is all the fruit?" he asked. "How can we say?" the two guards answered. "One of us is blind and cannot see it, and the other is crippled and cannot reach it."

The image of the resurrection embodies thus two significant ideas. The first is the consistent nature of the human person, body and soul, which I have just illustrated. The second I have alluded to; namely, that the resurrection is into a community, initially of the Jewish people. In the New Testament the community is of the kingdom of God or of heaven, and is more and more not of this world. Whether of earth or heaven, this means that the doctrine participates in the most persistent image of perfected humanity in the Scriptures: the redeemed city.

It is not without a checkered history. Not all Jews in the intertestamental period and at the time of Jesus believed in the resurrection or in any kind of personal existence after death. This was the point of the account in the New Testament of the Sadducees who came to Jesus describing the hypothetical problem of a woman who successively married seven brothers in accordance with the Deuteronomic Code (Deut. 25:5). The reason for the law was that if a man died without children it was believed that he could still "survive" through the children begotten by his brother of his wife. This was in lieu of any notion of personal, individual existence after death. The problem the Sadducees posed was: Given the truth of the resurrection, whose wife was she when they were all raised from the dead? Jesus' answer was to say that there is no marital relation in the resurrection (Matt. 22:23–30).

Perhaps we feel that Jesus gave the obvious and correct answer, but the Sadducees certainly held an older Jewish belief. When a man dies in the earlier tradition of the Old Testament, any possible individual survival is of a very shadowy, vague kind of state called *Sheol,* the abode of the departed (Ps. 16:8–11; Job 10:20–22; Isa. 5:14). *Sheol* is a place where nothing gets resolved. The theodicy question is separated from the problem of personal death, therefore, and the justification for a good life is found in the prosperity of the people of Israel. A pious Hebrew lived by the Law in order that Israel might survive in the "promised land."

What lay behind this understanding was the Hebrew concept of the corporate person: the individual embodies the community, and the community is responsible for the individual. In the notion of the corporate person there is no discrete individual, but a person is what he is by virtue of his membership in the community. If I cite a few examples, without any effort to exhaust the subject, of certain well-known biblical images dependent upon the idea of the corporate person, the reader may realize for himself the importance of this fundamental Hebrew understanding of man. For example: What possible justification could the Lord have for destroying the entire households of Dathan and Abiram, because these two men revolted against Moses (Num. 16:1–35)? Or again: What was the mind-set of the Israelites and the Philistines, that the battle at Socoh could be determined by two individuals, David and Goliath, each representing an army (1 Sam. 17:1–58)? Perhaps most dramatically: What is the dynamic of human nature that all die in Adam and all are made alive in Christ (1 Cor. 15:22)? The answer in each instance is the "corporate person."

Charles Williams, the English author and mystic, made a great point of the image of the city in Christian theology. He based the power of the image upon the fact that to be human is, as he put it, to coinhere, and that the power of salvation was the energy transmitted from one person to another—what he called "exchange" or "substitution"—made possible by our coinherence. Coinherence describes the condition of living in the redeemed city, and it is the "glue" of the corporate person.[4] To be human in Williams's thought is to live in a city, the heavenly city or new Jerusalem (Rev. 21:1–27). It is clearly a place in which the unity of man to God is established.

> I heard a loud voice proclaiming from the throne: "Now at last God has his dwelling among men! He will dwell among them and they shall be his people, and God himself shall be with them. He will wipe every tear from their eyes; there shall be an end to death" (Rev. 21:3–4).

It is a beautiful picture of the redeemed city, which not only answers the theodicy question, but speaks to the problem of death—something it can do because it is a "heavenly," not an "earthly," city into which we are resurrected. The image is parallel to the picture of the kingdom of God or heaven, for "kingdoms" in those days were possibly empires, but more likely were city-states, not much larger than a county. Our modern nation was not part of the ancient reality. People lived within the city walls, and only went out to farm, tend their herds, or to attack the adjoining city. To speak of the redeemed city is to take this visible and familiar image of the corporate person and think of him as fulfilled and with God.

In describing the city, Charles Williams says,

> In the last paragraph of the Apostles' Creed the City is defined. 'I believe in the Holy Ghost' is the first clause and the primal condition. If it is living, it lives so, and only so, towards Christ, in whom it already lives complete, having (by virtue of His substitution) 'the perfect and simultaneous possession of everlasting life.' Simultaneously all its citizens derive from all. 'The Holy Catholic Church' is its name. . . . But the other four clauses are . . . the four qualities of life: 'the Communion of Saints, the Forgiveness of Sins, the Resurrection of the Body, and the Life everlasting.'[5]

My point in introducing the insights of Williams has been to enforce the fact that the essential corporate nature of man, as caught up in the image of the city, is a culminating ingredient in the biblical notion of the perfected person. The redeemed city is a necessary part of each of us becoming human. Williams's relating the city to the last paragraph of the Apostles' Creed also provides an opportunity to develop its implications further.

Aristotle's statement that man is a "political animal" is to say that man by nature lives in a city or, to use the Greek, a *polis*—the word from which we get the words "politics," and "political." In this sense I would insist that the goal of the church's ministry is *political,* necessarily involving man's ontological dimension of community or the city, as Williams describes it. Man is born to coinhere with other men. He becomes himself in terms of the social reality.

Williams's description of the city, however, does not set it *over against* notions of man's true self as "soul" or "resurrected body." It sublates or catches up into the larger concept of the city the idea of the survival of the soul and the resurrection of the body. I think we can agree that the task of ministry is to "save souls," if we mean by that not to minister to the necessarily immortal soul-substance of Orphic-Pythagorean speculation, but rather to be concerned for the ultimate of God's gift of life. This would not run counter to the belief in the resurrection of the body, if we understand that the image of the resurrection is of the personal integrity of the *whole* man given new life by God. The resurrection of the body is, however, a resurrection into community. Therefore, what Williams calls "the four qualities of life" within the city are those of an open, loving community, in which each individual is an enlivened, integral part or member forever.

During World War II, Ronald Knox, the popular spokesman for English Roman Catholics, wrote somewhere that in heaven *all* "dog tags" (the metal identification tags worn by service personnel and others) carried the religious preference "RC." This kind of ecclesiastical triumphalism is, thankfully, less prevalent today than then; but Knox's point is not entirely without merit. Certainly in heaven there is an identifiable community, for the city requires identity by nature of its existence. Any sociologist would tell you that a social reality without boundaries is not a reality. Williams calls this city the Holy Catholic Church.

I would agree with Williams if we understand the unity with God and the coinherence with one another to be the destiny of all mankind, and that this is the church in its final dimensions. The visible, broken church of today is not the kingdom of God, but it is a very human witness, used by God, not only to work for the kingdom but to be a sacrament of that eschatological reality. The church is, by God's infinite mercy, a broken vessel, in which we may find a glimpse of the redeemed city. In this sense it is true that outside the church there is no salvation, because salvation or hominisation is political, and it is a gift of God.

The goal of ministry is then the perfection of man, which is the perfection of the church as the redeemed community.

THE MULTI-MODAL CITY

Certainly this kind of bold assertion is subject to all kinds of questions. The contemporary French lay theologian, Jacques Ellul, takes a different position in regard to the city, which requires us to qualify a simplistic acceptance of this image. His challenge, which I shall outline very briefly, can be met by examining what I call the modalities of the social reality.

Ellul points out that the city in the Bible is an expression of man's pride and presumption. Cain slays Abel and builds the first city. He surrenders security in God for a security of his own making. The tower of Babel (Babylon) evokes the anger of God and mankind is fragmented. As in Sodom, the city becomes a center for the accumulation of sin. For Ellul the city is a product of civilization, and it would appear that civilization itself is an expression of man's unwillingness to trust in God. Man would be better off in a primitive existence, as represented in the Garden of Eden, for the *polis* or city with its structures is necessarily alienating. City walls not only keep out the enemy, they keep out God.[6]

What Ellul has done, as I see it, is to narrow the definition of the city from that of Charles Williams. The city for Ellul is a social institution, created out of fear and for the sake of security, rooted in man's seeming conviction that if he is not in control, no one will be. Building a city is an expression of lack of faith in God, and the structures of that city are inevitably inhibiting to the awareness of and response to God's presence or grace.

I am not completely out of sympathy with what Ellul is suggesting. Ellul's theological presuppositions, however, are more individualistic and dualistic than mine. For example, Ellul never suggests that man is ontologically tied to community. He only says that Cain trades the security of God for a city of his own making. For Ellul the city, cleansed of its sin, can be at best a "neutral instrument" in the hands of God to call the power into judgment and repentance. When the notion of the redeemed city does appear in Ellul, it is something completely opposed to the earthly city. It is "absolutely free, unforeseeable, transcendent." It is of a different nature than man's cities.

This opposition of nature and supernature, the earthly city and the individual before God, does not seem to me very helpful, because it does not provide me with an adequate understanding of our experience. It makes more sense to begin by reaffirming the fact that man is always found existing in a reciprocal relationship with other men. This is another way of saying, with a different nuance, that it is of the nature of man to coinhere. We can then proceed to look at the forms of that reciprocity; and we can begin to move from the evidence that salvation is necessarily political to the discovery of the relation of the form of the city to its instrument of ministry; in the latter instance, the form a community takes speaks to the nature of the instrument and its effect in ministry.

The renowned French sociologist, Georges Gurvitch, developed an under-standing of social reality or, better, phenomena, which helps illuminate what I call the modalities of the city. In saying that Ellul has narrowed Williams's definition of the city to the point that it seems difficult to maintain the essential nature of community life as both the means and end of hominisation, I have in mind the kind of analysis that Gurvitch epitomizes.

Gurvitch divides the social phenomena into three large categories: micro-sociology, macrosociology, and global structures. Microsociology is a term applied to social bonds or what he calls "social electrons" that are based upon "we-relationships" that are astructural, infinitely varied, dynamically related, and the most abstract elements of social reality. These collectivities are bound together by symbols, as we shall see in subsequent chapters, which means that the bond reaches beneath the surface to engage the members at the deepest level of feeling. There is true communion here, which arises spontaneously and is not dependent upon external constraint.[7]

A fascinating point which Gurvitch makes is that the more profound the fusion within the social bond classified under microsociology the less pressure on the "I." I would assume from this that it follows that the deeper the commitment to the social bond the less destruction there is to the individual. It will be my contention through this study that this is true. Gurvitch divides the astructural, spontaneous, dynamic social bonds of microsociology into three categories: communion, community, and mass. There is less pressure on the "I" in communion than in community, and less in community than in mass. I would identify what the anthropologist, Victor Turner, calls "com-munitas" (see Chapter Five in particular) with Gurvitch's "communion," a category which is very important for this book.

Of course, when Ellul speaks of the city he does not have in mind micro-sociology, whereas Williams does. Gurvitch's second basic modality is more—although not in entirety—what Ellul has in mind, which he places under the category of macrosociology. By this he means social groupings (as opposed to bonds) which are more concrete (although only partially so), not reducible to their contents (the spontaneous fusion of a "we"), created out of shared attitudes, and moving toward structuration. Examples of such groups are an athletic team, a family, a political party, a band of partisans, a business co-op. These are obviously very different in some ways. For instance, they possess varying degrees of duration, structure, ease of admission, size, and so forth. Yet, on the one hand, they differ in the same way from the social bond of microsociology, and on the other hand, they have not achieved what Gurvitch means by a global structure.

The global structure possesses sovereign power, judicial and economic, over all groups within it. It has within itself a reciprocity or dialectical relationship between society (the institutions and their roles and statuses) and the culture (the civilization). Examples of the global structure run from the city of Cain to the Greek city-state, to the feudal society, to the capitalist nation, to the planned societies of state collectivism. There is no doubt, as we shall see, that global structures tend to be totalitarian and blind to transcendence; although Ellul's analysis seems overstated and insensitive to their value.

All the modalities of the city—microsociology, macrosociology, and global structures—are an inevitable and necessary part of the social phenomena and human ontology. Throughout this study this point will be reiterated in a variety of ways, which are important for the reader to grasp. This is because it appears that the categories of the social bond (microsociology) are central to that ministry of the church which would be particularly open to God's presence to us now. Therefore, the danger is that this modality of the "mountain-top experience" will be considered something to be cherished for its own sake, as Peter, James, and John would have done at the time of the Transfiguration (Mark 9:5).

There has been a tendency in man, particularly since the industrial revolution, to make odious comparisons between the spontaneous life of the social bond and the external constraints of social groupings, especially in global structures. The monastic movement of the third century is such a reaction, as was the rise of the mendicant orders in the thirteenth century. The Luddites, who smashed machinery in protest against the disappearance of the home-based artisan in the English Midlands (1811–1816), as well as John Ruskin (1819–1900) and his sensitive protest against the inhumanity of industrialism, are both expressions of a longing for a pristine, intimate life, characteristic of Gurvitch's communion. Lawrence Cunningham has described the relatively recent efforts of Eric Gill, the English artist, to establish at Ditchling a community that embodies the "return" to the pure spontaneous social bond of microsociology.[8] My purpose here is *not* to choose sides and to join in a simple reaction, but to suggest that this persistent quest of communion says something about the nature of man as a social reality, and, in particular, about the church.

There is a recurrencence of this theme of return to communion in much of the youth culture of the early 1970s and in the neopietism of present-day Christian life. (By neopietism I refer to the Jesus movement, the charismatic revival, and the spiritual sharing groups identified with "Faith Alive" or "Faith at Work" organizations. I am also implying that the etiology of these phenomena is closely related to a similar "enthusiastic" development in the late seventeenth and early eighteenth century.) The literature of the youth culture of the early 70s is filled with the lament over the loss of an intimate, spontaneous community in the face of contemporary technological society.

An illustration of the search for community among the young was provided me in a delightful way when I took from the shelves of our college library a copy of Charles Reich's *The Greening of America.* A student had written the words "like" and "good" beside those passages with which he especially concurred. They speak for themselves.

> Perhaps the culture just now being developed by the new generation—the new emphasis upon imagination, the senses, community, and the self—is the first real choice made by any Western people since the end of the Middle Ages.

> Thus, despite their bravery, they [the political radicals of the New Left] fail to offer an example of affirmative vision. Bob Dylan did what he wanted to do, lived his own life, and *incidentally* changed the world.

> To paint a Campbell's Soup can is to transcend that particular aspect of culture, to see it objectively rather than be dominated by it. That does not make the object "beautiful" but it does take away the object's power over man, and perhaps man may learn something from it, or get a little enjoyment from it. One can watch television, the news, the ads, the commentators, the dramas, and just laugh and laugh and laugh; all the power of television turns impotent and absurd.

> We lost the ability to control our lives or our society because we had placed ourselves excessively under the domination of the market and technology.[9]

Reich makes no secret of the fact that he is not a Christian; so the concluding marginal comment, written alongside Reich's disclaimer that the book has the faults and imperfections of it's author, is: "A man without Jesus Christ!"

I am not in complete accord with Reich, even chastened by Jesus. Yet there is a profound truth in the need to balance the all too obvious presence of the global structures with a renewed awareness of the social bonds that are a part of man's very being. James Sellers, an ethicist teaching at Rice University, has made the point that the best possible basis for a social ethic today is not so much the willy-nilly confrontation of the structures but a new sense of interdependence, fed by the kind of deep mutual caring that Gurvitch sees in communion and community.[10]

More important for the purposes of this book is Edward Farley's analysis of ecclesial man. Farley is arguing that, by all the criteria we know, man is a social or political being. Furthermore, faith becomes a possibility for him only in terms of a matrix of intersubjectivity that lies beneath the extrinsic constraints and structures. The ecclesia is the divinely chosen locus for the presence of God's redemptive activity. It is the communion and community of Gurvitch defined in terms of its transcendental possibilities. Farley speaks of this ecclesia as always possessing three things: the imagery of faith, the experience of an altered existence (redemption), and a specific cointentionality among the membership that can be identified apart from other communities.[11]

Again, Farley is not arguing against the fact that man moves to the structuration of his social world. He is identifying a modality of that world which is necessary for faith. From my understanding, he is correct in his analysis; and in the developing discussion of the experience of the word of God within the human community, I will be carrying out something of the implications of Farley's implicit theological commentary upon Gurvitch and other phenomenological sociologists. As I have already stated, the contention is that man must, if he is to achieve a full hominisation, live in a dialectical relation to the various modalities of the social reality.

I was grasping at this point somewhat intuitively in *The Future Shape of Ministry*. One of the ideas I offered there as a "trial balloon" was the notion of the Christian community as expressed in a "sect-church" relationship. I have been struck from the beginning by the response to this innovation, which has exceeded the positive support of any other particular suggestion. For the past two hundred years, the church has bet its survival on institutional structures, which is understandable. There is, however, a longing to balance this with a degree of spontaneous and less self-conscious corporate existence, the likes of which we have probably not seen since the medieval church.

This longing strikes me as being rooted in the very nature of man. As best we can tell, ninety-nine percent of the history of man and his immediate evolutionary ancestors was spent by the river bank in communities of about forty to sixty hunters and gatherers. It is not too farfetched to say that the human genotype is given most "naturally" to that kind of informal, intimate community, tied together by kinship, land, and need. It seems highly likely to me, without tying my thought too closely to particular theories of ethology, that man cannot escape his need, rooted in his history, for that social reality

26

of microsociology. Certainly anyone witnessing the exodus every Friday afternoon from the city to the country and the river banks and lake sides, to the
cabins in the woods or on the shore, does not have to stretch his imagination
too far to perceive *homo sapiens* returning to his natural habitat. I say this,
not to mock ourselves but to affirm our roots in the soil, in the forests and
fields, and more particularly in the intimate bond of the natural community.
In coming to this atavistic awareness, man has a possibility of confronting the
mystery that is the creative source of his history.

It is organization, however, that has made it possible for human existence
to advance in knowledge and to lift life above the merely tolerable. Man must
return on Sunday afternoon within the city. We cannot despise the technology
that saves us from living in brutish misery, nor can we reject the communication media which makes possible the sharing of human learning, nor may we
abrogate the law that spares us one continued exercise in the futility of tribal
chauvinism. In this sense society "humanizes" man, and in so doing deepens
the possibility of his knowing God in God's fullness.

The truth of the perfected city, we might say, is the truth of the multi-modal
city in which we must maintain our home. The point is to keep the road
passable and familiar between all modalities, for the dialogue is essential for
man's salvation. Ministry requires all modalities, for they are equal and yet
quite different, as this book shall unfold. As the church is the expression of
the divine calling of man's corporate self, so the church must hold within itself
in constant interaction man as bonded, grouped, and structured. The redeemed
city is both communion, social group, and global structure; it is many cities
in one.

FOUR VECTORS WITHIN THE CHURCH

There are all kinds of ways of describing the Church—One, Holy, Catholic,
and Apostolic; the locus of true preaching and rightly administered sacraments; a voluntary society; the Body of Christ, of which all baptized persons
are members—but I wish here to speak of it as an instrument of ministry and
a system possessing necessarily four vectors. As I have said, the goal of that
ministry is to enable us through God's action to become human. We have seen
that being human is to be a social self, which is enlivened and embodied. In
the last section we saw that the human collectivity possesses within it a tension,
hopefully held in some balance, between spontaneous bonds, groups, and
global structures. There is another way we can look at that same social reality
as it relates to the church, which reveals four vectors within the life of the

Christian community that are essential to its health and effectiveness as an instrument of ministry.

By a "vector" I mean an intervention which constitutes the field of social life. I could speak of "inputs" instead of "vectors," but the latter term is indicative of a more purposeful, dynamic quantity. In speaking of the church as a system, I understand it to be a network of relationships with a certain goal which these vectors engage. A system is teleological, at least in terms of the church, although its final cause is always subject to qualification by the life of the system itself. The relationships within the system consist, of course, of the members of the church and their various subgroups. The goal is, as I have said, the wholeness of man. It is as these four vectors intersect that it becomes possible for the church so to shape its life that it may fulfill its goal. I will argue that when any one or more vectors does not engage the membership, the ecclesial reality fails in its purpose.

A diagram will be found on page 29 which outlines the principal content of this section. Since this is pivotal material for the rationale of this book, it is of the utmost importance that the reader understands the two previous sections to have been leading up to this point, and that he realizes that the focus of this study will be only on one of the vectors described. Therefore, the function of the next few pages is to point out the main thrust of the book, setting it within the broader context of ministry studies.

The first vector is the *past* (number 1 in Figure 1). Dietrich Ritschl has argued that since Augustine of Hippo Western Christianity has been increasingly obsessed with the subjective experience of the salvific event of Calvary, an obsession which has had the effect of focusing the life of the church on the past.[12] There is in every religion a need to recapture the primal event, the dramatic occasion on which the adherents base the reason for the existence of their community, its worship, and its belief. This can easily slip into the notion that God spoke back then in a definitive manner and has not spoken since. Certainly those theological positions that speak of the closure of revelation as coincident with the final writing of the New Testament books give support to the idea that the church lives to confront the present with the past, and that nothing has happened since closure that can qualify the biblical authors' understanding of the experience of God. The author of the Letter of Jude speaks of preserving the faith "once for all delivered to the saints" (Jude 3). There is no doubt that he has in mind a body of content. From such thinking we get the image of the church as the "defender of the faith" and as a "shrine of the golden age."

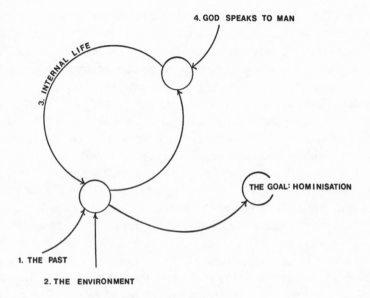

Figure 1

I have discussed the problem of history elsewhere.[13] The past is certain; it is not going to change. Therefore, to live in the past provides the illusion of security for some people. At the time of this writing I find myself drawn rather reluctantly into a debate, which is growing progressively more heated, over the nature and use of Confirmation in the Episcopal Church. One point of view holds very strongly that as part of our past the practice—and the interpretation of the meaning of that practice—of Confirmation is something from which we stray at the peril of the church's very existence, or at least of the existence of the episcopacy. The problem is that there is no consistent practice or interpretation in the history of the church. The reason for my "reluctance" is that I suspect this is an emotional issue, not a rational one. As with every problem of this kind, we cannot get the "faith" (as content) as one or more persons conceive it to fit any selected "golden age." A community that bases its security upon its past is only fooling itself.

At the same time, there is abroad today a largely ahistorical spirit, particularly in the youth culture, which ignores the past in favor of the inspiration of the moment. In the 60s we spoke of that break in the continuity of history, calling it the "generation gap." It seems to me that contemporary enthusiasm has given this a less rebellious twist by speaking of a "new beginning." The intention is the same: to avoid having to live under the burden of the past. I can appreciate this sometimes. Recently I led a seminar in human sexuality in which one woman questioned the use of the terms "masculine" and "feminine," because for her it was to divorce descriptions of intrapersonal symbols from a history of the stereotyping and dehumanizing of male and, more particularly, female persons. She was saying that the authority for what we do *now* is our feelings at the moment, not what was said or done *before*. My reply was that we must use language to communicate meaning and it does this, not in spite of its history but because of its history.

My criticism of this ahistorical attitude will appear in Chapter Four, when I seek to differentiate between imagination and fantasy. There I say an ahistorical attitude begets fantasy. For the present we need to keep in mind that fantasy is born of a desire to escape our true identity and is characteristic of the hopeless viewpoint of psychotic behavior, as opposed to the creative and hopeful power of the imagination.

The task of the Christian city in terms of the first vector is to live neither *in* the past *nor apart* from the past, but rather *out of* the past. The past gives us an identity. My children have asked me why we hang the pictures of our parents and grandparents in our home. I hope it is not an act of ancestor worship, but it does remind us from where we came. The act of knowing where we came from is a precondition for knowing where we might go. It is in the past that we find the promise for the future, which gives identity and clarity to our present experience.

The second vector is in the *environment,* social and natural (number 2 in Figure 1). The Christian understanding of nature has always been influenced by Greek notions of man as rational consciousness, and therefore we offer to set man over against nature. The fact that only in the last few years has any attempt been made to write a history of the church's relationship to the natural world, principally as a result of the ecological crisis, is a testimony to the lack of understanding we have in this dimension of the second vector. This has not been the case in terms of its relationship to social reality outside of itself.

The basic work in this area is that of Ernest Troeltsch, *The Social Teachings of the Christian Churches.* Troeltsch points out that the dialogue between the Christian institution and the commonweal over the last two thousand years is an immensely complicated and subtle issue. He argues that the kingdom proclaimed by Jesus was of another world. Here he would agree with Ellul. Therefore, the church's relationship to this world has to be, first, one of utter withdrawal. The church tried to shut itself off from the second vector, hoping for an immediate end of that world. Since this did not happen, it then had to settle for a form of compromise. The medieval compromise, second, was of an evolution from nature to grace, built upon the hierarchial ordering of the cosmos found in the scholastic synthesis. Third, the Calvinist or ascetic Protestant compromise was based on the notion of the holy community of the elect, whose privileged status was manifest by the character of their life in the world. The medieval compromise produced the constant power struggle between the papacy and the principal monarchs of Europe. As students of Max Weber will recall, there is a case for saying that ascetic Protestantism created a climate for radical individualism and the rise of capitalism.

Troeltsch believed that the kingdom of God is within us. Since he had no expectation of the immediate end of the world, the *eschaton,* he saw the only choice for the Church *vis-à-vis* the social order or the second vector to be a series of compromises, in which the church adjusted its life and response to the world in accord with what was reasonably possible.[14] His life overlapped the work of Washington Gladden and Walter Rauschenbush, the principal leaders of the American social gospel, who in effect disagreed with Troeltsch's belief that the kingdom of God could only exist within a man. The social gospel saw the revival of Old Testament prophecy and the effort to bring about the kingdom within the social order. The so-called theology of revolution, a kind of afterthought to the social activism of the 60s, was in some ways a revival in turn of the social gospel. Between Rauschenbush and the revolutionaries came Reinhold Niebuhr, with a much more sober, Troeltsch-like appraisal of what the relationship between the second vector and the ecclesial reality might be.

In all of this, however, we have seen the church seeking to grapple with the demands placed upon it by the environmental vector. This has, particularly in the last hundred years, become a searching concern of theologians and parish clergy as a whole. It is only right that it should. The alternative is to flee from this vector to become an ecclesiastical teahouse. If we do this, we simply abdicate the purpose of the church; to be God's instrument in making men whole. "Wholeness," as we have seen, has its essential political dimension.

The third vector is the relationship of the church to its own *internal life* (number 3 in Figure 1). The first record of any such concern might be found in Acts 15:6–29, in which the Christian leadership met at Jerusalem to determine the hold of the Mosaic Law over their membership. The contemporary concern for the internal dynamics of groups begins with the research of Kurt Lewin and his associates in this country about the time of World War II, although he in turn was dependent upon earlier Gestalt psychology. From this has come the human relations movement and its managerial offshoot, organizational development.

The importance of understanding the dynamics going on within a collectivity, particularly in regard to the nature of its leadership and the constructive management of conflict, cannot be underestimated. Although some church people have very negative feelings about "sensitivity training" and "T-groups," the attention to the interaction within the group is directly related to the effectiveness of the system's ability to achieve its goal. When we state the goal of a system, we are describing what we want to have happen as a result of that system's work. It is often true, however, that the internal life of the system makes the achievement of that goal impossible, and therefore adjustment is necessary.

It is not enough just to know what went on in the past and what is happening outside the church. For example, the whole man or saint can be justifiably described from New Testament sources as above all a person who loves (John 13:34; 1 Cor. 13:13; Eph. 5:2; 1 John 4:11–12). It can also be said on reasonable grounds that in order to love, a person has to be free, he has to make his own choices and be his own man (John 8:36; 1 Pet. 2:16; Gal. 5:1). He is accountable, and accountability in all justice requires responsibility (Matt. 25:14–28; Luke 19:12–27). It is very easy and quite prevalent for leadership styles to exist in the Christian collectivity which eat away at the person's responsibility, make his freedom an illusion, and consequently remove the possibility of love.[15] It is also quite possible for church members themselves, acting out of fear, to seek a quality of life within the church where they do not have to bear responsibility and be accountable, and hence surrender their freedom and think no more of love.[16]

Attention to the internal life of the church or the third vector is no mere fad or anti-Christian plot. It is an essential concern toward enabling ministry to fulfill its task. It begins with what a parish priest recently described for me as his most pressing ministry: "helping people to survive the night." It must, however, be much more than that. The internal life of the institution can become such that it, in fact, defeats the purpose of the church, and this needs to be identified and remedied, even when that task is frightening and painful.

Kurt Back has suggested, however, that the human relations movement in our time is a kind of secular religious quest or pilgrimage.[17] If we mean by "secular" at least a lack of awareness of the transcultural or transpersonal elements within our experience, this has been true in the movement within the church as well as without. The assumptions of radical theology are often implicit, although I think this is very often challenged today. Certainly the church's concern for the environment has been marked in the past by either a disregard for transcendence or an avowed rejection of it as a possibility for our experience. This has been a concern of mine, since at the heart of Christian ministry lies the incarnate Lord: the embodiment of transcendence.

I cannot settle, however, for saying that if we take into account the past of the church, we can remedy this lack. The problem is not one of simply not knowing our theology. Theology by itself, as necessary as I think it is, is the product of rational reflection upon a more inchoate meaning of the experience of God, as well as that experience itself.

The church cannot, therefore, be a communion, group, or structure embodying transcendence unless transcendence is an experience for it now. Without such experience it is either an archive or a museum or both, or a lobby for humanity, or a gigantic growth group, or combinations of all three. This is fine, but that is not what Christian commitment is all about. Christ is the sacrament of God, and the church continues that vocation. As "sacrament" I mean the context for the experience of God's presence within and in terms of our *present* history. There has to be a fourth vector: *God speaking to man* (number 4 in Figure 1).

My observation is that in going about the country and talking with clergy and/or lay groups, this statement—that the church is a community that experiences God now—meets with considerable approval. Over the last five or six years much of our society has come into what some call "the experience explosion," by which is meant the unwillingness to think of ourselves as spectators of life. What the experience explosion might be undoubtedly varies with those involved. The drug culture was part of the phenomenon. The various neopietistic movements (neo-Pentecostalism, Jesus people, Faith Alive) are part of it. The new interest in meditation, particularly in its Far Eastern forms, contribute. The whole fascination with nature, touching, play, fits in here. Whatever its form, the experience explosion expresses an unwillingness to settle for second-hand information, "canned interpretations," mere conceptual thinking, and a God afar off.

Morton Kelsey, an Episcopal priest teaching at the University of Notre Dame, has been a dedicated exponent of the possibility of the experience of God now. I am not altogether in sympathy with Kelsey's views on how this encounter is possible, nor with his prejudice against theologians like myself, but the fact that he writes and is read widely is indicative of a deep concern in Christian circles for the reality of the fourth vector.[18] God is to be encountered in the church now, Christ is present now, and the Holy Spirit moves among us now.

I want to be sure that I am clearly understood. The focus of this book is on the meaning of this fourth vector in the life of the church. It is crucial, because it is this vector which gives this particular group of people the right to call itself "Christian." In saying this and concerning myself primarily with this subject, I am in no sense implying any blanket condemnation of ministry studies in the area of the other three vectors. As those vectors are essential to the life of the church, so is the scholarly consideration of their meaning. I have and will be referring from time to time to some works in these other areas. The problem in reflecting upon the meaning of ministry is *not* that we have strayed in pursuing the meaning of these other vectors into disciplines that have no relation to theology or the church's ministry, but that we have not related them to the history of the church and set them within theological contexts.

SUMMARY

Ministry is the church's function to mediate the mystery of God to man, supremely revealed in Jesus Christ, in order that man might become that for which he is created. The wholeness of man demands life, body, and community. Therefore, the goal of ministry is political. Life in the church is a promise of the redeemed city.

This city has a number of modalities, each with their own value as well as their own problems. What we need is their interaction. Viewed another way, the ecclesial city has four vectors: the past, the environment, the internal relations, and the word of God. Both the modalities and vectors comprise necessary components in the total ecclesial reality, particularly as the church is not only a foretaste of the goal of ministry, but is the principal instrument of ministry.

My overall purpose in this chapter has been to set the discussion of ministry in the human enterprise itself, with an understanding of the fundamental nature of man's collective nature and God's use of the social phenomena. It was to the people of Israel that Jesus came, it was upon the community of a hundred and twenty that the Holy Spirit fell at Pentecost, and the Scriptures themselves are the books of the church. There is no such thing as the isolated whole man, any more than that ministry is what one person does to other people. If we are concerned for the Spirit speaking to man today, we must begin with a concern for the city of man.

2
THE MEANING

Immediately following the experience of Pentecost, Peter preached to the Jews, the same Jews who had just accused him and his associates of being drunk.

> Men of Israel, listen to me: I speak of Jesus of Nazareth, a man singled out by God and made known to you through miracles, portents, and signs, which God worked among you through him, as you know well. When he had been given up to you, by the deliberate will and plan of God, you used heathen men to crucify and kill him. . . . The Jesus we speak of has been raised by God, as we can all bear witness. Exalted thus with God's right hand, he received the Holy Spirit from the Father, as was promised, and all that you now see and hear flows from him (Acts 2:22–23, 32–33).

This selection of Peter's sermon, whether it be the recollection or the literary composition of Luke, is the first recorded act of ministry after the empowering of the church following the death and exaltation of Jesus. The sermon itself, as well as others in Acts, embodies the Petrine proclamation *(kerygma)* or Gospel. It is clearly a statement about Peter's understanding of the meaning of a common experience of those persons living in Jerusalem at that time: the event of the execution of the well-known teacher and miracle-worker, Jesus of Nazareth.

Over the past fifty years the ministry of the church has gone through some very painful self-examination. This is self-evident, even without the point having been made repeatedly. What is not quite so obvious is the relation of this identity crisis to the more general theological turmoil of the last hundred and fifty years and the problem of Christian meaning.

For example, the wide popularity of Carl Rogers' client-centered therapy in seminaries and in pastors' studies in the 50s was not just the evidence of the rise (and fall) of a particular mode of psychotherapy, but was the expression of a need at that time for ministry to find an identity which did not commit itself to some theological position that many found difficult to accept. "God talk" could be avoided in the name of good counseling.

The principal mentor of pastoral care at this time, and a man still rightly admired, was Seward Hiltner. In his profound influence upon ministry from the late 40s on, particularly in the clinical pastoral education movement, Hiltner and his associates were often used to support the notion that ministry involved no theological *a priori,* but that the act of ministering was one of listening, reflecting, and clarifying the content implicit in the pastoral event. The result was that *explicit* transcendence was removed from much ministry. Peter's sermon would have been considered a *bad* example of appropriate pastoral care, particularly with its very judgmental tones. Actually this position is not entirely what Hiltner advocates. He writes:

> When communicating the gospel is viewed in this way [*i.e.* in terms of field theory], two things become possible. First, that which is distinctive, unique, saving, and ultimate about the message can and must be emphasized, albeit with a humility fully aware that any man's knowledge and assimilation of it is limited. Second, all true human knowledge (and ways of receiving knowledge) can and must be examined for possible light they send upon our *reception* of saving truth over and above their autonomous significance.[1]

Hiltner did make shepherding the organization principle of all pastoral theology, and shepherding in his system is an operation-centered activity, rather than a logic-centered activity.[2] Given the temper of the times, with the battle raging between the heavy-handed theology of neoorthodoxy and the discovery of the human sciences in liberal Protestantism, it was almost inevitable that Hiltner's more balanced approach would be lost in the application of his priorities by his disciples.

Perhaps the problem was rendered more acute when Barth's theology and neo-orthodoxy lost its impetus, and in the 60s radical theology came in vogue. For example, in 1964 the World Student Christian Federation issued through its general committee the statement, "The Christian Community in the Academic World," which described the mission of the church to the higher education as one of *presence.* The committee described what it meant by "presence."

> It does not mean that we are simply there; it tries to describe the adventure of being there in the name of Christ, often anonymously, listening before we speak, hoping that men will recognize Jesus for what he is and stay where they are, involved in the fierce fight against all that dehumanizes, ready to act against

demonic powers, to identify with the outcast, merciless in ridiculing modern idols and new myths.[3]

Except for the regrettable reference to myth, there is nothing objectionable *per se* in this definition of presence, and much that is very good. It does not reveal a developed Christology, but it is certainly Christian in its commitment. Yet I heard this statement frequently used as a defense for divorcing ministry from explicit Christian witness; and debate raged for the next two volumes of *Student World* as to what "presence" might mean. There was a chronic identity crisis in theological circles which had the peculiar effect of emptying ministry of most transcendent meaning and sending it whoring after false gods —something to which ministry is still heir today.[4] Thomas Jackson's recent account of his disillusionment with his ministry, *Go Back, You Didn't Say May I,* strikes me as very much an illustration of this point.[5]

In a recent article in the *Christian Century,* Don Browning wrote: "The minister seems to be preoccupied with learning how to do *something* and the specialist with learning how to do *everything.* . . . Surely such promiscuous experimentation with method and technique betrays a lack of critical theological stability."[6] Browning is right. Theology has always been suspect and for good reason. It can easily become an end in itself, providing very little help to the Christian life. The alternative—no theology—however, is far worse. Richard Rolle (1300–1349) gave an eloquent protest over six hundred years ago to theology, which no anti-intellectual has surpassed since.

> An old woman can be more expert in the love of God—and less worldly too— than your theologian with his useless studying. He does it for vanity, to get a reputation, to obtain stipends and official positions. Such a fellow ought to be entitled not 'Doctor' but 'Fool'![7]

A contemporary equivalent of this was told me by a colleague at the University of the South. He related how he announced with excitement to an English rural vicar for whom he had worked for some two years that he was leaving to study theology. After an awkward pause, the vicar replied, "Yes, once before I knew a man who started a Christian and became a 'Doctor of Theology.' " I cannot speak for the vicar, but Rolle, like many people who abrogate theology, was a victim of his feelings, some of which were sublime, but most of which led him into a chronic dyspepsia. Religionists without theology generally become either dangerous enthusiasts, wrong-headed eccentrics, or cynics. Theology and the balanced systematic religious meaning it constitutes is essential for consistent, effective ministry.

By definition, ministry is tied to theology or, at least, what we understand the experience of God to mean. It is action based upon the meaning of God's presence in history. Peter's sermon is an explicit statement of his perception of the meaning of the events surrounding Jesus' death; which he understood not to end with his demise, but was followed by Jesus' resurrection, exaltation, and the sending forth of the Holy Spirit. This is a theological statement. The very fact that he was among those who appeared to be drunk, that as a Galilean fisherman he was preaching to the sophisticated citizens of Jerusalem, and that subsequently he would leave his family and go to the ends of the world to die a martyr's death—all of this was an action drawn from that perception of the meaning of Jesus' death. We may want to "demythologize" Peter's words about miracles, deliberate will, and the right hand of God—or we may not. This does not, however, take away from the fact that on the basis of what he preached, he acted, and his very actions were an expression of a certain meaning.

It is time we stopped talking about "imposing our meaning on others"; it is time we stopped feeling guilty about God-talk; and it is time we realize that there is no such thing as an empty presence. If behavior is more than the result of either our endocrine glands or our conditioning and has an element of will in it, then whatever we do—including being present at a hospital bed, manning a picket line, or working at the ladies' bazaar—is an expression of what we understand life to mean. In a very real sense what we do is inevitably an "imposition of meaning," "God-talk," and a presence full of meaning. If we do it as the church's ministry, then it has to do with what we understand Christ means, as experienced then and now.

We have all heard it said that it is not what a person thinks but what he does which is important or makes a difference. We identify truth somehow in behavior. The dichotomy is false and highly dangerous. A person does what he thinks, or at least what he holds as the meaning of the world of his experience. Seminarians who think all they need are practical courses, or authors who write that seminaries and their academic subjects are unnecessary for ministry, simply miss the point. Before we can act for Christ we have to know what Christ means to the Christian community—now, but also in the past, because the past provides much of the material for understanding Christ now.

In this chapter I shall begin with action as a class of human behavior under which falls ministry, and show how this is an expression of meaning. Secondly, I shall discuss the substance of meaning, relating it to the world in which we live. Finally, I shall speak to the source of meaning in experience, which will then tie in with the fourth vector of the ecclesial reality and lead to the next chapter on religious experience, or mystery. Perhaps some will recognize that I have discussed the same subject at much greater length and in a different order and with different emphasis in my book, *To Speak of God.*

ACTION OUT OF MEANING

Ministry is a species of action. We owe the classical definition of action to the German sociologist, Max Weber (1864–1920). "In 'action' is included all human behavior when and insofar as the acting individual attaches a subjective meaning to it. Action in this sense may be either overt or purely inward or subjective."[8] In other words, action is a choice of the willing subject, based upon the meaning he attaches to his experience. Not to do something is, therefore, as much an "action" as the process of doing something.

As scholasticism teaches, to know what something is you must first know what it is not. Action is not behavior that results from spontaneous electro-chemical messages within the central nervous system. Breathing is not an action, salivating is not an action, and a penile erection is not an action. Action is also not a behavior that results from conditioning. A phobic reaction to cats is not an action, the confusion of the identities of my two daughters, while disconcertingly frequent, is not an action, and my morning shower is often not an action.

Weber saw action as closely tied to rational subjectivity. In this book I will consider it the result of meaning as a whole, of which logical thinking or reason and its conceptual products are only a part. This means that action as a result of conscious willing slips into action which is less conscious, less choate, and more the result of a human will working out of feeling and intuition. What I mean by feeling and intuition, as well as thinking and a fourth category not yet mentioned, common sense, will become more evident in the next section. At this point an example of action out of feeling or intuition might help. If the smell of cape jasmine, a heavy-scented flowering shrub that grows in the South, leads me to a depressed demeanor that I identify with funerals and consequently I refuse to go to a party, the result is an action. If a dream I had the night before leads me to be particularly responsive to my daughter's departure from home that day, this also is an action. The first begins with a feeling, the second with an intuition.

Since action is subjectively willed, then the relationship of reasoned action to less choate action finds some explanation in the distinction that Leslie Farber has made between "first will" and "second will."[9] The first will relates to feeling and intuition. For example, we might insult our hostess at a party in the small morning hours after some extended drinking, having found her then and at previous meetings intolerably overbearing. Second will is related to reason or common sense. For example, after the party we awaken about noon to incredible remorse and the need to make amends, since we recall that we have offended the wife of our employer. Both wills beget action, and it is a possible consequence that ministry is not a result of just logical or even common-sense meaning, but of feeling and intuition.

In speaking of action as a result of the subjectivity of the actor I have inevitably referred to meaning, be it reason, common sense, feeling, or intuition. We need to make that necessary link between action and meaning now, leaving the further explication of meaning itself to the next section.

Action is something done, but first it is something planned. The subject projects a plan of doing into his future. Alfred Schutz, the German-American sociologist and phenomenologist, wrote: "An action is conscious in the sense that, before we carry it out, we have a picture in our mind of what we are going to do."[10] This is what planning is all about, whether or not we speak of the science of planning or ask our spouse at the breakfast table, "What are your plans for the day?"

But where does the plan or picture come from? *What we project in the future can only be that which lies within the meaning of our experience.* Put another way, we can only willfully do (act) in accordance with what sense we make of all that is going on within and around us. Columbus sailed across the Atlantic and opened the New World to European exploitation and settlement. Why did not someone do it centuries before? The technology was available. The Scandinavians made the trip, but nothing came of it. It can be argued that there *coalesced* in Columbus and his supporters an understanding of their world that made the trip, further trips, the settlement, and the trade all a possibility for action. There was enough in what Columbus understood of the world to make the action a possibility, as well as to inspire others to follow his initial action.

Action is the result of a projection into the future of a picture that is drawn from the interpretation of past experience. Breakthroughs such as Columbus's trip are the result more of intuitive planning—serendipity is a word for it—than reasoned planning. The happy convergence of images, perhaps never before put together, which while vague in their outline, offer sufficient promise to be pursued in detail—this is the intuition projection of an act. It is like viewing the purple mountains in the distance—with *imagined* cool forests and rippling brooks—across the parched desert. We pick our way carefully, willing to take the risk, not too sure of what we will find when we get there. This is as much action as following a computer program that gives us a detailed map of what to expect on the way and what we will find when we get "there." It is also just as much of an action as that based on common sense, such as knowing not to thrust a hand blindly into a waste container on a snake-infested golf course. (A bit of common-sense meaning that one unfortunate partner of mine lacked on a recent game on the golf course at the University of the South, resulting in a copperhead attached to his thumb.)

Action is a means of testing our meaning. If a person does something on the basis of what he understands is not only desirable but true, and that action fails, then "it's back to the drawing board." The "drawing board" is the locus for projecting action. If, for example, we understand the experience of warts to be the result of handling toads and that swamp water will remove them, and if we act accordingly and nothing happens, then a reasonable person will ask himself: Is it true that toads give warts and swamp water removes them? Perhaps the virus interpretation of the reason for warts is better and will lead us to do something different or to know that it is best to do nothing at all (which is still an action). As Thomas Kuhn suggests, new breakthroughs in scientific paradigms are the result of a building pressure produced by an increasing empirical residue or surds (*unexplained* things happening) during scientific operations or experimental action.[11]

While not all action has ethical implications, ethics—"the science which seeks to bring sensitivity and method to the human task of discovering moral value"[12]—is concerned with framing that understanding of our world which will give a basis for projecting a picture of what to do that our actions may further man's true end. This is why I would consider moral theology an explication of fundamental and systematic theology. The method of removing warts is not in itself an ethical question. The unwillingness to employ blacks is an action with profound ethical implications, related to our understanding of man *vis-à-vis* God.

It has become popular in recent years to speak of "consciousness raising" in the face of ethical issues. If I understand what is meant by this term, it correctly judges the source of ethical action as related to our *awareness* of what is happening about us. In the early days of the racial issue, as I experienced it in the "deep South," too often the opposing factions assaulted one another with programs for action. When we did have a rare quiet conversation to-gether, it became very apparent that what the world *meant* to each faction was remarkably different. The task became that of deepening the awareness in order to provide a picture which would make ethical action possible.

In traditional moral theology it has long been pointed out that we cannot judge an action purely upon the basis of observable behavior. This again illustrates the necessary link between what we do and what we understand of our meaning. One aspect of an ethical decision is the intention, which is the projected act as we see it accomplished. Many of us are familiar with Joseph Fletcher's illustrations of obvious exceptions to general norms, which he uses to argue against natural law. I am not concerned here for that particular debate, but Fletcher's illustrations can demonstrate my point. For example, a married German woman in a Russian prison camp after World War II had repeated sexual relations with another prisoner. This was an immoral act according to most standards. She knew, however, from what was happening around her and from what she heard from her husband and children back home, that this was one form of behavior which, if she became pregnant, could effect her release and her reunion with the family that needed her back home. We have to examine her intentions or the projected action as she pictured it in completion.

A crucial issue in action is, therefore, the meaning upon which it is based. At the same time, an ethical action is not only judged by its intentions, but also by its consequences. Is the completed action achieved and is it a good thing, or is our meaning inadequate to what is happening? Another Fletcher illustration is the woman staff member of a western European American embassy, who is asked by our government to become the mistress of an important Russian diplomat in order to obtain secrets. It sounds like a wonder-ful sacrifice of virtue for security; but are important Russian diplomats so stupid as not to foresee this possibility and to guard state secrets amid orgasmic ecstasy? The meaning seems to me very inadequate or poorly framed.

This is not a book on ethics, of course, but on ministry. Ministry has to do with ethics, as I shall discuss in the last chapter, but in this section I have been concerned that we understand that ministry is a species of action and that we see that action as necessarily linked to meaning. We cannot engage in ministry without *a priori* meaning. Since we are speaking of Christian ministry, that meaning must, to be true to itself, incarnate the transcendent. Certainly to speak of "incarnating the transcendent" is to say a great deal, which perhaps presents difficulties to some in a secular age. I do not, however, want it to say too much. I am speaking now of a process and not referring to any substantive forms of that incarnation.

PLAUSIBLE MEANING AND EFFECTIVE MINISTRY

Up to this point I have been speaking of meaning, assuming the reader had a general understanding of what I intend. We use the word in everyday language in a popular sense as what we interpret to be the significance, sense, or remembrance of our experience. I do not question the general definition, but I want the reader to understand that meaning is used also to describe a very specific thing: the product of the act of knowing. Meaning is the result of the subject's interaction with his environment—that is, the world of phenomena or sense data—and has an existence apart from the subject (as this written page exists apart from me) and from the environment it represents. We live out of our meaning. Without it, according to the Austrian psychotherapist, Viktor Frank, we become neurotic and incapable of constructive action. Yet meaning inevitably becomes reified. It becomes a thing in itself. Therefore, while meaning is the source of human action, it also can be less a servant and more a tyrant. This raises the issue of plausibility, which involves: 1) The relation between the apparent referent of meaning and the actual referent; 2) the freedom of the community to distinguish dead from living meaning; and 3) the skill to convey new meaning to the eternal experience of God.

At the beginning of this chapter I described Peter's initial act of ministry. He spoke to the "chosen people" of God, the children of Israel, concerning their God; but, they read his meaning as the language of a drunken man. They were captured in their own meaning, which said more about their pride than it did about the God they purported to worship. Peter, on the other hand, was free of the orthodoxy of the Pharisees which had brought so many of his fellow Jews to this lifeless expectation of God. And he was able to identify in the tradition those images that presented Jesus to his hearers in a new light, which not everybody judged "crazy," for, as we are told, some three thousand persons were baptized as a result of his words. Peter's meaning was both plausible and yet able to convey surprise.

The test of the plausibility of meaning is the effect of the action it begets in relation to the intention of the actor. What is the goal of ministry? In the first section of the last chapter I suggested that it is the freedom to become the whole man. Some Christian meaning can appear to the society in which we live as "crazy," but, in fact, it can serve God's purpose in freeing man from the slavery of a one-dimensional techno-barbaric culture. Other Christian meaning can be taken for granted in our culture, but in fact only contributes to the domestication of the God revealed in Christ and frees no one. It is no longer plausible, if it ever was, in terms of the original experience of Christian community. There is always the problem of talk of God that says nothing. Far worse is Christian meaning which is not plausible and which we do not know is killing us. There will be a running contrast between creatively "crazy" meaning and banal, destructive God-talk throughout this study.

Meaning is the product of the interaction of the subject with his environment or the objective world. It is the "sense" a person or persons make of what-is-happening-to-them in relation to meaning, under the name of "experience." In this section I am concerned specifically about meaning itself. For when we ask ourselves or others: What is true? What is real? we reply with meaning, to which we have given a life beyond and above ourselves or the succession of data impinging upon our sensorium. Meaning is congruent with what we believe is. This is neither idealism, which believes the real is within the consciousness of the subject, nor naïve realism, which holds that we have a direct perception and knowledge of the essence of the objective environment. It is sometimes known as "critical realism."

The infrastructure of meaning consists of an arrangement of images that represent the experience of the objective world by the subject. The nature of these representations I have discussed at some length in *To Speak of God,* but it is necessary to review them here.[13] I will be referring repeatedly to them in this book.

Representations consist of images, located within the environment, present or remembered, which are adopted and referred to the experience of an object or the relationship between objects as perceived through the senses of the subject, and which bestow an order upon that experience. If those images which constitute the representations of our experience and make up the infrastructure of our meaning have no ability to communicate the intended meaning to others, then the meaning itself lacks plausibility. A small child touches the element on the stove, experiences pain, and the mother says, "Hot!" "Hot" becomes an image from our language—language being a part of the cultural environment—which represents and orders that pain. It does it for almost anybody who speaks English. Later the representation becomes qualified by relating it to other images, which refines the referent. "Hot stove" is one thing; "hot tamale" is another very different thing.

Not all representations are of the same nature. This is a very important

44

point. They fall within a spectrum of reference, which have at the extreme poles a physiological terminal and an ideological terminal. I owe the basic conceptualization to the English-American anthropologist, Victor Turner, but I have altered it somewhat in the course of applying it to Western culture rather than primitive cultures.[14] As I have noted, representations run from a highly physiological pole to a highly ideological pole. The former are what I mean by "symbols," and the latter, in a pure or, as Turner says, "dissolved" form, are "signs." A single image can carry a symbol and sign quality at the same time; this is especially true of lexemes or words. For example, that ancient word of unquestioned Germanic origin, "shit," conveys far more than its synonym of Latin derivation, "excrement."

A sign is a representation that is precise or univocal, ideological, and inert. Signs are cultural or personal inventions. What I mean by this is that groups or individuals can and do bring them into being as representations of a given referent. To say that a sign is univocal indicates that it has a one-to-one relationship to its referent. It is precise, as is the function of computer language. This is to say that it has a digital quality as opposed to an analogical or metaphorical function. One of the debates my wife and I have as we "bird-watch" from the porch of our home is whether or not one of this summer's birds is a scarlet or a summer tanager. If we could get a clear enough look, we could settle the argument, because the bird book leaves no question. It is a book of signs.

Signs are ideological or normative. This is to say that they are the product of a given culture or have an acceptance of a given culture. Sometimes they are limited to groups within the culture. A sign is, therefore, rather "brittle," and the more limited it is the shorter the lifespan. It loses plausibility quicker than a symbol. Most language has sign value, although it may almost possess symbolic power, but then so do traffic signals, the "squiggles" in a mathematical equation, and certain gestures—what the officials do at a football or baseball game, Erving Goffman's interpersonal "tie-signs," and the gesticulations of the orchestra director.[15] Yet they are all ideological.

A sign is inert, which means that it does not partake of the life of its referent. It simply points. H_2O is the chemical sign for water. Reading it does not involve us in the life within water. Writing H_2O will never quench your thirst. Signs are powerless. If you can think of a sign with power, it has ceased to be a mere sign and has acquired some symbolic quality.

I think it is helpful to accept a differentiation among signs, with one major alteration made by Raymond Firth, an English anthropologist. That exception would be to disallow symbol as a species of sign. There are three kinds of signs: indices, signals, and icons.[16] An index exists where a sequential relation is inferred. Examples would be a signature at the end of a letter, the word "table" for all flat-topped pieces of furniture with legs, or David representing the Israelites. A signal points to a consequential response. A stoplight, a starter's pistol shot, or the "come hither" look of the attractive woman at the next table —these would be signals. An icon is the intention of a sensory likeness. The poems of Gerard Manley Hopkins were icons; but where "successful" they were also symbols, which reveals the tendency of icons to slip into symbolism. Vivaldi's *The Four Seasons* is an icon, according to Firth, as are all "icons" in the Eastern church's tradition.[17]

A symbol is a representation that is multivocal and multivalent, meaning that it is highly ambiguous. It is dynamic, and is not something made or invented. This last point is debated, but I would tend to say that for a sign to become a symbol it has to lose its cultural self-consciousness. For example, if the American flag is now a symbol, it was *not* that when George Washington got delivery from Betsy Ross.

The words "multivocal" and "multivalent" give problems. If we think of "multi" as signifying "many," then we need only note that "vocal" comes from the Latin word *vox,* meaning voice or speech or, by inference, that to which voice or speech refers; and "valent" comes from the Latin, *valentia,* meaning "strength" or "power." A symbol has many referents, some clearly denoted, and others only connoted. Water is a good illustration of multivocality. It denotes cleansing, life, fluidity, etc.; and it connotes birth, chaos, death, etc. A symbol also evokes many feelings. An automobile wreck, with bodies of dead or severely injured persons, is an example. We all know the fascination and the revulsion we feel before this sight. The multivalence of a symbol, as well as its multivocality, can be summed up by saying that a symbol is ambiguous. It embraces contradiction and paradox.

This means that a symbol is better able to acknowledge the fact that no meaning captures what it seeks to represent in what-is-happening-to-us, our experience. If "E" equals "experience" and "M" equals "meaning," it is *not* true that $M = E$ under any conditions. There is always a surd—literally that which is voiceless or cannot be given expression—that emerges in the attempt to constitute meaning. This surd is the result of our inability to be aware of all our experience, and the inability of the images available to give expression to that which we could, in fact, otherwise be aware of. Therefore, if "S" equals "surd," then the true equation is $S + M = E$. Symbols are much more capable of pointing to the surd!

A symbol is also physiological and tends to be related to the body, its feelings, needs, and mystery. The body is generally an ambiguous part of our environment, which is to say that we have mixed feelings about it and what it demands of us. I suspect the most powerful symbol in man's life is his sexuality, and certainly death and birth or the common meal are powerful body symbols as well. Not all symbols are this obviously physiological, and the less universal they are the more they are removed from the body. Yet they all do possess a tellurian or earthy quality bordering on the vulgar.

The ambiguity and physiological qualities of symbols are a key to their dynamic quality. As symbol is the means of participation in what they represent, Christ is the primal symbol of God; he is the means of participating in God. There is a life in a symbol, which is not just its own but its referent as well. There is a magnetic power in a symbol, which is to say that we are drawn or pulled into participation to the degree that we are open to that symbol. Whitehead has spoken of the symbolic as "the lure of feeling." The Sanskrit for symbol is *paroksa,* that which is "beyond the eye."

A symbol is a social event; that is, it emerges from various social configurations. Philip Wheelwright has said that symbols have five "grades of comprehensiveness" in regard to their social origin. I do not find his first category helpful: "the presiding image of a particular poem." Wheelwright is an English scholar, and perhaps that is why such a category appeals to him and not to me. The remaining four categories, it seems to me, do illuminate the nature of symbols.[18] Each one in turn has a greater universality, and consequently a greater performance, or lifespan and power. To the degree that the symbol is more comprehensive, its plausibility lasts longer.

First there is the personal symbol. The other day I was tending our tomato plants, and as I brushed against them an odor arose which immediately transformed me back to my childhood. I had all the feelings of a small boy, gardening beside his mother, and watching with pride the ripening tomatoes that she had encouraged him to plant. That odor is a personal symbol.

Second, there are the symbols of ancestral vitality. Mary Magdalene is a symbol of Christian literary tradition, which in turn partakes of a greater symbolic tradition. There is the persistent play in the Christian tradition of her as redeemed wanton and the sexual lover of Jesus. It was not in *Jesus Christ, Superstar* that this first surfaced, by any means.

Third, there is the symbol within the cultural range. Martin Luther King was carried to his grave on an old, flatbed wagon, pulled by two mules. For anyone brought up in the South the symbolic power of that image was without question. It spoke far more than all the oratory on that hot April day.

Fourth, there are the archetypal symbols. These are those most purely tellurian or physiological. They belong to the biogrammar or genetic inheritance of man. I have named three examples already: sexuality, death and birth, and the common meal.

My argument is that all meaning, be it a textbook in solid state physics or an Australian aborigine stroking his chirunga, is composed of a complex network of representations, possessing various degrees of signative and symbolic purpose. The balance within meaning of signs and symbols gives it a certain quality. Symbols are related to feeling and intuition or imagination. Signs are typical of common sense and are the essential tools of thinking.

Felt meaning is the powerful meaning. It is what motivates us. *Intuitive* meaning is the stuff of dreams—waking or sleeping—the hunch, the sudden breakthrough. This book is about intuitive meaning, as the title reveals. *Common-sense* meaning is "what everyone knows." It is the meaning mediated to us by the society without our questioning. It is the root of stereotypical or restricted meaning. *Thinking* is the act of reason, the logic and its product: the concept. All four of these are an essential part of any complete meaning, which I have discussed at some length in *To Speak of God.*[19]

What needs to be pursued further here is the fact that all representations are found as images within the environment we experience or have experienced and remembered. The value of a meaning is dependent upon the nature of its infrastructure *vis-à-vis* the images within a given society, and what those images are, in fact, intended to represent. Reality is a social construct. *The plausibility of a symbol or a sign is a function of the environment and the perception of its people.* This is a crucial principle, and one that many of us are very familiar with—at least in its application—from the revision of liturgical rites. A systematic grasp of the point is essential, however.

I have said that meaning and reality are synonymous, and that meaning and reality are subjective to the extent that they are the product of the subject's interaction with the objective environment. Peter Berger, to whom I owe the notion of the "plausibility structure," makes the observation; "The subjective reality of the world hangs on the thin thread of conversation."[20] In other words, the possibility of any clarity of meaning which can be shared is dependent on our willingness to draw on a common source of possible representations of our experience. In preaching to the Jews, Peter both did and did not do this, since some believed and others called him drunk. This does not mean that we must agree in our respective meanings, but that there is the possibility of leading each other to a new understanding which begets a fuller life. This is to say that our signs and symbols have a common ground.

In the face of this, two things need to be added, both of which relate to the content of meaning and its plausibility.

First, man is an historical being. Meaning is historical. Images are subject to change and so, therefore, are signs and symbols. For society and culture change constantly, although at different rates at different periods in history. Since all images are functions of society and culture as well as consciousness, not only are they born and die, *but they do so at differing rates.* If all representations had the same lifespan, we still would have a problem, but not as complex as the one we do have. For example, it seems to me quite obvious that liturgical revision is a response to the death of certain liturgical signs. Unfortunately, some revisions have done away with *symbols* that are still very much alive to many—the very *sounds* of Latin or sixteenth-century English prose.

This is even more complicated by the fact that meaning is a thing-in-itself having a life of its own. It is, as I have said, reified. Like a child of a mother and father, it lives on long after what has produced it is dead. This results in one of three possibilities: the death of meaning, the deflection of meaning, or the alienation of meaning.

The most harmless result is that meaning *dies.* For example, prohibition, the meaning begotten of post-frontier American Protestantism, died, and the twenty-first amendment was its obituary. It was no longer plausible to the American society to forbid the production and consumption of alcoholic beverages, for the social reality which made the idea plausible no longer prevailed as a dominant force in American culture.

The meaning can, however, also become *deflected.* I am using this word in a technical sense of my own making, referring to what seems to me a very important notion, often missed in ministry studies. It describes the phenomenon in which the same images that were used in a culture to represent the experience of one thing, or a configuration of certain things, come to be used to represent some other thing or a configuration quite different. To use a trivial example: What does the bride's feeding a piece of cake to the groom at a wedding reception represent? I asked a knowledgable friend and he suggested it indicates that she is now the "chief cook and bottle washer." It happens at almost every wedding, and I suspect most people only think of it as "cute." Its original referent, however, dating from the Roman republic, was the acceptance by the bride of the groom's hearth gods. Since every family had their own gods, the bride baked the cake on her husband's hearth and fed it to him to acknowledge her willingness to serve the gods of his hearth. It was the high point of the marital rite.

A far more serious deflection is represented in the contemporary expressions of American revivalism, as exemplified in the Billy Graham Crusade. I say "serious" because I think the effect of this deflection is to bind a large segment of American Christianity to a sectarianism which is ultimately self-defeating. Donald Clelland and his associates carried out a socioeconomic survey of the persons attending the Billy Graham Crusade in Knoxville, Tennessee, in 1970. They found a positive correlation there, as compared to a random sample of the Knoxville population, with the old middle class. Their conclusions were that the function of that "crusade" was to legitimate a life style that is "individualistic, nonintellectual, pietistic, familistic," and "definitely at odds with the cosmopolitanism of corporate and intellectual elites."[21] Those attending were, as a rule, wealthier and better educated than the norm, and yet apparently both their financial power and intellectual insight were employed only to seek to reinforce old answers to new problems.

My point is *not* to argue against this neofundamentalist core over against my own ideological commitments, but to suggest that what was done at those assemblies was not so much to confront people with the transcendent Gospel of Christ as to promote an ideological rally. Should one want to argue against the life style of the old middle class, as represented in that assembly, one would appear as arguing against God. This then faces us with a moral issue.

Finally, meaning can become *alienated,* by which I mean it becomes completely divorced from the life of any significant dimension of the culture. The separation between deflection and alienation is uncertain, but by the latter term I intend the existence of a meaning that, while dead, remains in the cultural consciousness or preconsciousness and putrifies and poisons the culture. As Alfred Whitehead once commented, "Knowledge does not keep any better than fish."[22] An example would be the idea that women are somehow subhuman—an interpretation inherited from Hellenistic cultural developments and perpetuated by the guilty conscience of the church. Its effect has been to corrupt justice and to destroy persons, while being something that obviously our culture cannot support in any positive way.

Shlomo Deshen, a social anthropologist at Tel Aviv University, provides a confirmation of this difficult point in regard to the death, deflection, and alienation of religious meaning. Working out of the phenomenon of religious change among the North African Jewish immigrants to Israel, Deshen identifies a fourfold typology of alteration within symbolic action in regard to

50

religious meaning. I find this particularly helpful, since he is striving for an abstraction that provides a basis for cross-cultural analysis and verification. Deshen's argument is that in religious change the symbol system constituting an existential order experiences 1) eradication, 2) creation, 3) innovation, and 4) profanation.* What he calls eradication I speak of as death. Innovation, which Deshen defines as "changing the range of experience in which a symbol applies," I have described as deflection. Profanation becomes my alienation. His definition of profanation is obscure, but his illustration is not. He tells how a maker of prayer shawls in contemporary Israel markets his wears in cheap polyethylene bags with a message imprinted on the bags implying that such containers must be treated as sacred objects. This is in the context of a growing interest in orthodoxy in that country. The justification of this is a nonsensical application of ritual law dependent upon the ignorance of the purchaser, which only serves the commercial interests of the manufacturer.

Deshen writes as an acknowledged agnostic, which may explain in part why his typology and my terms reveal a different orientation. I have an admitted commitment to a symbol system I think is being abused. Furthermore, his category of the creation of symbols (number two above), which does not relate either to death, deflection, or alienation, is also a particular investment of mine for which I am arguing throughout this study.

A second thing that needs to be said in relation to the content of meaning and its plausibility is that none of us lives within a homogeneous culture. The images that belong to one culture do not belong to another, and, therefore, signs and symbols that convey meaning in one setting are meaningless in another unless we make the effort to understand and translate them. In other words, pluralism is here to stay. We cannot pretend there is one true meaning to life even if we say there is one, true God who is above all mentality or thought. There are many meanings or, as Alfred Schutz says, "multiple realities" of relative truth in proportion to their participation in God's truth.[23] The effort of understanding and translating between "realities" is very enriching, but it requires a degree of sophistication that man, up until the time of rapid communication and ease of transportation—that is, within the last hundred years—has not had to confront.

Thomas Luckmann has argued that the effect of the multiplicity of reality is to reduce consensus in religious meaning to the level of the early Roman republic. The "sacred cosmos" or "canopy" that legitimates our life style at

*Shlomo Deshen and Moshe Shokeid, *The Predicament of Homecoming: Cultural and Social Life of North African Immigrants in Israel* (Ithaca: Cornell University Press, 1974), pp. 155–165.

the ultimate level extends not much further than the family. Everyone carries about his own familiar "gods," who can be quite different than the "gods" of his neighbor. Appeal to a common action based upon a common religious meaning becomes an exercise in frustration.[24] Consequently, the temptation is to seek some less transcendent lever on the behavior of our associates: self-interest, chauvinism, psychotherapeutic manipulation, fear.

This leads to the conclusion of this section, which is that for ministry to be effective in the sense of a Christian or incarnated and yet transcendent-in-referent ministry, it has to take account of the problems of plausibility. It cannot work out of a meaning whose signs and symbols are dead, deflected, or alienated from the culture. It must also take into account the pluralism of our times. It is therefore a ministry that is rooted as never before in a conscious reflection upon the meaning of religious experience for our times. In order to provide a continuity and communicability, this act of reflection has to be both sensitive to the past and responsive to the present cultural complexity. The art of building within the Christian collectivity a meaning whose infrastructure possesses representations that have viability within the culture becomes an overweening need. This act is further complicated by the fact that this reflective base of ministry has to take into account the function of both signs and symbols, constantly adjusting for the fact that the latter are more likely to have a longer lifespan than the former.

At the same time, that *plausibility* must not be confused with the *reduction* of meaning to the categories of the given sociocultural world. The infrastructure of religious meaning leans heavily upon the intuitive and symbolic, which a society may well judge as "crazy." Simultaneously, intuitive meaning can express the effervescence of the social phenomena in such a way that the open person of that culture is led to affirm and participate in a meaning that draws him to the horizon of his knowing and then beyond. Another way of putting it is to say that a meaning can be both plausible and account for the surd that lies outside of any cultural reduction. Religious meaning, which does *not* point to the surd becomes idolatry, confusing a finite construct with the infinite being.

In the seventh chapter, in which the subject of "story" is discussed, the distinction will be made between *closed* and *open* stories. One way of thinking of the difference is that a closed story is a reductionism, even to the point of ceasing to be plausible. An open story is plausible, even if "crazy," but never reduces its referent to the narrative. It is always a metaphor or symbol, not an analysis or a sign.

52

Ministry which divorces itself from this theological enterprise, in the sense of taking religious meaning seriously in all its forms (felt, common-sense, thinking, and intuitive), is courting disaster. It is surrendering the basis of all action of ministry to sentiment, undisciplined thought, and unexamined common sense. It is, therefore, extremely unfortunate that over the last fifty years this has been precisely what has been happening in some quarters. Such ministerial action is doomed to detach itself from the Christian Gospel: from transcendence become immanent or the incarnational presence of God.

Therefore, in discussing ministry as a species of action, rooted in the subjective meaning of the contemporary church, it must be said first that ministry requires a church that lives in its culture(s) with a sensitivity to those images and their relations to one another that can embody, clarify, and share an incarnational faith—which, in fact, summons us beyond the culture. We must have meaning before we can act effectively, but it must be a plausible meaning. This is, however, only one part of the question in regard to the church and the meaning of the Gospel. A second part must be covered in the last section.

THE OPENNESS OF ECCLESIAL MAN

We are surrounded by what-is-happening-to-us. Man lives in "a continuous coming-to-be and passing-away of heterogeneous qualities.[25] Think of ourselves bombarded by data amounting to thousands of sense impressions each second. The image that comes to my mind is the particles or waves of light that bathe the human organism on earth. All this that is "happening" to us is our *experience*. This is my specific use of that word, and its precise meaning is vital to this study.

Once we grasp the notion in abstract of these thousands-per-second sense impressions constituting our experience, then we need to realize that we are aware at any level of consciousness of only a small fraction of the total number of impressions. The human organism is in itself a *filter* which permits only a portion of what it experiences in the form of phenomena to break into its consciousness. Our meaning, therefore, is not just a function of the content possible in terms of our society and culture, as well as our memory, but it is also a function of what experience we discern in terms of the nature of the filter of our consciousness.

First of all, as I have said, ministry requires a church that lives in its culture(s). I am saying now that it also requires a church which possesses a filter of consciousness that is *open* to data in its experience that bespeaks God.

Obviously, it is not possible for us, as person or group of persons, ever to be aware of all our experience. The "noise" of what is happening around us would drive us very quickly to a psychotic break. There is a certain kind of hearing defect in which a person cannot distinguish what he wants to hear from the surrounding sounds. One can imagine the horror if this very troublesome disease were but an example of a situation where all our sense awareness was flooded by a cacophony of "noise"—sound, visual effects, odor, tactual impressions, and taste.

Some of our sense impressions are filtered out by the organism itself. For example, a dog whistle is based on the fact that dogs can hear a frequency of pitch inaudible to the human ear. So a man can blow the whistle and have his dog come without distracting the neighbors or himself. At the same time the human eye is limited in what it can see. It cannot determine inherent opacity of a substance, because it perceives the reflected and refracted light rather than the transmitted light. Gold appears yellow, for example, because it reflects yellow light, whereas the light it transmits is a bluish green. Our nose is also limited by nature. The ability of a bloodhound to pick up a scent is well known. No human of whom I have any knowledge has the sense of smell to discern the data of the lingering odor of one person, sufficient to follow a day-old trail, much less differentiate it from other odors.

It is equally true that the filter of our consciousness is also a function of our socialization. The perception of our experience is very much shaped for us by what the society, into which we are born and in which we are reared, trains us to perceive from that experience. The Headstart program, for example, which has sought over the last decade to take the children of the disadvantaged and to open for them new dimensions of their world, is based on the assumption that a child can only learn what he has been socialized to see. If a child has never seen an orange in his home, if his family has never spoken of an orange in the presence of this object, the child is not likely to "see" the orange when he confronts it in school.

The Whorf-Sapir hypothesis, named after Edward Sapir (1884–1939), a noted linguist and anthropologist, and his student, Benjamin Whorf (1897–1941), who by trade was a highly skilled fire prevention engineer, supports this contention. Their hypothesis is that language shapes the way in which we filter sense data. Whorf's study was done principally in a comparison between the American Indian tongue of Hopi and Standard Average European (SAE). Hopi does not place objects into spatial or time relations. SAE does. Whorf's thesis is, then, that a pure Hopi speaker will not see the world in spatial or chronological relations, as we do. For example, whether God is "up there," "down there," or "inside there," would not be an issue for a Hopi, as I judge Whorf's hypothesis, since there is no need in Hopi language for a thing to be "there" as opposed to "here" or "anywhere."

Most experiments seem to indicate only a weak validation of the Whorf-Sapir hypothesis, but certainly culture does shape our perceptions of things. For example, this lies at the root of a kind of depression, which not a few people know, resulting from a dislocality reaction. A person moves from one culture to another, and often, in almost unconscious ways, finds himself perceiving the world differently than the population as a whole. The energy expended and the sense of loneliness, in that we have to strain to think as those around us think and we feel rather alienated, can be attributed in large measure to this different socialization.

Max Weber spoke of our age as one of "disenchantment."[26] I would interpret this to mean that contemporary man does not discern in his experience any data that points to the sacred or transcendent. His filters are secularized. Francois Houtart, a French-Belgian Roman Catholic sociologist, has illustrated this in noting that the acceptance of divine instrumentality in our world has largely vanished. For example, he says that we find it incredible that Pius VII (1800–1823) condemned vaccination against smallpox on the grounds that the disease was a visitation of God upon us for our sins, and to thwart God's purpose is to side with Satan. This would be divine natural instrumentality. We also reject divine social instrumentality, Houtart says, but at a later period. No one today would take Pius X (1903–1914) seriously in his condemnation of a mildly socialist movement in France, *Le Sillon*. He objected to it on the grounds that God established the civil order and to advocate change in the governing structures is, therefore, to speak contrary to God's will.

Claims by theologians over the last ten or fifteen years that the very concept of God is meaningless, as well as Dietrich Bonhoeffer's statement that we no longer need a "God of the gaps" (the *deus ex machina*, who pulls man out of his insoluble problems), are illustrative of the disenchantment of our world. They go back as far as the Enlightenment, of which the great French astronomer, Pierre Simon de Laplace (1749–1827) is typical. Asked where God fit into his system, he is reported to have replied, "Sire, I have no need for that hypothesis." I am convinced that this attitude of disenchantment fits into the radical dislocation of the priest in our culture since the Enlightenment.

It is essential to see that my argument is that the "disenchantment" lies, not in experience itself but in the filter of our consciousness, which is a function of our socialization. This is very much related to Stanley Krippner's theory that a sensitivity to ESP is a result of a person's ability to transcend ordinary states of consciousness. The world is disenchanted, not necessarily because God has died, has withdrawn, or has been discovered to be an illusion, but because, among the large majority of people, that data which would lead us to conclude God is present in our experience is quite unconsciously, but effectively, not seen. God is not there because the society says he is not there just as surely as my son's "lost" textbooks are not where I clearly see them on his bed, because for reasons known only to God he cannot see them there.

This is not a new problem. The New Testament term for "clogged filters" is found in St. Mark's explanation of why the Jews did not understand the feeding of the five thousand and the stilling of the sea. Literally, the apostle says: "Their hearts were permanently petrified" (Mark 6:52; see also 8:17; John 12:40; Rom. 9:18; Heb. 3:8; 4:7). The New English Bible gets it closer to our idiom, although with less power, saying, "Their minds were closed." This was the ultimate answer to why so few of the Jews followed Jesus. They were not able, because of their Jewish socialization, to see him for what he really is. For example, in the Fourth Gospel the Jews hear Jesus with minds completely captured in their presuppositions. This is true particularly in 8:21–59, which concludes with the Jews trying to stone Jesus in the passion of frustration.

The opposite of the New Testament expression for possessing a permanently petrified heart—"heart" being a metonym for "mind"—is a Greek word, *anakrinō*, based upon the root *krinō* meaning "to separate, to choose, to judge," but is intensified by the addition of a prefix *(ana)* to the root. Paul speaks of the need to "discern the Body" in the eucharistic meal (1 Cor. 11:19), or he states that to be able to perceive the presence of God in the world one has to be able to "discern" or "judge" (as the New English Bible and Revised Standard Version translate it) by means of the Spirit's presence (1 Cor. 2:14–15). The power of being able to discern is a gift. As I shall argue later, while it is not synonymous with rational thought, it is not exclusive of it, and it is not something we achieve by "trying hard." It is the grace of sight.

It is the nature of man to be able to discern God in his experience. This is what the German Jesuit theologian, Karl Rahner, means when he defines man as *Geist im Welt,* "spirit in the world." This was the title of his first book, and the title of his second catches up the same theme. Man is created to be a "hearer of the word."[27] Man has within him the potentially open filter through which can pass into his consciousness the data that is expressive of the sacred or transcendent. The very act of knowing testifies to this. From the fact that man's horizon of knowledge is constantly expanding, it follows that there is to the best of our judgment an infinite realm of experience and its data to be known. The implication of "infinity"—experience posited as limitless—is indicative of the presence of God, the infinite one, to man. Another way of putting this is that we cannot perceive a limit upon man's potential to know, and, therefore, any assumptions as to the limits of the filter of man's consciousness are precluded. It follows that to be human is to possess a cognitive drive which is, of necessity, open to the world of knowable being, and to live within constantly expanding horizons of knowledge. This is not intended as a "proof" for the existence of God, but as a description of the cognitive process in man as we know it, and as a suggestion that it implies the existence of an experience that transcends man and his environment and which is available to be known.[28]

The ministry of the church, therefore, not only needs to act out of a meaning that possesses a symbol-sign infrastructure that is capable of embodying an incarnated message for our present age, it needs also to implement and to be expressive of a filter of consciousness within the Christian community and society that is open to the experience of God and capable of discerning his presence in that experience. The title of this section "The Openness of Ecclesial Man," was intended to describe this posture of the church. Man is not a mere individual, but is his community. The man in Christ is ontologically bound to the ecclesial reality. His openness to the experience of God is an ecclesial openness. Ministry, as action out of meaning and as the expression of a faith that God is present in history, now means that ecclesial man is vector-four man (see Fig 1, p. 29).

SUMMARY

The fundamental contention of this chapter is that ministry is a species of action rooted in the church's meaning of the experience of God in Christ. When ministry is examined, it is seen to be the projection of that meaning; and that meaning, in turn, is derived from the Christian community's awareness of God's presence in its life. At the beginning of this chapter I illustrated this point by calling attention to Peter's sermon after the experience at Pentecost. Peter was a man of action, but what he did was clearly rooted in his and his community's construction of the meaning of Jesus' life and work, seen through the very intuitive eyes of this Galilean fisherman.

In the analysis of the construction of meaning, two aspects of its construc-

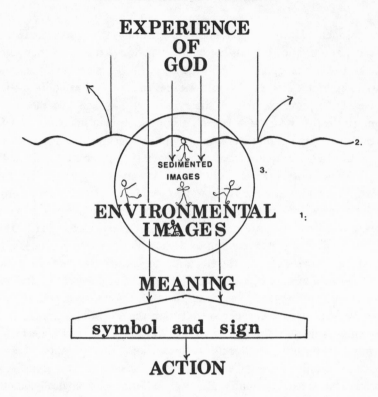

Figure 2

tion have been emphasized. In Figure 2 (page 58), I offer a diagram of the content of this chapter, particularly the last two sections. The movement listed as 1, which is related to the second section of this chapter, illustrates the appropriation of images within the environment with the potential of embodying the meaning of the church's experience. The step identified as 2, which corresponds to the last section of this chapter, depicts the opening of the filters of our consciousness to the degree that it is possible to discern the transcendent present.

In the diagram a third movement is suggested. I have only touched lightly on this with an occasional reference to "memory." This item is actually a concern of the first vector of ministry, the past. For no one comes empty to experience. He brings his inherited representations, some of which still find resonance in the environment and some which do not. In constructing the meaning of our experience in order to ground our ministry in the coherent sense of what God is to our world, we inevitably relate those *sedimented* images—representations which have come to rest in our memories as the waters of history have flowed over us—to the images that lie both within the internal and external environment. The degree to which we are willing to call into question the sediment of our corporate and individual memory, by the presence or absence of related images existing in the environment, has a great deal to say about how plausible is our meaning and how effective is our action of ministry.

When I was in seminary in the early fifties we were told to read *The Parson's Handbook* by Percy Dearmer. The instructor felt that it was a solid guide to effective ministry. The edition then in print, however, still suggested that every parish should keep sheep to provide a trim lawn and that every cleric should wear a nightcap to avoid catching "his death of cold." I do not remember anything else Dearmer said, because on these two counts his pastoral advice was so obviously implausible that I could "hear" nothing else.

The point is that, granting the truth of the first section of the chapter that ministry is rooted in meaning, sensitivity to all three terms of the construction of meaning, as identified in the diagram in Figure 2, (p. 58) is a prior condition of effective ministry. Such sensitivity is, of course, the business of the fourth vector of ministry, which is the immediate concern of this study.

It would seem clear that the next move is to discover how that sensitivity works. There is, however, one area of Figure 2 that can profitably be explored for our purposes first: the meaning of the religious experience. Ministry is ultimately rooted in the mystery that is God and in the affirmation of its ultimate ineffability. As Bonhoeffer has said, our meaning can only speak the penultimate word.[29] Ultimately the community's action rests on simple faith that all will be resolved in the infinite wisdom of him whom we serve. It is essential, therefore, for the purposes of this book that we spend some thought on the nature of the experience of that mystery.

3

THE MYSTERY

Over the past few generations the debate has raged over the relation of religion to Christianity. Beginning with Karl Barth, the contemporary discussion found focus in Dietrich Bonhoeffer's opposition of Christian faith to religious striving.[1] Religion is understood by Barth and Bonhoeffer as man's presumptive attempts to achieve the knowledge of God, and by implication to make God subject to man's will. Paul Tillich's criticism of incarnational theology would appear to stand in the same tradition. It conceives of God as becoming somehow the "captive" of man.[2] In such an understanding of religion, the possibility of a Christian speaking of or anticipating a "religious experience" falls into serious question.

It is my personal conviction that the case for the opposition of religion and faith has been overstated. In saying this, I have in mind both a theological and semantic disagreement with Barth, Bonhoeffer, and, to a lesser degree, Tillich. The theological disagreement has been and shall continue to be implicit throughout this book. Here the semantic problem needs to be stated. "Religion," as I use the term, is a *condition* of man. The word itself comes from either one or two Latin roots: *religere,* meaning "to reflect deeply, to contemplate with awe, or to act out of a sense of duty;" or *religare,* meaning "to tie securely, to moor [as a boat]." It describes the *process,* natural to man, of pondering the meaning of his experience out of a persistent need to make sense of his world.

In this context the question, "What is your religion?" is meaningless. It is the same kind of question as "What is your thirst?" or "What is your lust?" We can legitimately ask, "What are the results of your religion?" just as we can ask, "What did you drink as a result of your thirst?" or "With whom are you sleeping?" The point is that religion is not an object or collection of stuff, but it is a state of existence.

This state of existence has been variously described. Augustine of Hippo wrote in the opening of his *Confessions:* "Our heart is restless until it rests in you."[3] Marx described religion as the "sigh of the oppressed," meaning something quite different by the word and much more in accord with my meaning than the "opiate of the people." Clifford Geertz has spoken of religion as the alternative to madness, the inevitable result for man of an ultimately meaningless world.[4] The religious man is, as I understand him, man who is seeking, man who with his whole being craves the unity of all things and yet prays that the source of unity will always be greater than he. Again, as Augustine said: "Let us seek so as to find and let us find so as to continue to seek."[5] The religious nature of man is his openness to the word of God. To act upon the basis of our religious nature is to have faith, to be confidently assured (Heb. 11:1) that our inquietude of mind is not simply a human malady, as Paschal once suggested, but the capacity to act in the knowledge of God's purpose.[6]

"Knowledge" is a key word in all of this. This is understandable. When we are open to the word of God, and indeed are confronted by that word, this is not perceived in terms of an *object* within our experience, but as a *consciousness* of the meaning of God who lies beyond and yet communicates himself through the data of our experience. No one has a visual, tactual, audial, savorous, or olfactory relationship to the divine essence. Yet there are levels of awareness that a person may possess which he identifies with the presence of God "speaking" to him. This does not have to be something he has conjured up by his own power, but in the Christian tradition it can be that which he "knows" only because of God's action. This is a religious or transcendental experience.

Such an experience has been defined as the occasion of a perceived spontaneous expansion or elevation of consciousness in which the knowledge given is not the result of our labors, but is of the nature of a gift outside ourselves. The "knowledge" is more *felt* meaning than *thinking* meaning. Such mystical experiences are described by William James as possessing four marks. Ineffability and a noetic quality are the primary marks, and relate to the sense of knowing and yet not being able to tell. The less sharply defined marks, transiency and passivity, will become apparent in further discussion.[7]

The introduction of William James into the discussion gives me occasion for pointing out that over the last decade or so there has been a renewed interest in James and the study of religious or transcendent experience as open to scientific—particularly psychological and sociological—analysis. Abraham

Maslow, one of the leading humanist psychologists of the last generation, wrote extensively about what he called "peak experiences," a synonym for transcendental, mystical, or religious experiences. Maslow, while eminently worth reading, is not easy to reduce to a few simple sentences. At the risk of doing his analysis an injustice, I would describe what he means by a peak experience as the consciousness of being overwhelmed by a self*less* love, in which one is completely absorbed in being. It is a holistic, nonevaluating, creative experience in which the self is transcended. Time, space, justification, will, polarities, fears—and dichotomies between inner and outer, subject and object—all disappear. It is both a godlike and childlike fulfillment of one's esthetic perceptions, in which a self-authenticating person feels his most creative.[8] It is worth noting for future reference that Maslow specifically says that the peak experience is akin to a "second naïvete," using a term coined by the French theologian, Paul Ricoeur.[9]

Some of Maslow's analysis of the peak experience has been paralleled by the work on ecstasy of Marghanita Laski in England. Her writing style is even less epigrammatic than Maslow's, but I gather that what she calls "ecstasy" are "experiences characterized by being joyful, transitory, unexpected, rare, valued, and extraordinary to the point of often seeming as if derived from a preternatural source."[10] Laski sees these experiences as of two kinds: withdrawal experiences and intensity experiences.[11] She does not accept as universal James's four marks of the mystical experience.

The thing that needs to be noted about both Maslow and Laski is that neither one sees peak experiences or ecstasies as a validation of a transcendental referent. In fact, they say the exact opposite: they are "natural," which is to say they have nothing to do with God.[12] This raises a point that the reader needs to keep in mind. The relationship of theology to the human sciences is not divided between those who deny the reality of the experience of symbolic meaning and those who affirm symbols and God. There is clearly an intermediary group who admit the phenomena of the symbolic experience while utterly *un*convinced of the reality of its transcendent referent.

Linda Bourque, who did an analysis of the frequency of transcendental experiences among Americans, came up with the conclusion that the majority of Americans have such experiences, even if only a small majority (56.7 percent); and that most of those who have them do so in terms of a secular imagery (music, nature, sex). People who have "religious" transcendental experiences tend to be less educated.[13] This last bit of data could be interpreted as a "put down" of religionists. I myself believe it can just as well be interpreted as a symptom of the reification and alienation of the traditional symbols of early modern Christianity.

I am sure it is obvious to the reader that the claim of Laski or Maslow, as well as the persons reported by Bourque, that such transcendental experiences are *not* indicative of God is, of course, symptomatic of their own perceptual filters. What they are saying is that since "we all know" there is no God, when some people experience what seems like God, it is not God. Laski calls this the "we all know" rationalism.[14] I would describe it as a particular form of crippling socialization.

However, my intention in this study is not to focus on the call for faith. My purpose is to say that ministry must take the religious or transcendental experience seriously if it is to see itself as related to the Incarnation. The transcendental experience is a fact of life which is, to my understanding, neither demonic, as I think some Barthians might imply, nor simply naturalistic, as Maslow and Laski suggest, but is expressive of the religious process *within* or the openness of man *to* the present word of God. My suspicion is that ministry studies tend to look upon transcendental experiences through either Barthian or secular eyes, and my hope is that we will cease to do this, but will look at religious experience, as analyzed by the scientists and yet affirmed by the man of faith, as an essential focus for understanding what it is to minister today. This is not to say that ministry needs to be gullible and take all reports of such experiences at their face value; but that we need to understand man at the point of his interface with the mystery of being.

To that end, in this chapter I will first seek to describe that experience more deeply. Second, I want to touch upon the relation of this discussion to revelation. It is most important that we see revelation as a concept that safeguards the relation between man as religious and the Christian Gospel as grace. Finally, I will relate it to the structured life of the church, particularly as regards liturgy.

THE EXPERIENCE OF MYSTERY

Medieval man saw God everywhere. Anything out of the ordinary—a deformed person, a plague, a comet, the convenient demise of a tyrant, a psychotic break—was interpreted as evidence of God's presence. His enchanted reality was subsumed with divine instrumentality on the natural and social levels.

The early modern man (from the sixteenth into the eighteenth centuries) was somewhat different. The growing rationalism and Puritanism of the late Middle Ages, beginning with the scholastics, blossomed into an obsession with logical thought that had several manifestations and imposed a certain self-consciousness upon pure esthetic delight in mystery. One such manifestation of early modern rationalism—of which Rene Descartes (1576–1650), Benedict Spinoza (1632–1677), and Gottfried Leibniz (1646–1716) were the most renowned spokesmen—was the argument that man grasped in the mind the essence of God's being by the power of reason. In this sense God was considered an object of our experience. This theory collapsed under the onslaught of David Hume (1711–1776) and Immanuel Kant (1724–1804)—at least in the minds of many theologians today. As a consequence, Christian ministry was left with little upon which to build a theological understanding of its purpose, aside from the warm feelings of the Pietists, who, as a rule, abrogated theology. The church was faced with an apologetic and evangelistic crisis, from which it has yet to recover.

It was the task of the early nineteenth-century theologians to attempt to recoup the church's self-understanding. From that time, the response to this task has been, very generally speaking, in terms of several intellectual movements: a philosophy of consciousness or romanticism (as in Ralph Waldo Emerson (1803–1882)); a postcritical rationalism or, more particularly, idealism (as in G. W. F. Hegel (1770–1831)); an attitude of the abnegation of humanism (as in Søren Kierkegaard (1813–1858)); and a secular scepticism (as in Auguste Comte (1798–1857)). I use these terms in a nonpejorative sense. For these men, somewhat loosely associated with the terms, are to be admired for their deep devotion to truth, which they may have only served in part. Furthermore, the agenda to which they were speaking, the theological ground of ministry today, is still very much before us. For that reason we have to go back to the beginning.

If we acknowledge the religious nature of man as the restless quest for a unifying sense to all of his experience as perceived by him, then we have to ask ourselves: *At what point is there a level of awareness* that there is a resolution to this quest? Hegel grounded this in the experience of the process of coming into consciousness, identical with the process of history. This is a kind of detached intellectualism in which the Absolute Spirit is the Absolute Mind. It tends to become pantheistic, depending on how one reads Hegel, with no possibility of a transcendental experience. Hegel may be, as some argue, a forerunner of pan*en*theism (the belief that the "all" is in God, but that God is infinitely "more"), but it is difficult to discern how God in Hegel is anything more than the evolution of self-consciousness, divorced from the objective world.

I would rather focus the possibility of an answer to this fundamental question on the work of Friedrich Schleiermacher (1768–1834), Rudolf Otto (1869–1937), and Max Scheler (1874–1928). Pastoral theology over the last fifty years is much the poorer for failing to take these men with greater seriousness. They all might be classified as in some sense of the philosophy of consciousness, although it would be a mistake to lump them with romantics such as Wordsworth, Whitman, or Ruskin. What they affirm is the reality of the religious experience or the sense of God's presence, and they do it at the level of a felt *and* intuitive meaning.

Schleiermacher came out of a pietistic (Moravian) background, and was influenced by the Romanticism of the early nineteenth century. His concern was for the basis of faith among those who found the classical dogmas of the church difficult to accept. In his theology, contrary to some popular opinion, he took Christ and the church with the utmost seriousness. Yet he believed that we engage the presence of God at a much more primary level; namely, in a sense of unconditioned dependence. "True religion," he wrote in 1799, "is sense and taste for the Infinite."[15] By 1830 he described this sense as a feeling *(Gefühl)* related to self-consciousness, in which one is aware of the self as self-caused, and of the self as dependent upon that which has caused it to be. This is the *feeling of unqualified dependence*[16] *(Das schlechthinnige Abhangig-keitsgefühl).*

This feeling of dependence becomes the focus of man's awareness that he stands in the presence of God. It is important to look closer at what Schleiermacher means by it. It is not a special kind of feeling designating the extraordinary condition under which God is to be met, nor is it a special faculty in man. It is, as I think Maslow and Laski suggest, the entire person's sense of the wholeness of life and the unity of the self within that wholeness: the intuitive grasp of the end of the religious quest, the many made one, power, and ultimate worth.

It would be incorrect to identify *Gefühl,* Schleiermacher's feeling, with raw emotion. The word can also mean consciousness. It would be equally incorrect to say, as some have, that *Gefühl* has no emotional component. It is emotional and intuitive, and it leads to thought. Ricoeur speaks of Schleiermacher as an early pioneer in the "revivification of philosophy through contact with the fundamental symbols of consciousness" (for example, the "second naviete").[17] *Gefühl* is perhaps the obverse of another German word, made popular in the writings of C. S. Lewis, *Sehnsucht,* a longing or yearning for the recovery of a unity which bespeaks man's creatureliness. *Gefühl* in Schleiermacher is the immediate sense of one's existence as related.

Related to what? Otto criticized Schleiermacher for not seeing in the feeling of absolute dependence that it is a sense utterly unique in man, *sui generis,* and that the sense of creatureliness is primary. There is no other feeling like it and it has a referent outside itself. It is a sense of the *numinous (das Gefühl des uberweltlichen).* In this feeling of the presence of the holy, Otto identified two paradoxical elements. There is an element of being confronted with over-whelming power and the fear or awe associated with that, as well as an element of fascination or attraction of the uncanny. The *mysterium tremendum,* as Otto terms the former, is the deepest and most fundamental element.[18] In other words, the multivalency that I have identified with a symbol is a part of the experience of the numinous, as seen by Otto, as is Laski's two dimensions of ecstasy.

Max Scheler—the father of the sociology of knowledge; a student of Husserl, the founder of phenomenology; and a friend and admirer of Otto—believed that there is an *a priori* structure in the whole of man which enables him to experience God as Otto described. He is particularly sensitive to man's crea-ture-feeling, a sense of being nothing apart from God, and the need to satisfy his capacity for religious value. Scheler describes the "eternal" in man as his permanent possibility for the religious experience that fulfills this need. In this *a priori* there is a kind of internal logic, the kind of which Pascal spoke when he wrote: "The heart has its own reasons which reason does not know . . . the heart loves the universal Being naturally, and itself naturally."[19]

This particular epigram of Paschal sums up for a number of theologians a description of man's point of awareness of God's presence in the religious experience. This is to speak of the certainty in man of God's address to him which lies outside of the univocal categories of reason or common sense. Pascal obviously relates this to a feeling of love, as does the Canadian Roman Catholic philosophical theologian, Bernard Lonergan, who in quoting Pascal speaks of love as the content of faith.[20] Both men are reminiscent of the unknown late fourteenth-century author of *The Cloud of Unknowing,* who wrote: "only to our intellect is he [God] incomprehensible: not to our love."[21]

Perhaps Otto, Scheler, and other phenomenologists of religion are a bit more accurate in giving a less domesticated flavor to love by stating that God's presence in religious experience is sensed as power and value. What we are aware of as a fulfillment of our religious quest on the primary level is the ambiguous feeling of both fear and love. We find ourselves gazing into a mystery, which would seem to engage us as an overweening power and yet flood us with an unimaginable assurance of worth. Such experience is not of equal impact in all individuals. Laski described ecstasies of withdrawal and intensity; and perhaps one person is more aware of their smallness and alienation before the mystery, while another is rewarded with the gift of wholeness and unity. At the same time, I do know that reporters as different as St. Teresa of Avila (1515–1582) and the contemporary American anthropologist, Carlos Castaneda, describe mystical or transcendental experiences in which there is an intense level of pain and delight at the same time.

This leads to a key point in this discussion. The awareness of the numinous, to use Otto's term, which we call a transcendental experience, generally involves an encounter which is seemingly incongruous. This is to say that the categories of our logic, common sense, or rational thought, are not able to "explain" the data of the experience in a secular fashion. There is "more" there than we can reduce to our theories; there is a gap between our explanation and our awareness. Dorothy Sayers has said somewhere that it was the incongruity of Jesus that was his power. He does not "fit."

Another way of saying the same thing is to say that the religious experience is always a surprise. "A real surprise," writes Robert Neale, "destroys our self understanding and our understanding of the world."[22] Neale's thesis is that surprise at first horrifies us, then, when the anxiety is over, it strikes us as humorous. Yet the greatest surprise is that of Christ himself, "that incongruous juxtaposition of the holy and profane."[23] The fact that Christ is the primal sacrament or symbol of God fits this understanding, since to be a symbol is to be an image that is ambiguous and incongruous.

It is vital, then, for the principal thesis of this book, for the reader to understand the nature of the religious experience as the encounter with that which is not reducible to the univocal categories provided by the structures of society. Religious experience begins at the level of symbol, with all that means for feeling and intuition; and the signative forms of meaning, common sense and thinking, only follow upon it. Religion begins with feeling, not intellectual conviction. I recall a survey made in the 50s of adult confirmands in the Diocese of Louisiana. One question was: What motivated you to seek Confirmation? The answers, in order of importance, were the liturgy, a close friend or family member, or a clergyman. All these are relationships that work themselves out on a level of feeling and intuition.

If Lonergan can say that love is the content of faith and that faith precedes theology, as he does again and again, we have a pristine intellectual justification for the belief that the knowledge of God is prior to our conceptualization of him. This is, of course, an internal experience, in some ways intensely personal. In the last section I will argue that it is not the experience of the individual over against the community, as some suggest, but the experience of the individual within the community. Yet the sense of the presence of God comes as a feeling of power and value at a very inchoate level. Its symbolization is basic and deeply rooted in the penumbra that lies beyond the horizon of our consciousness. As this feeling takes on greater clarity and precision, it shares more in the external world of the one who has experienced it. At the same time, it loses something of its ability to move us to action and the sense of being a free, unqualified gift. The raw fear and the orgasmic love are diminished.

This brings us face-to-face with two traditions of criticism of religious experience, as I have outlined it in the succession of Schleiermacher, Otto, and Scheler. The first is typified in Kierkegaard, who is roughly Schleiermacher's contemporary. There is a danger in Schleiermacher, which is true of the liberal Protestantism that followed him, which is that the object of religion becomes religion itself and not God, who is lost in all the welter of feeling. The truth of religion becomes the experience or feeling within man, which he possesses by virtue of his inwardness. Somehow the transcendental reference (God) is lost, if he was ever perceived there in the first place.

There is a current theory in theological circles that the study of symbols is a very good thing, but that one does not necessarily have to imply there is anything "out there" to which the symbol points. Current enthusiasts for the writings of C. G. Jung, the German-Swiss founder of analytical psychology, for whom I have a profound admiration, need to beware that his theories do not leave them in this naturalistic philosophy. Certainly this is where Maslow and Laski are to be located.

Søren Kierkegaard, a theological conservative, called the Christian away from this form of seduction. While he and Schleiermacher undoubtedly agreed that subjectivity is truth, Kierkegaard did a better job of pointing out that the dread one experiences before the numinous is the surrender of presumption about the self and the precondition of any sense of love as a gift of God. The experience is of the "wholly other." Therefore, while I would agree with Otto —who also worked to save Schleiermacher's theories from naturalism—that the "wholly other" cannot be totally "other," I think we need to heed the *caveat* of Kierkegaard. "If I am of infinitely, infinitely little importance," says Kierkegaard, "if in my wretchedness I feel myself to be the most miserable of all: then it is eternally, eternally certain that God loves me."[24]

There are some indications on several sides that contemporary theology is taking a renewed and welcome interest in Schleiermacher.[25] Hopefully, pastoral theology will build on this. There is a real risk, however, that scholars in the field of pastoral care, with their understandable concern for acceptance as scientifically respectable by their colleagues in the so-called "helping professions," will allow themselves to focus on the phenomena of the feeling and intuition of religious experience, and not make adequate account of the referent of that experience: God. Kierkegaard offers a solid antidote to this.

The other tradition of criticism is epitomized in Samuel Taylor Coleridge (1772–1834). Coleridge, whom we are more inclined to remember as the author of *The Rime of the Ancient Mariner,* was one of the notable theological thinkers of nineteenth-century England. He took Kant seriously and tried to work out some understanding as to the nature of religious knowledge. He was, however, rather sceptical of Schleiermacher's solution in the feeling of dependence. Coleridge was a rationalist, in the sense that he believed that reason, particularly what he called "higher reason," led to the knowledge of God. The "higher reason" seems in some sense to be related to Kant's "transcendentals" and, consequently, to the transcendental method of Karl Rahner, Bernard Lonergan, and others. In this sense, Coleridge was far ahead of his time. At the same time, unlike Rahner and Lonergan, Coleridge was very suspicious of basing too much on feeling or mystical experience. He had that English inability to see the "unfitting" as anything but a nuisance or bad taste. He spoke of Schleiermacher as the founder of the "pietistic school" of theology.[26] Coleridge wrote: "The exercise of the reasoning and reflecting powers, increasing insight, and enlarging views, are requisite to keep alive the substantial faith of the heart."[27]

I doubt very much that anyone would question the validity of Coleridge's sentiment. The edition of his works which I am using has written in the flyleaf the autograph of its original owner, "W. P. DuBose," one of the great theologians of the Episcopal Church, and second Dean of the School of Theology where I now serve. DuBose once wrote: "Right reason is to know God as the eternal reason, meaning, and purpose of all things, as of ourselves; and so to know God is for us eternal life."[28] This is true, and the great danger to which we expose ourselves by focusing on the feeling and intuition of God is to forget that and to lose God in a welter of sentimentality.

At the same time meaning begins with feeling, and when it is creative, it moves from there to intuition and on to thinking or rational analysis. As

Ricoeur says: "The symbol gives rise to the thought."[29] The very nature of religious thought is grounded in religious experience, which is an encounter with the mystery that is God. Our first premonitions of this are very inchoate and perceived only as the feeling of something uncanny or weird, upon which, when all is said and done, our very selves depend. It is upon the sensitivity to this weak signal that the whole possibility of a transcendent destiny for man seems to lie.

REVELATION AS MEETING

A number of theologians (Wolfhart Pannenberg, Gabriel Moran, Gerhard Ebeling, and others) have said that the fundamental question in modern theology is the problem of revelation, the self-disclosure of God to man. If I am right in contending that Christian ministry is action rooted in Christian meaning, and that in some sense it is legitimate to differentiate Christianity from a myriad of philosophies and other religions as "revealed," then this fundamental question for theology is also a primary issue for ministry. The whole matter of the nature of religious or transcendental experience as it relates to pastoral care only gives substance to that issue.

Avery Dulles, S.J., has suggested that there are three "mentalities" in the theological understanding of revelation. The first is that which concentrates on revelation as a concrete event, and speaks of a biblical or kerygmatic revelation. The focus of revelation is the story of salvation history, perhaps beginning with Adam or, more likely, Moses, working on down to Christ, and then recounting the life of the church. The second mentality thinks of revelation as a body of doctrine, conceptual abstractions obtained by rational reflection upon the data. The third mentality depicts revelation as an ineffable encounter with the sacred, either in terms of its immanent or transcendent presence.[30]

Probably most of us stand in the tradition of the second mentality. This is more of a personal reminiscence, perhaps, than a statement based on hard data. I do think, however, that the tradition of confessional Christianity among the Reformed and Lutheran communions, and of "manual theology" (as in C. B. Moss's *The Christian Faith,* F. J. Hall's *Theological Outlines,* or Christian Peschi's *Praelectiones Dogmaticae*) in the Anglican and Roman Catholic communions, is well ingrained in our thinking. The problem is that such propositional and systematic material is highly subject to reification and alienation of meaning, and appeals to the "inner meaning" of dogma can become so vague

70

as to leave one wondering why one bothers with the system in the first place.

In the final analysis this is the identification of God's self-disclosure with language: words about God and his relationship to man. It is difficult to see how it is possible to divorce language from culture and to discern what is trans-historical in such a revelation. God becomes a fifth-century Neo-Platonist, a thirteenth-century scholastic, a sixteenth-century lawyer, or a twentieth-century phenomenologist. Revelation becomes identified with the content of the mind and, as a consequence, is incredibly intellectualistic.[31]

Undoubtedly we are aware that ministry has backed off from the implications of this understanding of revelation for some time. No one is converted to Christianity, to wholeness, or to the ethical life by writing or preaching essays, even if we label them "revealed truth." Systematic and rational thought is essential to human existence and to Christian experience, but to speak of it as "revealed," even if agreed upon by an assembly of bishops, is to bind the self-disclosure of God to the language of a given era. We have all heard jokes about whether or not God speaks Hebrew, Greek, or Latin; but logically this becomes no laughing matter if a proposition becomes confused with the word of God. We have to distinguish between the experience of God in the core of a person and any effort to objectify that experience.

The issues lie at the interface between man's finite and historical existence and whatever we may mean by the transcendence and infinite understanding of God. At what point do the images within human discernment lie *within* the being of God? Is the nature of man and the nature of God mutually exclusive? Certainly classical theology, which has affirmed the *total otherness* of God, would answer in the affirmative. There is nothing in the essence of man which God shares. The Christological struggle is an example of this problem. Despite Chalcedon, how is it possible that the person, Jesus of Nazareth, can be both God and man at the same time in more than a logical juxtaposition? If Jesus were God according to the classical understanding of God, then he was completely aware of his future. If he were man in any sense that we understand humanity, then he was not conscious of his future. There is no way of having it both ways, which is expressive of apparent utter incompatibility between the divine mentality and the human.

Dulles's description of the first mentality, revelation as event rather than system, does offer more promise in meeting this dilemma. First we have to define what we mean by "event," however. It can refer to the event of the life, death, and resurrection of Jesus, and only that (as in Bultmann, Fuchs, Ebeling), in which we participate by one means or another. On the other hand, it can refer to the totality of our experience, in which the event of Jesus is unique and/or normative in some sense (as in Pannenberg and Moltmann). Revelation then becomes God's self-disclosure, not only in Christ but in all of history.

Revelation as event, to continue to use Dulles's term, is conveyed not so much, as in doctrine, by an analytical system, but as in story. In Chapter Seven I will be discussing the role of story in man's experience of God, and so it is important to call attention to the relationship between this second mentality and the sweep of the whole second part of this book. Story can, of course, take the form of literally telling some kind of tale (as in a myth, folk story, or fairy tale), or it can fall under the category of proclamation (as in kerygma or preaching). The whole thrust of the "new hermeneutic" sees preaching as a word-event, which makes present now the saving power of the original story of Jesus.

Because the first mentality deals with the activity of God in the lives of people—instead of reducing it to language that becomes the report of that activity and hence the report of revelation—it overcomes the brittle nature of signative systems and has the greater flexibility of a symbolic narrative. At the same time, there is the implicit suggestion that God is not so much "totally other" as classical theology, begotten of the Hellenistic notions of absolute being, might suggest. God becomes more personal, and there seems to be the possibility of some mutuality between man and God. This is not to denigrate the Scriptures, the creeds, or something as magnificent as Augustine's *De Trinitate;* but it is to say that the second mentality is a step removed from the first in being described as revelation.

There is a problem of revelation in the first mentality, however. If we acknowledge that God's self-disclosure is an event—and more than one event —but something that is true for all of experience, and that the event of Jesus is somehow unique and normative within that totality, and that this self-disclosure is discerned by man in the midst of his history, then why is it that God is visible to some and not to others? This is to pose the problem with which St. Paul wrestled. Why is it that the Jews did not accept Christ (Rom. 9–11)?

The answer some give, which is really not an answer, is to speak of a special experience or salvation history given to a particular people. A cruder way of putting it is to say that God wants to save some people and not others, so he chooses to whom he will reveal himself. If God is an arbitrary oriental despot, who needs no sufficient reason for his action other than personal whim, then perhaps this would be acceptable. It is certainly not in accord with the unique and normative event of revelation, Jesus, whose very uniqueness demands that God be present in all of experience as the creator of all our environment. What follows from this, of course, without going into the reams of discussion it would require to explicate the point in detail, is that God does not stand over against our history, entering as he will, but that our environment and our history is *within* God, although he be *infinitely more* than his creation. So the solution to the problem of why only some discern God's self-disclosure has to be resolved apart from any notion of God's *selective* revelation of himself.

Before passing on to discuss an alternative, it needs to be said here that ministry has discovered revelation as event. The problem is that the majesty of the insight is often quickly trivialized, if I may quote a rather indelicate phrase of a friend of mine, into confusing "balloons and grabass" for the "still small voice" or, as the New English Bible puts it, into "a low murmuring sound" (1 Kings 19:12). If the notion of event is not trivialized, it is made so ponderous that we only substitute boredom for nausea. Those who speak most eloquently of the power of preaching often confuse poetry with homiletical essays. Somehow I miss the point when the German theologians, of whom Austin Farrar, the English metaphysician, once aptly wrote: ". . . set their eyeballs and pronounce the terrific words: He speaks to thee! *(Er redet dich an!).* "[32]

It seems to me that the problem is not whether God speaks, but whether or not we are capable of hearing. Dulles's third mentality, toward which he seems to have a rather sceptical attitude, is helpful here. This is revelation as relationship, the relationship between man and his experience as understood to enfold the presence of another subject, God. God discloses himself in the experience of man, and by responding to that self-disclosure man participates in God. This is to *know* God, not as one knows the doctrine of the Trinity but as Adam knew Eve. Revelation is an intersubjective experience of the nature of sexual intercourse.

This is to oppose sexual intercourse, as an act of love, to coital behavior, which is an act of use or abuse, as expressed in the word "screw." Intercourse denotes a spontaneous participation with another at a level of involvement far deeper than intellectual contemplation. There is a difference between making love and reading Masters and Johnson on *Human Sexual Inadequacy.* Intercourse is a process and not an object or thing in itself. No explanation can exhaust the experience of intercourse, which is to say that we recognize its ineffability. We can be thankful for that, since it is difficult to imagine the confusion involved in being able to convey the experience to another of making

73

love to one's spouse in the fullness of its meaning by words. Intercourse is an interaction between two subjects that is grounded in mystery. We are aware that whatever it is, it is more than we can explain. The surd is self-evident.

This is as good an analogy as there is of revelation as relationship, since the content of faith is love, and it is this that grounds the belief of man in God and his relation to him. Clearly I have opposed faith, as the open expectancy of man toward God, to belief, which is the substance of what he understands to be the meaning of that relationship. If I grasp the difficult style of Gabriel Moran correctly, he seems to be agreeing when he says that the relationship between God and man *illuminates* man's entire existence, so that revelation is not a body of knowledge but the presence of God enabling man to see as God and to live as God would have him live.[33] Moran says in this connection that revelation is the power of growing interaction between the two subjects, God and man. In this sense, he finds common cause with Ray Hart, who describes revelation as God's solicitation of man into being by virtue of man's union with him and man's participation in God's vision of the finality of the created order.[34] Revelation is in some sense the experience of hominisation.

Of course, there is still a major problem in our analogy. Unlike our partner in sexual intercourse, God is not an object of our experience; that is, he is not a *direct* object. If he were not at least an *indirect* object, it would be impossible to speak of a continuing revelation, which is clearly my assumption. Jaspers attempts to preserve the absolute nature of transcendence to existence by saying that this participation is through "ciphers," which are *not* embodiments of transcendence but the possibilities or promises of a hidden transcendence that enables us to capture transcendence for our reality.[35] Jaspers seems to be seeking to preserve the preapprehension of transcendence in the face of its ultimate unknowability. To know God is to know that we do not know him except as hidden; but unless we had some interaction with him as not limited by our knowing, we could not even know that he is hidden.

Ciphers appear to be the internal divine logic of symbols. They are a point of energy which becomes realized in the symbolic. One possible understanding of Carl Jung's archetypes—namely, as presymbolic—is related to ciphers. "Ritualism and sacramentalism are possible," says Jaspers, "in a life of ciphers."[36] Symbols and symbolic narratives or myths are those images or their relationships within our awareness that clearly draw us beyond the horizon of our consciousness into a world of precognition, into the mystery which, in present terms, can only be described as "nothingness." Our world of meaning becomes nothing before the mystery, and yet we preapprehend, according to

Rahner, a meaning to be there. Husserl writes in a similar vein of apprehension, which includes appresentation, where the subject completes or fills by way of intentions what he does not sense directly. One way of seeing Jaspers's analysis is that at our end of discernment these images are symbols, and at God's end are, for us, ciphers. God can be indirectly known in the environment that is his creation, as we know a lover, but in that he is more than his creation, he is a cipher.

Christ as divine man is the primal symbol or sacrament of God. It is in terms of him that we interpret the divine intention for history and its possible end. It is, however, at the level of his humanity that we engage him. His divinity is for us a cipher, rooted in the mystery, which is God's reality and ultimately ours if we participate in him. Even as symbol, however, there is a transhistorical presence to him. This means that Christ judges. He calls into question our present reality and the action based upon it. He also saves us, which is to say that he solicits us into becoming more than what our history would make us.

Revelation is to understand religious experience as the act of God disclosing himself to us in such a way that we can embody that self-disclosure in the images of our history so that it bears some relationship to the God who is ultimately hidden from us. Revelation then becomes the basis of action which is in accord with God's vision for his creation. Obviously ministry has to have a fundamental, continuing concern for revelation, and whatever it takes to enable the Christian city to be open to this resource of Christian action. It is the purpose of this study to explicate what that means for ministry.

MYSTERY WITHIN THE CITY

Every religion involves a communion and community in which is found rite and myth. This is not to say much more about the nature of that association than that it always exists, and that it does not identify myth with theology. In some primitive forms of religion the city of the gods would appear to be identical with the commonweal; in others, it would appear to be opposed. Despite the early history of the church and later millennial movements, it needs to be made clear that in the final analysis no ecclesial reality can be set over against the culture in which it lives by creating its own isolated world for its membership, even though it may effect the illusion of doing this. Simon Stylites had to live in a culture that would support his curious retreat. There are sects that attempt this isolation, however, and their members live in this style often without realizing their dependence upon the culture they despise (as, for example, in the use of language), and by virtue of the willingness of that culture to tolerate or even support their existence (as, for example, in the ruling of the Supreme Court that the Amish may terminate the education of their children at the eighth grade).

The openness of a contemporary person to God's word is made possible within the context of the world in which we live. As already noted, the church can no longer convince its members that we exist in a world where smallpox is to be considered God's retribution for our sins. Furthermore, as said in the last chapter, the images that make up the meaning of the church must have some plausibility within the prevailing culture, even though all parts of that culture may not find them acceptable. Witches are an interesting example. I received recently a brochure inviting me to a conference on witches, which I consider a "put on" or nonsense. Obviously some take them more seriously than I, but I am confident that I represent the majority within my culture and that no matter how many conferences we have, witches are not going to achieve a comeback in the Christian stock of images in the foreseeable future.

To recall some of the material we covered in the first two chapters, it follows from that discussion that religious experience always has a collective context and expression. This is not to identify God with any society or the ecclesial reality with the social system, but to hold that, both in regard to the filter of our consciousness and the infrastructure of our religious meaning, the religious collectivity is an integral function. The church was originally constituted by a perception of the presence of God in the life, death, and resurrection of Jesus. The fact is, however, that those persons who so discerned the mission of Christ were members of a religious body, the Jews, which enabled them to be open to this possibility and gave them the language for giving meaning to that possibility—at least in the initial stages of interpreting the meaning of Jesus. Furthermore, the continued experience of the life, death, and resurrection of Jesus remains a possibility because of the community which exists to reenact that experience.

Therefore, what is being said is that the ecclesial reality is integral to the revelatory experience in two ways. First of all, it socializes its members so that the filters of their consciousness are open to the possibility of the transcendent experience; and once open to that experience, it provides the images from which to identify, clarify, and share that experience. Then, secondly, it exists because of that experience and for the sake of making it continually available to its membership.

Lets take a look at the first point. Most of my ministry has involved higher education, and I have discussed the priestly vocation with many persons. In the 50s no one ever said to me: "I have a call from God," much less did they suggest that, like Samuel in the presence of Eli (1 Sam. 3:1–21), the Lord spoke directly to them. To them, the ministry was a career with real promise, a career in which they would spend most of their time solving parishioners' personal problems. In the 60s the pattern changed. Persons wanted to enter the priesthood either to save the world from capitalism or to escape the war in Vietnam, but there was even less mention of divine summons. (There was one man who told me in utmost confidence that he had seen Jesus on the altar, but he never made it through the psychiatric exam.) Now in the midst of the 70s people are getting "calls" repeatedly. At a recent clergy conference on the priestly vocation, in which I participated, the passage on Samuel and Eli was read at the Eucharist with the point of illustrating this very conviction. A priest who is approximately a contemporary of mine, remarked in reporting on an interview of a perspective student for the seminary: "The only thing that worried me about him was that he spoke of being called." What the priest does not realize is that this is "okay" now.

What do I mean by saying it is "okay" *now?* I mean that the church allows people to have a literal "call" now, whereas it did not seem to support this ten or twenty years ago. Certainly people are experiencing transcendent calls, but they are also, perhaps, experiencing them because the church says it is "okay" to have them. In other words, the ecclesial reality promotes the kind of filter of consciousness that lets this sort of data be identified. If it did not, I doubt very much that many people, if any, would be aware of such "calls."

This is not a cynical observation on my part. It does not mean that conditioning is all there is to it. God speaks, and he can make himself heard in spite of our deaf ears, as Isaiah once suggested (Isa. 9:8–10:11). Yet he has to be heard as a "still small voice."

To continue with this first point, we express the content of our religious experience in the images of the religious collectivity. Buddhists do not have visions of Christ and Presbyterians do not have visions of Buddha or, as Roman Catholics may, of the Virgin Mary. God does not tell Teresa of Avila to go and serve as a temple prostitute, but he did tell her to reform the Carmelites. I think anyone who handles poisonous snakes under any circumstances is foolish; but I am sure that those who do so in the name of Jesus are equally puzzled by my fondness for sixteenth-century polyphany. Is an experience any less transcendental because it is expressed in the paganism of Indian animism, as in the writings of Carlos Castaneda, than in the ecstatic experience

77

of Dag Hammarskjöld?[37] Please notice that I did not say any less "creative" or "true" or "Christian," words or categories that I might apply to the analysis of the meaning of and the object of the experience.

Bernard Lonergan is fond of speaking of the theologian as working within a collaborative community. He is, of course, speaking more about the sharing of the substance of the tradition as a theological resource, the need for a belief which the collectivity legitimates, and the value of the ongoing discourse among theologians sharing this common tradition and belief. However, he certainly does not preclude the dimension of transcendental experience. It is a general rule in the Roman Catholic Church to test claims for such experience within the context of the community, from which it follows that such experiences are expected. Whereas there is something deadening in a legal entity stamping its approval upon the ecstasies of its members, I do think there is legitimacy in seeing that the substance of the revelatory experience is located within the ecclesial city, because the possibility of the awareness of God's presence among us is a function of our community.

The second basic point of this section is that the church exists because of the primal event of Jesus' life, death, and resurrection; and that it lives in order to make that experience a living reality in the present. As one commentator on the relationship of the social structures to religious experience has written: "A religious community is a group of members who try to share and reenact the same religious experiences."[38] This is a very different thing from suggesting that it is a character-building organization, a debate club, or a therapy group —as good as ethics, philosophy, and counseling undoubtedly are, and as valuable as they might be as programmatic adjuncts to the local parish. This sharing and reenactment are the functions of ritual and myth.

It is difficult to say which comes first, ritual or myth. My own inclination would be to vote for the former, but certainly they exist among the membership in a dialogic relationship within the life of any religious city. Between them they carry the symbolic power to make present the primal event that constituted the coming together of the members; and consequently they are the *sine qua non* of the church's life.

Margaret Mead concurs that ritual has a vital role in the life of faith, and has described ritual as the repetitive pattern of activity, designed to evoke a feeling which is a *re*presentation of the feeling identified with the primal event. In other words, every ritual is an "anamnesis." Both Baptism and the Eucharist are rituals that seek to recall the participant to his share in the death and resurrection of Christ, and thereby to become one with the new order that this historical event inaugurated. We are baptized with Christ in his death as we are buried beneath the water, and we become partakers of his resurrection as we rise from the life-giving water (Rom. 6:4; Col. 2:12). When we eat and drink the body and blood of Christ we recall his death and look forward to the heavenly banquet, which we shall share with the Lord (John 6:33–46; 1 Cor. 11:26).

One definition of a ritual is a bundle of symbols. An analogy of a ritual, which expands this image, is that it is like a lead envelope, such as that in which radioisotopes are carried. In this "lead envelope" of the ritual are found the symbols, which by their very nature are risky and powerful. The repetitive patterns of the rite make the symbols available to us in a usable and nondestructive form. For example, we can speak of the experience of the death and resurrection of Jesus in the eating and drinking of his body and blood in the context of the ritual, whereas to evoke them outside of that patterned form would indeed involve the kind of threat that such images might normally invoke. It was this threat that brought the Romans to accuse the early Christians of being "cannibals," an accusation that would be justified outside of the ritual. The power of the ritual depends, of course, on its possession of such potentially dangerous threatening symbols. It is perhaps just this realization which led M. D. Chenu, the French Dominican liturgiologist, to say that true liturgy (ritual) needs to border on the vulgar.[39]

Rituals are of all kinds and are subject to various classifications. Their universal goal is the transformation of the participant. The experience of the reenactment of the primal event is intended to change the members so as to draw them more closely into union with God and break down that which separates or inhibits them from realizing their divine purpose. A ritual is anything but the result of an obsessive-compulsive neurotic pattern. It is *not* intended to soothe the anxious person but to heighten and expand the consciousness of God in man. This may well make that person more anxious. The effect of the heightened consciousness, however, is to draw the participants together in community, as they share the same awareness of the nature of the religious experience. It is from this point that it becomes the nucleus of meaning for the church as a community of moral discourse and action. In this sense ritual is a source of order and coherence.

The myth interprets the ritual. It is the narrative of what is properly and fully expressed in ritual. The reader needs to dismiss as best he can the popular meaning of the English word "myth"—a fanciful, perhaps grotesque, and certainly untrue tale. The Greek word *mythos* comes from a verb meaning "to

79

speak," and is used by Greeks to denote fictional stories as opposed to true stories *(mythoi* versus *logoi).* In this spirit the German literary scholar, Karl Muller (1779–1840), spoke of myth as the "disease of language." In the history of religions and theology, however, a myth is a *true* story about God and his relationship to man, particularly but not exclusively in regard to man's beginnings. Myths are not, however, primarily intended to explain causes; they are not specifically etiological. They are usually not historical, although I would argue that some have historical elements, and that some of the Christian myths, being true stories enabling us to participate in a truth about God and his relationship to us, are historical, as in the account of the death and resurrection of Jesus. There are only so many kinds of myths, and their basic motifs are larger than a given culture.

Myth is a species of religious story. By "religious story" I mean a narrative that is related and gives substance to man's religious needs. I will discuss further religious stories, including myths, in Chapter Seven. For the time being it is important just to note that a myth is a narrative symbol. It establishes order in the structure of existence, an order which has divine authority. Therefore, it is an extremely powerful source of motivation, guiding human action in ways of which we are only partially conscious. It is a mode of being in the world. This makes the identification of the operant myths in our life most important. They depict for us what "really is" at a very fundamental level, for they tell us what it is to be "me" within the world of my experience, and they suggest how I may fulfill my "whatness."

Myths are related to time, the *illud tempus* or "great time." There are two kinds of time in myths: cosmic time and historical time. Myths of cosmic time call us back, referring to some "golden age" in which everything was wonderful and as it should be. They are characteristic of pagan religion, in which the primal event is the moment of creation, and the mythic structure summons us back to the "navel of the world." Some churchmen fall into this mythic structure: the sixteenth century was the "golden age" and Geneva is the "navel"; or the thirteenth century was the "golden age" and Rome is the "navel"; or the eighth century was the "golden age" and Constantinople is the "navel"; or the year 4004 B.C. is the "golden age" and we just have to keep looking for the Garden of Eden or the Ark. Myths of historic time are eschatological or forward looking, which is generally the tradition of the Judaeo-Christian faith—as well, incidentally, as Marxism. This mythic structure is utopian in some sense.

Myths are, as I have said, related to cult or ritual. This is not always the apparent case, but is so clearly the usual case as to say they are bound to one another. The myth is the prototypical exegesis of the ritual. I mean by this that it explains the ritual in a powerful way; but at the same time the myth itself may need explanation (which is what theology is all about), or it may leave unexplained portions of the ritual that will have to be understood in other than a symbolic narrative.

Those other manners of explaining a ritual can be found in what a ritual does (operational) or in terms of the position of the symbols in the ritual to other symbols (positional). For example, what goes on at a Billy Graham Crusade is clearly a ritual, however much the anti-ritualists may disclaim this. As we noted in Chapter Two, what the revival ritual does is legitimate the old middle class in its style of life, despite its identification with the exegetical myth of the death and resurrection of Jesus. Positionally, it is closely identified with symbols of American individualism: flags, hymns of the nineteenth century, sports arenas (Richard Nixon at "Billy Graham Day" in Charlotte, N. C., in 1970 drew the appropriate analogy between football and Graham).

I spoke of ritual as being the source of order, meaning, and moral coherence. It provides a certain regulation and restraint to the lives of its participants. Myths, to put what I have said in slightly different language, are the repetition of an exemplary scenario; they are ideal statements about social categories and their interrelationships. As theists we believe that in performing this function they are rooted in the mystery that is God's presence to us, and within the ecclesial reality they form the fundamental substance of the bridge between revelation and ministry. The central meaning of the people of the city of God lies in the symbols of God's transcendent presence conveyed in a *living* ritual or liturgy and myth.

To say that ritual and myth are fundamental to both the religious experience and the action that follows from such meaning, which we know as ministry, is *not* to claim too much for either. They are not sufficient in themselves in our very complex world, despite what persons like Joseph Campbell suggest, nor am I pleading for any specific liturgic or mythic interpretation. What I do believe, however, is that Rudolf Bultmann is essentially wrong in saying we must demythologize the Gospel. To a degree we may have to *re*mythologize, just as we must recover the *depth* of liturgical experience, and not just a superficial "relevance." Ministry in its fullness and practical sense must look for its impetus and shaping purpose in liturgy and in the recounting of the religious story. For in this way will ministry serve the fourth vector: attention to the mystery of being.

While I have slipped this point in at the end of the chapter, it must not be overlooked. The whole argument of these three sections has been directed to this climax. In fact all of Part One—beginning with the discussion of ministry and the city and moving to its relationship to meaning and, inevitably, to mystery—has led to this conclusion. The ministry of the church is the action of a people, whose reason for being is celebrated and recovered in the ritual and myth of God's incarnation in Jesus Christ. What follows in the rest of this book will assume this truth.

SUMMARY

In closing I would anticipate a discomfort some may have with this chapter. Abraham Maslow and others, in their studies of transcendental experiences, have argued that this is something one does alone. The "peaker," as Maslow calls such a person, is a self-sufficient, self-authenticating *individual.* There is something very private about the experience of the mystery. As Kierkegaard wrote: "The knight of faith is obliged to rely upon himself alone."[40] It is as if Whitehead's definition of religion, as that which a person does with his solitariness, encompasses the total focus of the transcendental experience, shutting such a person off from a concern for the world and action to better that world.

In asserting as I have that undergirding the church's ministry, if that ministry be true to the Christian perception of God's relation to man, is the ongoing experience of God's presence among us, I am not suggesting a return to some insensitive individualism. Not only is there no necessary relation between an inwardness and a lack of concern for the suffering world, but there is no true experience of God without compassion for the world. The individual nature of the transcendental experience, *properly understood,* is inextricably bound and is a necessary prelude to the corporate life of the redeeming ecclesial reality. The author of the Letter of James speaks to this in saying that faith, man's commitment in love to the God he experiences within him, "if it does not lead to action, it is in itself a lifeless thing" (James 2:17). We must have faith, but if it is a faith in a living God it will necessarily be a living faith, inward in its inception but always moving outward to serve the suffering of man.

This is evident in the lives and writings of the great contemporary Christian mystics, men and women who have experienced what I have described in this chapter. John of the Cross (1542–1591) says somewhere: "The Word of God is the effect on the soul." If we seek to identify God's presence, we must find its effect as evidence in the saving action of persons in the world.

It is the American Trappist, Thomas Merton, who has perhaps done the most in our time to demonstrate the "respectability" of a life given over to prayer and contemplation. Yet he saw this style of life as a prelude to creative action. Merton believed that Christianity seeks to bring about "a transformation of man's consciousness."[41] Yet in his Cistercian tradition, rooted as it is in Benedictine piety, there was an inseparable movement from prayer to work. Action, as I have argued on this point, is the inevitable result of our consciousness. Merton wrote in the same spirit, only far more eloquently: "The contemplative life must always provide an area, a space of liberty, of silence, in which possibilities are allowed to surface and new choices—beyond routine choice—become manifest."[42]

To experience God is to find the possibility for creative action, a new action, which may draw the world about us and ourselves that much closer to the unity of all things in God. This perception of the new will be tested in our doing. This is what Dag Hammarskjöld believed. "In our era," he wrote, "the road to holiness necessarily passes through the world of action."[43] Hammarskjöld was certainly a contemplative of the Christian tradition, despite his professed discomfort with the label. My only discomfort with this particular saying, now popular on Christian "banner-art," is the qualification. It is not a truth unique to our era, but is eternally true.

The embodiment of this truth can be no better exemplified for us than in the Christian martyr, Martin Luther King. What many people do not realize about King was that his most influential teacher, George Washington Davis at Crozer Seminary, was a theologian deeply influenced by Protestant mysticism. Anyone who reads or has heard King with this mind quickly recognizes the higher consciousness born of the experience of the mystery behind the action. This is generally true in the image that dominated King's thought, the "beloved community," the heavenly city, the same community of which I spoke in the first chapter. It is particularly true, and obvious to the discerning reader, in one of his best known public statements at the Lincoln Memorial, on August 28, 1963.

> I say to you today, my friends, though, even though we face difficulties today and tomorrow, I still have a dream. It is a dream deeply rooted in the American dream. I have a dream that one day this nation will rise up, live out the true meaning of its creed: "We hold these truths to be self-evident, that all men are created equal."

I have a dream today. . . . The glory of the Lord shall be revealed, and all flesh shall see it together. This is our hope. This is the faith that I go back to the South with. With this faith we will be able to hew out of the mountain of despair a stone of hope.

When we allow freedom to ring . . . we will be able to join hands and song in the words of that old Negro spiritual, "Free at last, Free at last, Great God almighty, We are free at last."[44]

PART TWO

TOWARD A CONTEMPORARY PIETY

4

HE WHO IMAGES

"We live in a rainbow, not a pure white light of truth."[1] Carlos Castenada quotes his Yaqui shaman as saying, "To believe that the world is only as you think it is, is stupid. The world is a mysterious place. Especially in the twilight."[2] The remarkable fact of our time is that we are coming to know that what these statements affirm—both that attributed to Goethe, a product of the eighteenth-century Enlightenment, and that attributed to the primitive shaman of northwestern Mexico, Don Juan—is in fact true. It seems to me ironic that the recovery of this truth does not come from those who ought to be most interested in it: the church.

It is the character of the fourth vector of the ecclesial reality to be open to the possibility of the new. This is what the transcendental experience and revelation are all about. If God is present to us, as we believe he is, there is no limit to what we may find and what may take shape in our world as man and God enter into dialogue. God speaks to us of the infinite possibilities that lie within his vision for creation; and as man responds to God and shares his vision, he becomes the co-creator with God of the actuality of that vision. The style here is one of experiencing, imagining, conceptualizing, judging, and acting. It moves from an expectant passivity to confident action.

My interest in this chapter is the act of imagination, or "imaging" as a methodology of the experience of my story and the construction of its meaning. Having outlined in the previous three chapters the nature of ministry in regard to the city, meaning, and mystery, we now turn to discuss the style of ministry as focused in the fourth vector of the church's life. This is to speak of the spirituality of the church, in the sense that Karl Rahner refers to the nature of man as *Geist* or "spirit," man as created open to God. It is to speak of a piety, by which I mean a disciplined attending to God (in the classical sense). We are all aware of the negative or vacuous feelings attached to words like "spirituality" and "piety" in our society and in the life of the church; but unless someone can come forward with better terms for the same thing, the reader needs to do his best to put aside the unpleasant associations attached over the years to those words, and to look at them in their original intent.

The style of spirituality or piety is one of imagination. If the church is to be open to the presence of God in Christ now, it has to live a life of imagination. This is to say that imagination is not a "faculty" in man, but a posture of the whole man toward his experience. Man as he who images is not the same as man as he who merely feels or thinks logically; nor is he the same man who simply moves with the stereotypical thinking of his social world. This is not to deprecate any of these other ways of developing the meaning of our experience, but to say that they do not lend themselves to a discernment of God's presence in our experience, making all things new. The life style of the fourth vector has to be one of imagination or, to introduce two words that are to me synonymous, of intuition or of wonder. The fact that religious experience is considered so rare a thing among us—although, as Bourque indicated, it is really not that unusual—does not mean that God is no longer present, but that in our Western culture we have made so little of imagination, intuition, and wonder to discern within our own culture the presence of God.

We all know how to dismiss some unlikely suggestion of an opponent. "He is only imagining it," we say, as if to imagine is to conjure up an unreal thing. We pass beyond the childlike by saying, "It is all in his imagination," as if to locate the consciousness of an experience in the imagination is to exile it to oblivion. The truth is that if the horizons of our understanding of our experience are to expand, they will only do so through the intuitive dimension of man's knowing. The very nature of the imagination requires that no preconditions be set on what is possible within our experience.

The purpose of this chapter is, therefore, to begin the exploration of ministry as a new piety by examining what it means to be-in-the-world-as-one-who-images. It is my conviction that this is the primary agenda of ministry today; to recover for itself that meaning. It would follow that we accept the truth of what Goethe and Don Juan say—truth is a rainbow, and the world is a mysterious place—and that we so live as to explore the possibilities of this in our experience. I am hardly the first to suggest this in recent years, as the citations in the rest of the chapter in this second part of the book will testify. My own contribution to the discussion, however, is intended to set the research within the practicalities of ministry as such, and also to call attention to these new or recovered insights as one committed to the church as the Body of Christ and to its mission.

The organization of the chapter is this. First of all we can profitably ground our discussion in some research in the psychology of intuition. Following this, it is important that we draw together some of the recent discussion of the imagination in philosophical and theological writing. Third, a distinction then needs to be drawn between imagination and fantasy. This will be a crucial point. Finally, there is the question of what we do with the imagination.

These four sections in this chapter will not be complete in themselves, since the three chapters that follow will provide a different and yet supplementary approach to the same concern: ministry as a new piety. The insight then that I intend for the reader to begin to develop here will, I hope, be greatly sharpened in the subsequent chapters.

THINKING WITH THE LEFT HAND

I first discovered the image of "thinking with the left hand" as representative of intuitive or imaginative thought in a series of essays by the American educational psychologist, Jerome Bruner.[3] This collection of Bruner's is not a systematic treatise, as befits the subject, but a gathering together of a number of reflections upon a unified theme. The theme, metaphorically expressed in the image of the left hand, is that way of knowing "that grows happy hunches and 'lucky' guesses, that is stirred into connective activity by the poet and the necromancer looking sideways rather than directly. Their hunches and intuitions generate a grammar of their own."[4] The essays discuss creativity, myth, the modern novel, art, the art of discovery, learning mathematics, fate, among others.

Of course, as we shall see, Bruner did not invent the image of the left hand to stand for man's intuitive or imaginative approach to knowing. It weaves its way throughout the history of man for reasons that shall become clear, and has attached to it all sorts of fascinating implications. What Bruner is pointing out is that the frontal assault upon the data of our experience is only one way of knowing, although a necessary one. Just as essential, however, is the less antiseptic and more oblique approach, identified with symbol and myth, the poetic and the artistic. Bruner writes about the role of the "effective surprise" in creativity, which, as I have previously said, is a dimension of the religious experience and which he sees as a condition of thinking with the left hand or imagination.

Robert Ornstein, who cites Bruner frequently, has devoted his career as a psychologist to a further exploration of the meaning of thinking with the left hand. More than a metaphor to him, his argument is that such thinking is a biological fact. Ornstein argues that the human brain has two sides, and when these two sides are divided from one another, as in certain surgery to treat epileptic seizure, each side functions as if it were a *separate* brain. It is, of course, reasonably well known that the left hemisphere controls the right hand side of the body and the right hemisphere the left hand side. Therefore, what we normally relate to the left side is ultimately tied in with the right hemisphere of the brain. This theory of Ornstein and others, it should be noted, is not an established, generally accepted hypothesis. It is presently challenged in part, if not in its entirety, by other psychologists.

Ornstein points out that the left cerebral hemisphere operates well in an analytical manner, processing verbal information and expressing itself in a rational manner. It is related to performance of a task. The right hemisphere, however, possesses certain capacities lacking to the left hemisphere. For example, it has a better grasp of spatial relationships. It is more aware of emotional reactions to experience *prior* to analysis, causing us to identify such consciousness with the reasons of the heart. The heart, of course, is located on our left side. Ornstein believes that duality of consciousness is characteristic of all men, and that the different function of the two cerebral hemispheres is the clear explanation of all of this.[5]

Some characteristics of thinking with the left hand, as drawn together by Ornstein from a number of sources, include its identification with darkness, sensuality, timelessness, receptivity, tacit knowing (as in Michael Polanyi), nonlinear thinking, simultaneity, diffuseness, the earth, acausality, and femininity.[6] I would note that all these characteristics bespeak a certain ambiguity. Right-hand thinking reduces our experience to a series of time-related units or events, from which we develop a linear logic of causality. Piaget calls it operational thinking, be it concrete or formal. Intuitive thinking is associative or transductive, where discrete images, representing bits of experience, may be arranged almost at will to formulate possible meaning. We are not coerced by the meaning that is ours, we are stimulated and awakened into possibilities. This is the ambiguity of that consciousness which is begotten of the right cerebral hemisphere.

To illustrate what I mean, we can draw on a point made by Bruner. Art is thinking with the left hand. He calls our attention to the paintings of Christ by Giotto. The power of these paintings is that he combines that which cannot be logically joined; the image of a medieval peasant in pain upon the Cross, which at the same time is God eternally offering himself for all mankind. Metaphor, the language of the right cerebral hemisphere, Bruner says, "joins dissimilar experiences by finding the image or the symbol that unites them at some deeper emotional level of meaning. Its effect depends upon its capacity for getting past the literal mode of connecting."[7] Its power is its incongruity, which clearly relates it to symbolic meaning.

Ornstein's research is very important, if for no other reason than that it ties in man-as-he-who-images with the biological nature of man himself. To document in any sense the intuitive capacities of man's right cerebral hemisphere does not, of course, "prove" the existence of God. It does indicate that it is the very nature of man to exercise a creative imagination, which imagination I have suggested is the appropriate posture of the Christian collectivity in the fourth vector. Man as "spirit in the world," in Rahner's sense, takes on a neurological respectability. So much for Ornstein for the moment. We shall have occasion to return to him.

The metaphor of thinking with the left hand, which we now perceive is much more than just a metaphor, has a long history. The relationship of the right hemisphere of the brain to the left side of man, inasmuch as it is an ingredient of man's biogrammar (the biological built-in structure of human intentionality), would be expected to flow throughout human cultural history, and so it does. There is great value in touching upon this fact, for it gives some idea of man's discomfort with this capacity of himself, and consequently begins to build both a picture of what it is like to "think with the left hand" and an understanding of why man, particularly contemporary man, has shrunk from this dimension of his existence.

One way to jump into the data, historically speaking, is to begin with the Latin word for "left," *sinister*. The English that is based on this word and its secondary Latin meaning quickly draws our attention to all the connotations of the left hand or side. The left symbolizes ambiguity, suspicion of perversity, uncertainty of intention, paradox, and even evil. The "bar sinister" is well known as the heraldic device, borne by those whose conception was illegitimate. In primitive tribes over the world left-handed children were put to death as threatening to the social system, and even today we see parents who strive to change their left-handed children for no apparent reason. All those things which Ornstein associated with the right cerebral hemisphere are a part of the feeling and thinking content of the sinister.

The Greek language offers an interesting twist on the symbol of the left hand. One word for "left" is *euonumos,* which literally means the "well-

named" one. For the Greeks, whose language was in its inception very concrete, names have power. If you bestow upon that of which you are fearful a
complimentary name, then you may stay on the good side of the power it
represents.

I have written elsewhere about the relationship of the feminine to the left
hand.[8] The association is, as far as I can tell, universal. All the connotations
of femininity, particularly as expressed in the intuitive character of the feminine symbol, are conveyed by the left hand: contradictory meaning between
creativity and wanton destructiveness, darkness and reflected light, uncontrolled and uncontrollable passion, lack of predictability. This is the substance
of the consciousness identified by Ornstein with the right hemisphere of the
brain.

The well-trained man of the classical world approached his neighbor with
his right hand exposed and his left hand covered amid his garments (as if "in
his pocket").[9] Books on the social life of the ancient world will tell you that
the right hand was revealed to show that the person carried no weapon. Why,
however, was the left hand covered? There was something *obscene* in this in
the literal sense of that word, "unfitting." For similar reasons one "shakes
hands" today with the right hand, and to use the left hand is considered not
quite proper. All this seems to lie in the fact that the left hand is associated
with the earthy and hidden dimensions of human existence. My father, an
internationally known scholar of medieval social life, repeatedly told me that
medieval man always cleansed himself with his left hand after defecation, and
that it was forbidden to eat with this hand. The use of the left hand for toilet
functions was also true among the Hindus and the American Mohave Indians.
Ancient man, whom I assume probably followed the same customs in regard
to calls of nature, lay on his left side for formal meals, thereby incapacitating
the left hand for eating. In polite circles today we keep our left hands in our
laps while dining.[10]

Of course, all this identifies the left hand or side as "bad," as with darkness or blackness, and many cultures have chosen this univocal conclusion.
Actually it is not that simple. The left is also the artistic side, and while
many people are genuinely suspicious or afraid of artists, they are a vital part
of culture and the perception of the new. The Hopi Indians believed that
language belonged to the right hand and music to the left. (I wonder if it is
purely coincidental that the artists's colony in Paris is located on the "left
bank" of the Seine.) Jerome Bruner, as I have already mentioned, clearly
identifies painting, music, sculpture, literature, etc., with "thinking with the

92

left hand." The artist is the person of integral awareness, and this is both frightening and yet the source of a foreseeable future. Life does follow art, and we only pray that it is true art. Robert Bellah, the American sociologist, has suggested that the problem with America today is that it lacks meaning for its existence, and that this will only return when art is rescued from the periphery of our existence.[11]

What needs to be kept in mind, however, is something I will be saying for the rest of this book, and that I have at least implied before. All the symbolic associations of the left hand carry a certain feeling. The feeling is one of the unknown, the ambiguous, the risky, the unpredictable, and the uncontrolled. Man's efforts are always to get things under control. Mary Douglas, a distinguished English anthropologist, has pointed out that the concept of pollution is the control of chaos. What is forbidden in dietary laws, for example, is that which "does not fit."[12]

Control is necessary for man. The movement from thinking with the left hand to thinking with the right hand, to continue this image, is essential for our sanity. It is also inversely proportionate, however, to creative thinking and an awareness of the mystery from which God speaks. It is in terms of the imagination, with all its fearsome ambiguity and risk, that we come to identify the contemporary word of God. We cannot let the right side of our brain atrophy for lack of use and expect to have any sense of the presence of God among us. Yet that right cerebral hemisphere will develop a consciousness that will leave us in fear and trembling (Phil. 2:12). Jacob, in his vision of the ladder reaching to heaven (a powerful, common symbol in the ancient world), awoke saying, "How fearsome is this place" (Gen. 28:16). Indeed, it must have been. Yet that was and is no reason for avoiding it.

The thesis of this study, if we accept Ornstein's model of the brain, is that to be wholly human one exercises one's entire brain. Man images and, in so doing, becomes aware of the presence of God in his life. This is dangerous, but no one promised anything else. Our "God is a devouring fire" (Deut. 4:24).

SEEING RATHER THAN LOOKING

If we move from the psychological identification of the intuitive posture of man to describe what in effect imagination is, it helps to develop some clear verbal image of what we mean. What happens when we imagine? One answer can be found as the principal theme of Carlos Castaneda's second book on his Yaqui

93

shaman, *A Separate Reality: Further Conversations with Don Juan.* There Castaneda speaks of his struggle to become a "man of knowledge": one who *sees,* rather than merely *looks.*

The first point that Don Juan makes to Castaneda is that seeing is *not* achieved by clarity of analytical thought but by waiting. It has nothing to do with manipulation of oneself or the environment. Consequently, it is the opposite of technology, which partially explains why Castaneda was so popular in the youth culture of the late sixties. It is a feeling experienced as a result of detachment from the common-sense world of our society. Castaneda quotes Don Juan as saying,

> Upon learning to *see* a man becomes everything by becoming nothing. He, so to speak, vanishes and yet he's there. I would say that this is the time when a man can be or get anything he desires. But he desires nothing, and instead of playing with his fellow men, like they were toys, he meets them in the midst of their folly. The only difference between them is that a man who *sees* controls his folly, while his fellow men can't. A man who *sees* has no longer an active interest in his fellow men. *Seeing* has already detached him from absolutely everything he knew before."[13]

Clearly I will not claim for this statement that it meets the demand of the Christian ethic, because its appeal to detachment seems to call for a passivity before injustice. At the same time, the sense of nothingness, the embracing of our foolishness, and a detachment from the world's values is indeed biblical, and relates to whatever Castaneda understands seeing to be.

Of course, the image of a visual discernment that gets behind the *appearance* of things is not original with the Yaqui shaman. Such images abound in the New Testament: "Now we see *(blepomen)* only puzzling reflections in a mirror, but then we shall see *(blepomen)* face to face" (1 Cor. 13:12); "then will you see clearly *(diablepseis)* to take the speck out of your brother's [eye]" (Matt. 7:5); "His [God's] invisible attributes . . . have been visible . . . to the eye of reason *(tois poiemasin nooumena kathopatai)* (Rom. 1:20); "Also he was seen *(ophthe)* by Cephas, and then by the Twelve" (1 Cor. 15:5, translation mine). As can be readily discovered, no one Greek word carries the particular meaning, but clearly the context implies a kind of seeing that gets beyond the phenomena.

In Aristotelian terms this would mean that the one who sees gets behind the attributes of the object perceived to the substance. E. L. Mascall, the English Thomistic theologian, speaks of this discernment of actual being as a "cointuition."[14] I do not agree with Mascall that the knowing subject has a direct experience of Being, for which we can argue to the analogy of Being. He is locating the act of seeing on the left cerebral hemisphere, and I believe that it lies within the jurisdiction of the right cerebral hemisphere. Having disagreed to that point, however, I would go on to say that Mascall is accurately describing the act of seeing. Goethe has suggested that what is seen is the *Urphänomen* the "primal phenomenon," or the *Urpflanze,* the "primal scion"; in other words, the creative seed that gives birth to that cluster of phenomena at which we look. (It is interesting to speculate on the relationship of the *Urphänomen* to Jaspers's "cipher.")

As we pursue the meaning of seeing as the act of the imagination, in contrast to mere looking, it is helpful to reflect on the theories of the English Jesuit poet of the last century, Gerard Manley Hopkins. Hopkins speaks of the perception of the "inscape," as opposed to the "landscape." One *looks at* a landscape; I would say one *sees* the inscape. The very word "inscape" is ultimately rooted in the Greek *skopei,* meaning "to look" or "to keep one's eyes on" something or somebody; as well as the noun, *skopos,* meaning a "mark." The feeling of the word is the mark to which one ultimately looks, the heart of the matter. "This mark is," Hopkins says, " 'the species or scape of any object, as of sight, sound, taste, smell' found in the 'intellectual imagination.' "[15] To discern the inscape is to see the God through whom the object experienced came to be. It is to intuit Being, but clearly in the sense of the imaginative.

The inscape for Hopkins is a convergence (a "tacit knowing" pointing toward God), a coming together of the phenomena of our experience into a unity of their source. We become aware of this through what he calls the "instress," the force or impact of the inscape, as perceived by our senses. It seems to me that the instress is first discerned as feeling, awaking the imaginative powers to see the inscape. In his journal Hopkins speaks of the inscape as perceived most frequently by a detailed feeling of nature. At one point he relates how he caused a duck to keep its head down by placing it on a table and drawing a white chalk line across the table from its beak. He explains this phenomenon as "most likely the fascinating instress of the straight white stroke."[16]

Elsewhere in his journal Hopkins writes:

> In the snow, flat-topped hillocks and shoulders outlined with wavy edges, ridge below ridge, very like the grain of wood in line and in projection, like relief maps. These the wind makes I think and of course drifts, which are in fact snow waves. The sharp nape of a drift sometimes broken by slant flutes or channels. I think this must be when the wind after shaping the drift first changed and cast waves

in the body of the wave itself. All the world is full of inscape and chance left free
to act falls into an order as well as a purpose.[17]

The beauty of the passage is the ability of the author to convey the feeling
of beauty in the experience, which is the instress, pointing to the inscape. The
fact that he moves from intuition and wonder to analysis and logic and back
again twice illustrates what we all do. The power of what he says is its message
to the imagination, often conveyed in the sound of the words and fleeting
metaphors.

Hopkins wrote his poetry (as apart from mere "verse") as the speech of
inscape. It sought to enable us, by so shaping the instress perceived in reading
or hearing the poem, to see that we are drawn to the unity of all things. The
classic example of Hopkins's understanding of poetry as the language of inscape, the same poetry which we have already seen is the language of the right
hemisphere of the brain, is "The Wreck of the Deutschland." It was written
to commemorate the death of five Franciscan nuns, whose ship on route from
Germany to America, foundered on the shores of Kent. It deals with the
subject of death, and the inscape is Christ. One has to read the entire poem
of thirty-five stanzas, however, to get the feel of the instress, leading to this
proclamation:

> But how shall I . . . make no room there:
>   Reach me a . . . Fancy, come faster—
> Strike you the sight of it? look at it loom there,
>   Thing that she . . . there then! the Master,
> *Ipse,* the only one, Christ, King, Head:
> He was to cure the extremity where he had cast her;
>   Do, deal, lord it with living and dead;
> Let him ride, her pride, in his triumph, despatch and
>   have done with his doom there.

Long before Thass-Thienemann and others described the emotional power
of words, and consequently their symbolic force, and Noam Chomsky discussed the "deep grammar" of language, Hopkins had sensed that there is a
force to the arrangement of language that draws us beyond the univocal,
surface denotations of words to an inherent meaning behind them.[18] Read the
stanza I have quoted from "The Wreck of the Deutschland" aloud or, better
yet, read the whole poem, and perhaps in hearing you will see and not just look.

To see is to engage the inscape, the convergence that lies behind the
phenomena. If we only look we just know the landscape, the phenomena
themselves. Let us analyze that a bit further. Owen Barfield, an English

solicitor and friend to C. S. Lewis, offers considerable help here. Barfield calls our attention to Plato's statement that there are three degrees of knowledge, which result in turn from simple observation, observation with explanation, and participation in the divine mind. The first Barfield calls "figuration," which is simply converting phenomena into "things," the second is alpha-thinking, and the third is beta-thinking, which is reflective thinking.

Barfield's first fundamental point is that the primitive mind does not engage in alpha-thinking, much less beta-thinking, but participates in the phenomena of its experience. Perhaps there are a few primitive minds still around today. This level of thinking Barfield calls "original participation." He defines it as follows:

> The essence of *original* participation is that there stands behind the phenomena, *and on the other side of them from me,* a represented which is of the same nature as me . . . the perceiving self inasmuch as it is not mechanical or accidental, but psychic and voluntary.[19]

What is perceived is the same as the inscape, but we need to keep a little loose to this conclusion for the moment. Because it is alpha-thinking which made original participation no longer possible, and the culture is *irrevocably* committed to alpha-thinking. In other words, there is no way to go back to the mind of an Australian aborigine, an African of the sixteenth century, or a Navaho of a hundred years ago.

What Barfield does believe is that in detaching ourselves from our experience, as we have done in alpha-thinking, and explaining what we observe in conceptual language—which is what "saving the appearances" (a term used by Simplicus in the sixth century A.D. in his commentary on Aristotle's *De Caelo,* "Concerning the Heaven") in the title of Barfield's book means—we have made idols out of our explanations. We have become the slaves of our own scientific paradigms, which have become reified and alienated. Rubem Alves, a "third world" theologian, is saying the same thing when he suggests that the reality which Western culture has rationalized is really an illusion.[20] We have to get beyond saving the appearances, beyond our detached paradigms, to perceive once again what lies beyond the phenomena. This requires contemporary man to move, not only through alpha-thinking but also through thinking about thinking, beta-thinking.

Barfield calls this going beyond saving the appearances "final participation," and considers it an act of the imagination. It is very much the same as Ricoeur's "second naïvete." The imagination is for Barfield that capacity in man to make the material an image of the immaterial or spiritual. With this definition in mind the following two quotations from Barfield are most helpful.

> Beta-thinking can go thus far. It can convince us itself that, just as for original participation potential existence was something quite different from not-being, so, for the kind of participation at which we have arrived today, the potentially phenomenal is not the same as nothing.... Let us call this ... *final participation*.[21]

> To be *able* to experience the representations as idols, and then to be able also to perform the act of figuration consciously, so as to experience them as participated, that is imagination.[22]

What this means is that we cannot go back to some kind of "paleolithic revival," to quote Robert Bellah, which Barfield believes only ends up in pantheism, spiritualism, and occultism. We have to explain what we observe, but that is not all. It is quite possible to see a unifying subjectivity lying behind the phenomena, which is potentially there and is not mere nothingness just because its presence is not evident on the surface. As we convert the phenomena into "things" it is possible to see the subject on the other side of the phenomena. This is to exercise, consciously and with sophistication, the imagination. It is to perceive what Goethe called the *Urphänomen*, the source of or primal phenomenon.

I think it was Jacob Burkhardt, the great Renaissance historian, who said that religion without imagination would become either magic or sentimentality. He is right, because religion that has no sense of the immediate presence of God either attempts to conjure up that presence by man's cunning or reduces piety to nostalgia and "being sweet." Ray Hart, an American theologian teaching at the University of Montana, has taken Burkhardt's admonition seriously and has done a systematic job of building on Barfield's insights. He offers an epistemological rationale of the imagination, which undergirds what I have described as "seeing."

Hart describes a process of the extension and intention of knowing, which is very much like a dialogic movement between the left and right cerebral hemispheres, looking and seeing, landscape and inscape, and "saving the appearances" and "final participation." It also seems related to the journey back and forth between the structures and antistructures we will discuss in the next chapter. He argues that to understand our experience we have to participate in it ("be" with it) as well as detach ourselves from it and analyze it. Most of us are good at analysis. We are not so good at being or participation.

Two key concepts in Hart are those of the "hermeneutical spiral" and the "imaginative shock." Hermeneutics, as some immediately recognize, is the art of interpretation, the understanding and articulation of our experience in its integrity. The hermeneutical spiral—an image Hart offers in place of the often discussed "hermeneutical circle"—describes the action of *intensive* and *extensive* knowing. By this is meant the dialogue between participation in our experience (intensive knowing) and the objective knowledge of that experience (extensive knowing). It is descriptive of an entering into the experience for the sake of being, and a purposeful detachment from the experience for the sake of knowing. The act of knowing, however, never encompasses or captures the act of being, and consequently we return to participate again and to withdraw again for the sake of greater knowledge. Hence we have an ascending spiral of knowing or interpretation of experiences.

The movement into the experience is one of imagination. Hart describes the imagination in several ways. It is "light (in the mind), in search of enlightenment (in events)," "the seat of connection between perception and thinking," "a way of being human," and "the very alembic [that which refines or purifies] of creative energy."[23] The imagination is always active, as well as contagious. To be an educated person is to have a developed imagination. It is the posture of man as he is coming to be, for it is the dominant characteristic of the fourth vector, our openness to revelation and God's solicitation of us into being. To see God on the other side of the phenomena, to participate in a final way, is to imagine new possibilities for our being and to move into them.

The "imaginative shock" is that which gets the hermeneutical spiral going. It awakens man to the inscape of life and calls him out to participate in being. It is a correlate of Tillich's "ontological shock," which is "the jarring of one's reality-sense, the conviction that one's disposition is cheating himself of his ownmost possibilities of being. By the act, active imagination is thrown into gear in quest of just what those potencies are."[24] It is the same thing as the "shock" Amos Wilder identifies in the Gospel parables.[25] The "imaginative shock" is the same as a striking awareness that our categories do not fit our experience.

On the basis of this definition, Jesus was an imaginative shock to those he called to follow him. Paul's experience on the road to Damascus was an imaginative shock. Certainly the small child's voice which Augustine of Hippo, while sitting in his garden, heard saying "Take up and read," served as an imaginative shock. I remember the Baptism of the agnostic chairman of the philosophy department at my university, which was provoked by an emergency appendectomy. This bodily threat was an imaginative shock, even though it may also have been a case of "fox-hole Christianity." Don Juan's comment to Castaneda that he fed him hallucinogenic plants because "there was no other way to jolt you," is a tall illustration of the imaginative shock.[26] My own move in 1966 from the French culture of South Louisiana a thousand miles north to the German culture of Milwaukee was a painful imaginative shock which lasted a year. The point is that the imagination begins to work and we come to see as we never did before.

Castaneda describes seeing as "stopping the world." To stop the world is to collapse the illusion of reality the world imposes upon us—a very important concept that I will develop more systematically in the next chapter—in order to see new possibilities. A state of fear, awe, power, and death are ideal, according to Don Juan, for stopping the world.[27] Castaneda describes something of what one sees when he stops the world. By an active passivity he sees the holes in the world, which means he literally sees the space between the phenomena of which he is customarily conscious at some level. When he looks *through* these holes, it would appear that he would find on the other side a subjective presence, which Castaneda translates as an "ally."[28] Here lies Goethe's *Urphänomen.*

If we look at this in Hart's language, as well as that of Barfield, the imaginative shock stops the world. The imagination then can move beyond the collective representations, the socially imposed filters, by a conscious willed act, to participate in the being that undergirds the phenomena. This is what Barfield means by final participation. It is to see, not just to look, which means that we transcend what the society tells us is there in order to find out for ourselves. Imagination is what is lacking in the rich young man who asked Jesus what he had to do to enter into life, and "went away with a heavy heart; for he was a man of great wealth" (Matt. 19:22). It is also the difference between the many who are invited and the few who are chosen (Matt. 22:14).

FANTASY AND IMAGINATION

Both R. D. Laing, an English psychiatrist, and Joseph Campbell, an American scholar of mythology, have suggested that a psychotic break may well sharpen our ability to see. We usually describe as "crazy" those whose reality and subsequent action does not conform to the reality and action of the society of which they are a part. This is to say that, at least to a degree, insanity is a definition imposed upon meaning and action by a culture, and is not something discrete and identifiable apart from its social context. The Soviet Union has been known to hospitalize political deviants as insane. This is, I suspect, only a more calloused form of what might happen in America. Thomas Szasz, the American psychologist, has documented in a convincing manner our own ideological definition of mental illness.[29]

Of course, there is a genuine, destructive mental illness, which stifles the creativity of a person and makes him a hazard to his freedom and the freedom of society. The issue is the line between a truly destructive reality and behavior, rooted in a confused perception of experience, and what is nonconformist because of the subject's perception of that which the society itself cannot see. Often it is the movement into the "holes," the spaces between the phenomena, or what Laing calls the "cracks," that we label "psychotic." Campbell writes of two kinds of schizophrenia: "essential" or creative, and "paranoid" or destructive. In the former the subject falls into the chaos of the psychotic break and swims to shore. In the latter the subject drowns.[30] This is a good image, whose very ambiguity reveals once more the risky character of imagination.

Following this lead, it is helpful to look at the claim the American existential psychologist, William Lynch, S.J., who argues that the mentally ill person is just he who does *not* possess imagination. Lynch says that confusion is a necessary part of existence, but amid his confusion man must have hope. I would say that this hope is the source of meaning and his confusion, which can form the basis of a purposeful life. Hope depends on the ability to wish, and that requires a developed imagination. The mentally ill person is one who is hopeless amid the confused world, and because he lacks imagination and cannot wish, he is left only to fantasize.[31]

Obviously Lynch is making a distinction between imagination and fantasy, and it is an important one, which I share in this study. The reader who finds himself uncomfortable in the thought that this chapter is suggesting that ministry calls on us to "dream at will" about unicorns, gods from outer space, or white supremacy needs to attend carefully to the distinction Lynch develops and which is implied in what Campbell says.

Lynch states that fantasy fails to live in the world of facts, truth, and reality.[32] Fantasy is more a hostile rejection or a gnostic escape from that world. These three words, facts, truth, and reality, all synonyms really, describe the *reasoned judgment* of *what is* in the context of an ongoing community of collaboration. This judgment is not absolute, because we do not possess the mind of God; but it is the best we can do at this moment. For example, there may have been a time when to speak of unicorns was not all that fantastic, but contemporary reasoned judgment would say that it is not true that unicorns exist. It is pure fantasy, despite the efforts of past decades, for me to suggest that because my skin is white I am superior to my neighbor whose skin happens to be black. There is no data in our experience, of which we are aware, that is not subject to a simpler solution. The same thing goes for the recently popularized notion about gods coming among us in primeval times from outer space, although I would be willing to say that this is a more open question.

Imagination *builds* on facts, truth, and reality. Unlike fantasy, it does not break completely with the continuum of man's understanding of his environment, but moves forward by a judicious selection and reshaping of the representations of experience that make up our meaning. Alfred North Whitehead wrote:

> Imagination is not to be divorced from the facts: it is a way of illuminating the facts. It works by eliciting the general principles which apply to the facts, as they exist, and then by an intellectual survey of alternative possibilities which are consistent with those principles. It enables men to construct an intellectual vision of a new world, and it preserves the zest of life by the suggestion of satisfying purposes.[33]

That is a most helpful statement from a man for whose imagination theology today is in great debt. He also says, "Fools act on imagination without knowledge; pedants act on knowledge without imagination."[34] Imagination creates perspective, which results from seeing, not apart from the phenomena but through and beyond the phenomena. As Barfield has said, it is imagination that unites the world of matter and spirit—Descartes lacked imagination, as did the Puritans—and requires them both.[35] Polanyi speaks of the movement from the *proximal* to the *distal* in tacit knowing, and what I am saying here is related to the thought that when imagination fails that "movement" breaks down.[36]

Obviously, imagination, in all that I have said, is kept from fantasy by reason. Charles Williams was a prolific and inspired student of the imagination, but he was also committed to truth and wanted to distinguish imagination from what Lynch and I have called fantasy. For Williams, the discipline of imagery by reason involved three criteria. First, imagination uses images as representations. The image must be appropriate within its own natural limits to the referent. $E = MC^2$ can represent relativity, but not the God of the New Testament. Second, there needs to be a pattern of consistent thought discernible in the product of the imagination. God cannot be both a vindictive despot *and* a loving creator. Third, we do not confuse the representation with its referent. The Christ is not the "prisoner of the tabernacle," meaning that he is not identical with the reserved sacrament that symbolically represents him.[37]

Certainly the line between imagination and fantasy is not neat. This implies what I have suggested several times already, there are no guarantees in the life of the imagination. It is a risky business. The risk is compounded when we reflect that, if Lynch is right and to avoid imagination is to fall backwards into fantasy, the more we attempt to avoid the uncertainties of the imagination the more likely we are to lapse into the fantastic.

It took imagination to perceive the nature of Jesus of Nazareth, and that involved all kinds of risk. Whitehead, always the master of the epigram, wrote, "Imagination . . . is a dangerous gift, which has started many a conflagration."[38] Imagination is, however, creative. Fantasy is not, and yet it often has even more tragic endings than imagination. For example, Jesus and those who had the imagination to see him for what he was changed the world. Those Jews who failed to exercise their imagination in regard to Jesus shortly afterwards engaged in two acts of fantasy, the first and second Jewish wars against the Romans in A.D. 69–70 and in A.D. 135, which only ended in the destruction of the Jewish state in Palestine.

Fantasy can be corporate, as in the case of the first- and second-century Palestinian Jews. An active community of discourse within which we imagine is a very positive counter to fantasy and does, in fact, feed the imagination. A true community often finds itself able to image more than the sum of the images brought to it by its membership (called "equifinality"), and yet at the same time there is more likely to be in that group a check upon the fantasies of individuals or subgroups within it. This is particularly true when there is a conscious and continuing acknowledgement of the community's history. Imagination is possible for the individual or community which knows its past and, therefore, knows who or what it is.

In the conclusion of *Fiddler on the Roof* the question is asked from off stage, "What holds him [the fiddler on the roof] up?" The answer is heard, "Tradition." This is what I mean. The creativity of "fiddling around" is possible when it is done within the ongoing self-consciousness of a community, which we call tradition. It is the sense of identity, handed down through time (the Greek word for tradition, *paradosis,* means to "hand down"), which gives us the imagery and the security to think the new.

THE ACT OF IMAGINATION

Whitehead said that the imagination is youthful. It is more than that; it is *childlike*. Jesus said, "Unless you turn around and become like children you will never enter the kingdom of Heaven" (Matt. 18:3). He is talking about the capacity of the little child, aged three to seven, to think associatively or, to use Jean Piaget's word, transductively, rather than reducing all meaning to a logical operation imposed by society's categories of reality. To imagine is to escape the procrustean bed of the given culture's collective representation of experience.

In the Gospels, the opposite of the childlike person is the man with the hardened heart. In Mark's Gospel, after the miracle of feeding the four thousand, the Pharisees challenge Jesus. They seem to have no idea as to the meaning of the miracle. Jesus says to them, "Have you no inkling yet? Do you still not understand? Are your minds closed?" (Mark 8:17). Literally, the last question reads: "Do you have the heart of all of you permanently hardened?" The reasons of the heart are not possible for these men, and consequently they cannot perceive the inscape of the event of the feeding. The Pharisees were sincere persons, trapped in the collective representation of their particular Jewish sect.

Of course, this can happen to any of us when we lose the child's ability to play. Among a few books, I remember one from my early school days. Its contemporary is a Dr. Seuss book, one entitled *And To Think That I Saw It on Mulberry Street.* It is about a little boy who, while walking home, "sees" a wonderful circus parade coming down his home street. He reports this all to his father in marvelous, vivid detail. As the plot unfolds, the father slowly wears the boy down to the "truth," which is that all he actually saw was "a plain horse and wagon on Mulberry Street." Technological thinking wins out in the end and the little boy can grow up to be a "good American."

I contrast this with Castaneda's account of a visit to Don Juan's house in 1971, when he found Don Juan's friend, a Mazatec Indian sorcerer, Don Genaro. Don Juan and Don Genaro make great fun of Castaneda and they literally play with him. Finally, Don Genaro announces that he will take away the car in which Castaneda drove to Don Juan's house, and when Castaneda returns to where he parked, it is indeed gone. The whole scene is one of great hilarity. Later Don Juan explains to Castaneda, "Genaro wanted to soften your certainty."[39] He could just as well have said, "soften your heart."

A young child can perceive the phenomena of his experience, identify random images within the data, and associate them without having to follow some univocal set of rules. The filters of his mind are suspectible to change, and phenomena which we might not see he does. Can we be sure that there was no circus parade on Mulberry Street? Is that any more fantastic than the "disappearance" of Castaneda's car? Why did not the Pharisees see the meaning of the feeding of the four thousand? And why did Peter know Jesus to be the promised Messiah, the Son of the Living God (Matt. 16:17)? I am suggesting that the difference is the ability to play, to look at our experience in terms of "what if."

This is to say that the act of the imagination is not the result of being terribly serious about the culture's imposed reality, of straining to be consistent, or of wanting to be in control. It is really the opposite of all these things. Northrop Frye, the Canadian William Blake scholar, has written:

> In the imagination anything goes that can be imagined, and the limit of the imagination is a totally human world. Here we recapture, in full consciousness, that original lost sense of identity with our surroundings, where there is nothing outside the mind of man, or something identical with the mind of man.[40]

How does one associate what is outside the mind with the mind? Frye believes one does this by possessing a mind rich in the images of literature and the other arts. The imagination is something we *train* by saturating ourselves with the imaginative works of others. "The fundamental job of the imagination in ordinary life, then," Frye goes on to say, "is to produce, out of the society we have to live in, a vision of the society we want to live in."[41] The imagination is the only solution to a life lived as a victim of our collective, socialized representations.

Sam Keen, the American prophet of play, speaks of the imagination as the sense of wonder. I find his list of the elements of wonder in children very helpful in describing for us what the imagination is in action. Wonder possesses a sense of immediacy or spontaneous delight, unjaded by a pessimism and detachment born of dejection over the ephemeral nature of all life. There is a lack of necessity, Keen argues, in wonder. The rules of the game in play can change. Also, rather than being lost in the abstraction of experience, the child enjoys a concrete sense of the particular without requiring universal solutions. There is an intimacy and personal feeling to the experience of wonder. There is a challenge there, which calls for the child to master the experience and to act. There is no sense of prior defeat, but a kind of chastened optimism.[42]

There is no reason why the development of the rational powers has to be accompanied by a loss of this sense of wonder or imagination. The artist, the rare person who has retained his wonder, can still balance his check book, write a textbook on painting, or pass a driver's license test. Recent theological writings, such as those of Keen, Harvey Cox, and Rubem Alves, have often been interpreted on the popular scene as advocating Dionysian play to the denial of Apollonian thought. This is not what I am suggesting, and neither does anyone else who stops to think. The point is that we need to practice the styles of both sides of the brain. We need both the childlike, associative thought, as well as formal, operational thought. Play and logic are both an essential part of the pursuit of truth. The problem is we do not know how to play.

One way of assisting in play is to approach it in a structured manner. Best, I suspect, is that play just happens, but we have a cultural complex against admitting the value of anything that "just happens." Therefore, I would take a look at one method of pursuing the use of the imagination in a very analytical, right-handed approach. I describe it as the "four Ds," and you will notice that it moves from the Dionysian to the Apollonian (another way of speaking of the movement between the two hemispheres of the brain in the structure and antistructure of the next chapter), or engages in a hermeneutical spiral.[42] The four Ds are: description, discovery, development, and discipline.[43]

In most classical forms of Christian meditation we begin by trying to picture a scene. Frequently, this is from the life of Jesus as recorded in the Gospels. The art of such picturing is very difficult if we want to let it flow into our consciousness without imposing upon it what we want to find. All kinds of detective stories are built around the fact that people have to work to see the scene of the crime, because they either ignore detail or actually block the unpleasant or unusual. Edgar Allen Poe made much of this in the account of *The Purloined Letter.* When we can recall our dreams, they are often uncensored descriptions of something. The problem of *description* is the problem of opening the filters of consciousness to let as complete a picture of an experience as possible form on our mind. It is a passive and innocent act, in which judgment is suspended and we are willing to be informed.

The next step is *discovery.* Do you remember the puzzles in children's magazines and comic books? My mother brought them to me when I was sick, and I always loved those with pictures of great detail: gnarled trees, thick bushes, long vistas, and much shading of light and shadow. Underneath would be a question such as: "How many squirrels are in this picture?" It was a test of your ability to let the images emerge in your peripheral vision. It was an exploration in the visual sense of Michael Polanyi's "tacit knowing." Polanyi, the author of *Personal Knowledge,* is a distinguished American philosopher, who takes that knowledge and engages the person from outside the point of his concentration and control.

The act of discovering the significant images in our picture or description of experience requires a certain oblique seeing. Castaneda is told by Don Juan that to see is *not doing.* "Shadows are like doors," Don Juan says, "the doors of *not-doing.* "[44] Elsewhere he talks about looking for the holes in the world or listening to the space between sounds. It is as if he understood that man imposes the categories upon the phenomena, and only when we look "between the phenomena" do we escape the categories and have the possibility of perceiving images that are implicit within the description and are not our own preconditioned constructs.

There is a watercolor that hangs in my office, painted by a friend of some years ago. Its title is *The Sting of Death.* That is perhaps what it means for the artist. It has none of this for me, although I love the painting for the images that illuminate my own unconscious. Actually, it was a painting-description of a recurring childhood dream of the artist, and "the sting of death" is one image he finds in it. I find others. I only deplore those who, after asking what is it "supposed" to be, say after a few moments contemplation, "Oh yes, I see now. It is the painting of a wolf's head."

Barbara Myerhoff, an anthropologist teaching at the University of Southern California, has related to me an experience she once had under the influence of peyote. She was working among the Huichol Indians in Mexico. In her peyote vision she first saw the *mara'akame,* the Huiochol priest-shaman, in various birdlike manifestations, and then she saw a yarn painting such as the Huichols love to make. She looked closely at the painting hoping to see what it meant, but could discover nothing until the last moment. Then, she told me, out of the corner of her eye she saw a little animal "escape" from the center of the painting. When she awoke, the *mara'akame* came into the hut, and in great excitement she described what she saw. Then, not satisfied with the mystery itself, she asked him what it meant. In great disgust, he turned and stomped out of the hut.

The point is that a discovery of this kind is a function of our peripheral vision, the uncontrolled presence. As one person has told me, "God appears somewhere over my left shoulder." For this reason, in moving to the third step, *development,* which follows upon discovery, it is important that we still see ourselves as engaged in a very ambiguous performance, where to press the meaning is to lose it.

The emergent images of our imagination do, however, need to be related;

not in any certain way, but associated so as to test for interrelated patterns that illuminate ourselves within experience. This could be called a search for insight. I describe it here as *development*. Development can be seen as a very abstract and theoretical dimension of the cognitive process, or it can be illustrated in terms well known to us all. I choose the latter and refer the reader to the child's love of ghost stories and the male (usually) adult's delight in scatological tales. The former depend on their power for the ability to frighten or even terrify, and the latter for their humor. Both terror and humor depend, as we have seen (see page 67), upon incongruity.

Ghost stories, as they are told by children, require the combination of images, all of which are supposed to point to strange and unnatural events—severed hands that walk in pursuit of their enemy, the dead who return to claim a lost lover, spirits of the departed bound to haunt certain places. As these stories are told, the skill is in elaborating them, binding a spell over the hearers through free association of images to create something new, strange, and incongruous. The better we develop the tale, the better we tell ghost stories.

Ribald humor is the same, except that it seeks to amuse rather than horrify, and is generally considered more socially acceptable among adults—intellectually speaking, if not socially. The images of body functions, racial attributes, promiscuous relationships are all played upon in free association again to paint an absurd, incongruous picture. Perhaps those who suggest that such stories are symptoms of their own unconscious fears are correct, but this does not gainsay—rather it supports—my contention that they are an illustration of the act of developing the images within the environment through a playful association, and are not based upon a socialized logical system. Think of your favorite "dirty joke" and it is obvious that it is absurd, at least in the eyes of formal thought. Yet we all tell them, and those who tell them best are those who can share and stimulate the free association of images best.

I was recently told a "good news, bad news" joke, a popular *genre* at the moment, which on the face of it is utterly absurd. Parents of a boy at college are phoned by the dean of men, who tells them, "I have some bad news and some good news about your son." "Oh my," they respond, "what is the bad news?" "Well," says the dean, "we have absolute proof your son is a practicing homosexual." Horrified, the parents ask for the "good news." The dean replies, "We are so proud of him. He has just been elected May queen."

The joke, if that is what it is, combined all kinds of association of incongruous ideas. Homosexuality is incongruous to many people in our culture, and either frightens or amuses, or both. The notion of a male student as "May queen," a kind of latter-day, sterilized temple prostitute, builds the incongruity. Even the possibility of a dean of men making such a phone call today approaches nonsense. The hearers are challenged, however, in all kinds of ways to further associate, and we know the string of stories that this kind of humor begets.

The fourth step, *discipline*, is the sudden leap into the "cold water" of analysis. It is a movement from intuition, and I only list it here because I think it is important that we see both its necessity and limitations. We all have had the experience in an English class of being asked what a poem "really means." This is an effort to reduce art to a conceptual clarity, which enables us to identify in some usable form what we have learned from it and how it might shape our action. In this way, ethics follows aesthetics, which I think is a much-needed understanding of the good.

At the same time, I am reminded of the story of the reporters who came to Martha Graham, the founder of modern dance, and asked her, "Miss Graham, what does your dance mean?" She is said to have replied, "Darlings, if I could tell you I would not have danced it!" The movement from imagination to thinking is always restrictive and limiting, as necessary as it must be. Only when we acknowledge the loss in that movement can we appreciate fully the power of the act of imagination.

SUMMARY

This concludes the first phase of the discussion of the dynamic of man as one who waits on God, the fourth vector of the Christian city. There is much more to be said, and there is far more that there is no way to express; but this much has been stated.

Man is not just a creature who thinks analytically and logically, but his very biology indicates that he has the capacity to exercise a creative imagination. We can speak of the effect of this imagination in terms of *seeing* the deeper meaning of our experience, as opposed to merely looking upon the surface. This becomes a context for perceiving God's self-disclosure or revelation. The imagination is an activity that must be separated from fantasy, for the latter is as destructive as the former is productive. Finally, to live intuitively or in the spirit of wonder is to retain the childlike capacity to identify and associate images in a playful manner within our experience.

One caveat is appropriate as we leave this particular dimension of the discussion of a new piety. In seeking to define the immediate kind of knowing that I have described in this chapter, Edward Farley expresses some concern about the use of the term "intuition." Its common definition, he suggests, appears to point toward mere spontaneous feeling without any relation to evidence. Farley prefers the word "apprehension," of which the appresentation (to which I refer in the third chapter) is a part.[45] I sense that Farley is reacting against and protecting his own discussion from a kind of mindless fantasizing that we have inherited from the youth culture of the last decade. In concluding this chapter I wish to make common cause with him and say that imagination and apprehension are roughly equivalent, although I would emphasize the emotional component, as I did in the discussion of *Gefühl* (see Chapter Three) more than perhaps Farley does.

My overall intention so far has been to make the function of the imagination in ministry not only acceptable, but to enable the reader to begin to sense its central place in the service of Christ. The next task will be to move on to the analysis of the land of the imagination, which I hope will fill out this initial description.

5

THE PLACE OF IMAGING

The Jewish Feast of Sukkoth, perhaps more commonly known among Gentiles as the Feast of Booths or Tabernacles, is the setting for the triumphal entry of Jesus into Jerusalem as recorded in the Gospels (Matt. 21:1-9; Mark 11:1-10; Luke 19:28-28; John 12:12-25). If this is a historical recollection, the event itself did not then occur the Sunday before our Lord's crucifixion, but in the fall, when the Feast of Sukkoth was observed.

My interest is not, however, in the New Testament account, but in this curious feast itself. Sukkoth is an agricultural festival of thanksgiving for the grape and olive harvest, and of petitions for continuing good crops. It lasts eight days, during which time the faithful are expected to live in huts, thatched with branches of palm and other trees, outside the city walls. The huts not only hark back to the shelters on the sides of fields, common to ancient agriculture at the times of harvest, but they also bespeak the wilderness experience of the Hebrews. These eight days are a *pilgrimage* feast, an *anamnesis* of the search for the Promised Land.

For this period the worshipers lived as nomads outside the city; they returned to a simpler form of existence. Here some scholars have argued that they renewed the covenant first made in the wilderness at Mt. Sinai. Indeed, a cultic theophany of Yahweh was expected. On the first day of the feast there was revelry and dancing, recalling a kind of Dionysian spirit, and there were prayers for a good future harvest. These rites were associated with rain-making, and they also heralded the coming of the messianic days. On the seventh day there was a procession about the city, in which the participants carried tree branches and sung psalms, particularly psalms 111-118.

> Blessed in the name of the Lord are all who come;
> we bless you from the house of the Lord.
> The Lord is God; he has given light to us,
> the ordered line of pilgrims by the horns of the altar."
>
> Ps. 118:26–27

Light and water were particular symbols of Sukkoth, images of which Jesus the Messiah makes much in the Fourth Gospel (John 8:12; 4:13–15). It can be readily seen how the Gospel writers identified this feast with the discernment of the Christ, the light of the world who gives us living water.

The Feast of Sukkoth provides a concrete illustration of the subject of this chapter, which has a familiar expression in Jesus' life. Sukkoth was the primordial feast of the Jews. It called them back to their nomadic roots, it summoned them from the cities they built in later centuries, and demanded of them that they live close to the earth for a period of days as a communion (to recall Gurvitch's categories in Chapter One). The intention was that they might experience again the glory of Yahweh's presence among them, calling them into the covenant relationship with him and promising them a time when all should be fulfilled. In calling them back, Sukkoth actually called them forward to a time of knowledge and life, when they would truly experience God and be one with him in the Promised Land.

In a society like ours, which so self-consciously avoids the ritualization of our past (save in the kind of *kitsch* celebration surrounding the bicentennial), perhaps because as one people we have no one past, there is no such ritual as Sukkoth. We are the poorer for the lack of a self-conscious remembrance of our primordial existence. I would suggest, however, that we have a very common, unconscious, and yet powerful recollection of this same existence. I have already spoken of the Friday evening spectacle of the highways extending from any major city in the United States filled with a stream of cars carrying their occupants out of the city to the forests, the lakes, the ocean shore, the hills, and the mountains. Why do we spend our leisure time, usually in far more "primitive" living conditions than we have back in the city, huddled together in some rural setting? The answer is, as I have previously suggested, that it is a return to our roots, to our "natural" existence; for it is on the banks of some stream or lake, in bands of forty to sixty persons, that *homo sapiens* and his forebears lived more than ninety-nine percent of their history.

The differentiation of human existence has effectively enabled man to assume responsibility for his world. This has come, however, at a very high price. It has required him to focus his attention in such a way, to center his activities and to organize his relationships by such a means, that he has lost contact with the ground of his being. I speak of the "ground of being" not just as a Tillichian synonym for God, but for the whole evolutionary process and the present environment through which God himself gives life to man and in terms of which God speaks to man.

It is my contention that the place of imaging—I find the verbal form carries my meaning better than the nominative "imagination"—is a Sukkoth-like experience. People leave the city, either consciously or without direct intent, in order to reconstitute their intuitive selves. Yet the world of Sukkoth and its meaning are not that easily perceived. It will be the purpose of this chapter to unfold it somewhat, and in so doing to build still further a notion of a new piety based upon the gift to man of imagination.

The first section will develop the manner in which the institutions of man, the necessary objectivations of his experience, reduce his self-image to univocal and secular categories. In the second section I will call for a new appreciation of the awareness of chaos. My thesis is that political man has also to be chaotic man. Then, in the third section, the language of the pilgrim experience, the movement out of the city into chaos, will be discussed. The chapter will close with a fourth section on the dangers of the place of imaging, for man has always been afraid of chaos, just as he fears God. Both fears are justified, but for different reasons.

THE EFFECTS OF MAN'S STRUCTURAL DEFINITION

To be a man is to be in relationship. I have discussed this in the analysis of the city. All the modalities, running from the spontaneous life of communion to global structures, have the purpose of enabling and defining that relationship. My concern in this section is more for groups and structures. There is often an illusion of freedom that accompanies the political (in that word's root sense) definition of man, and I have found in discussing this issue some confusion and not infrequent denial in stating that we are what the city has socialized us to be. Yet surely, after racial conflict, women's liberation, and the "gay" movement, we know what people mean when they say that they are the prisoners of the stereotypical image imposed upon them by society.

George Herbert Mead, a philosopher at the University of Chicago during the first quarter of this century, has had a profound influence upon social psychology and sociology far out of proportion to the volume of his writing. Typical of his insight is this statement.

> The individual possesses a self only in relation to the selves of the other members of his social group; and the structure of his self expresses or reflects the general behavior pattern of this social group to which he belongs, just as does the structure of the self of every other individual belonging to this social group.[1]

What Mead means by the "self" is that in human consciousness which is an object to itself. This is not the body. The self is reflexive. We can experience it as a whole. It is our consciousness of being a person. This self, Mead insists, is constructed from the reflection of our behavior in society as a whole; what we see of ourselves in terms of the "generalized other." There is no content to the individual by virtue of his individuality, only consciousness or thought. The content belongs to the society. Society is then necessarily prior to the individual self.

This means that Mead would agree with the existential phenomenologists, like Merleau-Ponty, who say that man does not *have* a city, he *is* his city or social fact. As the self becomes differentiated from the mere physical organism —becomes more than the body it is—it emerges in the shape of the community responsible for its socialization. The individual is a focus of awareness or intention within the body, the past, *and the community* that it is. As Mead suggests, the individual is the responsible "I," reacting to his awareness of his "me"; that is, his self perceived as reflected in the generalized other.[2] Whereas ethologists or analytical psychologists might suggest that there is some content to the self by virtue of *inherited* genetic structure or by means of the collective unconscious *within* the person, this is not George Herbert Mead's belief.

This self, what is perceived in the response in the other to the action of the individual organism, is structured according to the institutionalized expectations of society. Institutions are the basic structures of any social system or society. They are a universal reality in the life of every one of us from birth, whether we like it or not. Institutions consist of (1) a regularized pattern of objectivated behavior (2) according to a definite, continuous, organized pattern 3) which is upheld by norms and sanctions within the society. The self is, then, at least in major part, a function of the institutions of the social system of which it is a member. We need to understand this clearly both to see the problem of living an imaginative life and to work toward some possible solutions to enabling such a life.

It is, first of all, important for individuals to live together predictably. If you have ever tried driving on the left hand side of the road in the United Kingdom after living all your life in the United States, you know the problem of coping in a situation where behavior is not in a predictable, regularized pattern. It

114

makes interaction with other individuals difficult, if not destructive. How well I recall being "trapped" in a roundabout at the Wellington monument in London, where I did not know how I could get out without a monstrous crash. The predictability of parents is essential for the emotional well-being of children, of church services for the assurance of the worshipers, of government for the stability of world peace, and of language for the possibility of communication. Perhaps the reader remembers the old joke about the Frenchman who gets on the American streetcar and asks the conductor why it is running late. The reply utterly confuses him because two words are used in an apparently contradictory and unpredictable manner: "The car in front is behind!"

This leads to a second point, which harks back to Mead. The definite pattern of behavior in an institution is organized and continuous. There are rules to the game, which, unlike children's play, do not change arbitrarily, and they require that we accept what is understood by the group as responsible behavior within the activity of the group or to those outside the group. It is the difference between several five-year-olds playing "doctor" and a professional football team. Our activity is not spontaneous but learned, and any change requires legislative process or revolution.

Thirdly, this means that an institution operates by norms. There is a normative behavior expected of its members, and when they fail to act in that manner there are sanctions against them. One norm in the United States is that anyone earning money within the borders of the country is expected to pay income tax according to certain schedules. If he does not, he is sentenced to pay a fine and, perhaps, serve a prison term. That is a sanction. All healthy institutions have norms and sanctions.

The reader should now have some idea of examples of institutions. The family or kinship group is one class; political institutions, including the armed services, are another. There are economic institutions, religious institutions, and cultural institutions (including language). This regular, continuous pattern of behavior within an institution can be analyzed in terms of status-sets and role-sets. In so doing we define much more clearly the manner in which the society shapes the individual.

A status-set refers to "a position in a social system, with its distinctive array of designated rights and obligations."[3] Everyone has, according to Robert Merton, a number of statuses, and within each status he has a role-set. A role refers to behavior "that is oriented toward the patterned expectations of others (who accord the rights and exact the obligations (identified with status))."[4] In other words, the status of rector or pastor of a parish involves certain role expectations. There are the expectations of the youth, the vestry, the older people, and the principal supporters (overlapping groups, but identifiable in each category). There are also the expectations of the rector's seminary faculty, his bishop, and his peers or fellow presbyters. This fan of role expectations sets up the role-set within the status of rector or pastor. He also, however, has the status within his family, which has its different role-set of expectations from wife, parents, and children.

The more complicated the social system, the more varied our statuses and the greater the role-sets. A person within such a society has the immense task of organizing the demands made upon him. It is no wonder that we often hear people complain that their lives are not their own and they are "nothing more than a number." It is possible to raise the question as to whether in any society at any time a person's life has ever been "his own," since it would appear that it is more a reflection of the status bestowed upon him by the social system and the role expectations laid upon him by the society's institutions.

The effect of this shaping of the self in the reflection of the generalized other, or the perceived expectations of behavior, is to reduce the understanding of the individual, within the world into which he is thrown, to a univocal, one-to-one, common-sense meaning. This is most important to understand. Socialization does not encourage—in fact, it has sanctions *against*—intuitive thinking, which might lead the individual to behave in other than a predictable, patterned, normative manner. Sociologists call unpredictable, idiosyncratic actions "deviant behavior," and many a person is in a mental hospital, behind bars, or ostracized for giving way to such urges. Everyone is *expected* to do his part, and the society tells each person what "his part" is; and to fail to do his part is to create a dysfunctional situation. The effect of intuitive thought on the part of too many people—every society can endure a *few* "kooks"— is that the social system does not perform as it should. People are hurt because someone is "out of step" at a crucial time.

If the reader could accept the notion that the individual is *completely* a function of the social fact, which is prior to the individual and the creator of the personal self, then he would approve the notion that there is nothing more to life than social life, and the better that is organized for the good of all, the better it is. He would see that personal imagination only threatens the *summum bonum,* the social reality. Totalitarianism would become a doctrine of salvation, as some already understand it to be. It becomes an issue between a good and a bad totalitarianism.

If the individual cannot accept this sweeping point of view, as I cannot, perhaps he can see that, given its partial truth, there is a constant pressure in the life of every individual to reduce his life to the definition found within the roles and statuses of social institutions, with a consequent emphasis upon the benefits of living in the light of common sense. There are "benefits" of course, and to a large degree it is only right that we live within our institutional expectations. The effect of this is, however, to *encapsulate* the awareness of the person within the social structures, and to reduce the possibilities for his perceptual filters.

A good friend of mine, with whom I have shared some of the thought reflected in this section, described to me a fairly common experience illustrative of the stultifying power of life within the social system, which also points to where this discussion must lead. He had spent a week in Los Angeles in a hotel, attending a professional meeting. It was one of those particularly bad times in southern California, when the smog hung over the city in an oppressive, thick, yellow cloud: the result of the economic institutions of our technological age. He left Los Angeles by plane at night. As the plane lifted off the ground, it moved through this noxious layer of particulate, and suddenly, as it rose above the clouds, he and his fellow travelers became aware as if for the first time of a world of translucent beauty, filled with a quarter moon, stars, and distant lightning. Not until he had moved above the smog did he realize how the by-products of our industrial system had closed in his whole perception of the world, and that his understanding of his experience was subject to such a degree to the system within which he lived.

This is a chapter about the "place of imaging," and the reader is probably sensing where I want to take him. I think it is essential, as previous discussions of this material have convinced me, that before we move any further in that direction it be clear what I am *not* suggesting in this chapter. I will not *oppose* some kind of pristine "golden age" of innocent savagery—irrespective of whether or not Jean-Jacques Rousseau ever did—to the "horrors" of political and economic structures, technology, and urban sprawl. This book is *not* a call to return to Walden, either "one" or "two," or to advocate the theories of the Luddites or John Ruskin. It is not even an unqualified endorsement of the youth culture. Social structures are good and necessary, and hominisation, in a non-specific-species creature such as man, cannot proceed without them. They are an expression of that *ordering process,* which is an expression of man's creation in the image of God.

Furthermore, to return to the analogy of the plane rising through the layers of smog, I would point out that the plane must *return* to the earth, to society, and to the life in the city. We all spend very little of our time above the clouds, and if existence is somewhat more bearable or even enjoyable because of those trips, the work of getting on with the human enterprise requires the return. There are no "mountain-top" experiences where we can simply "build three shelters" that we might stay and worship (Luke 9:33). We have to come down.

It is important for us to realize that the social system, with its institutions and their statuses and roles, reduced the meaning of our experience to one- and two-dimensional categories. The meaning of our experience moves with great difficulty into a three-dimensional world of feeling, common sense, and thinking; and everything works against that fourth dimension of intuition and imagination. The effect of this, *in a society which is secular, disenchanted, and oriented to production and consumption,* is to make the ministry of the transcendent extremely difficult. Therefore, care for experience which is not to all intents and purposes filtered by the structures of the social system is *particularly* crucial in our culture.

One very clear illustration of this need is seen in a survey conducted in 1973 by a team of clergy and social scientists to determine what is "spiritual maturity" in this present time. In talking with these researchers, it is my impression that they were attempting to define the substance of sainthood, as the churches perceive it, for the late twentieth century. The subjects of their interviews were chosen by priests, pastors, and rabbis. The results of the survey were, in one sense, very disappointing. In another sense, they were most revealing. The persons chosen by the clergy, with the exception of some black subjects, were not to be noted for their keen sense of the presence of God in their lives as a mysterious but evident power, but for their place as effective members of the society. They were, on the whole, "successful people" as the social system judges success.[5] The word "spiritual" seemed to have little content to the judges, and they heard "maturity" as defined by effective behavior in terms of the standards of this sociocultural world.

This is, perhaps, all right; but the fourth vector of ministry has become lost in our passion for creative adjustment. The Pharisees were "spiritually mature" in this sense, and they crucified Jesus as a blasphemer (social deviant). There has to be some way of getting apart from the inevitable tendency of the socialization process to "harden the heart," so that we might see. At the end of *A Separate Reality,* Carlos Castaneda tells of Don Juan's causing him to see the same leaf falling from a tree three times over (like a television rerun); and Castaneda insists, "It is impossible." Don Juan's retort is, "You're chained. You're chained to your reason."[6] The problem at hand is to become "unchained."

118

THE ENCOUNTER WITH CHAOS

Sukkoth, which I described in the introduction to this chapter, is a clue to the process of unchaining. It is an institutionalized act of moving outside the institutions, represented by the city walls, into a more primal order. It is a structuring of what Victor Turner has called the "anti-structure."[7] Sukkoth as a kind of antistructure is a time when the people are invited to open their perceptual filters to see their experience in a way that life in the city does not permit. It is anticipated that in this light they shall perhaps see the Messiah whom they would never recognize within the walls. (It is suggestive to me that the crowds hailed Jesus as "Messiah" while standing *outside* the city, and cried for his crucifixion while *within* the city. They could only *see* him for who he was outside the structures.)

Turner's thesis concerning the antistructure, of which Sukkoth is a ritual example, is based on the belief that there is more to human experience than the experience mediated by the city, whatever its modality. While Sukkoth seems to me to be a ritualized heading back to an elemental primitive community, which still had a simple, internal structure—perhaps characterized by the division of labor between men and women and some sort of tribal government —Turner is suggesting even something more "radical" than this: an utterly undifferentiated kind of existence. In order to avoid confusing it with primitive societies called "natural communities" possessing some basic internal structure, Turner calls such existence "communitas."[8] It is akin to Gurvitch's "communion."

I have discussed in *The Future Shape of Ministry,* and in several subsequent essays, some preliminary reflections upon Turner's development of the notion of liminality as a state of existence outside the structured institutions of the social system.[9] In one of his most recent writings Turner defines liminality as "the midpoint of transition in a status-sequence between two positions."[10] The definition has the value of not only pointing out that to be liminal means not to "fit" the institutional definition, but to be in the process of *passage* between institutional definitions, which is necessary to the ordering function of man's religious quest.

In Turner's thought, communitas and liminality are *not* the same thing. The latter is a sphere of action which, as a number of persons have suggested to me, requires a certain solitary condition. The solitude of the priest is a function of his liminality. (Henri Nouwen's distinction between the value of such solitude, which he calls "receptive," and the destructive nature of "suffocating" loneliness is helpful.)[11] Communitas is a social modality, yet it is one that, like liminality, exists in the antistructural. It is undifferentiated, equalitarian, direct, and nonrational (not *ir*rational). It is, as Turner says, the sphere of the "Essential We" in the sense of Martin Buber.[12] Communitas is the expression of the bond of our common humanity and nothing more.

Because communitas is an existence where the differentiations necessitated by the ordering process are consciously avoided, the nature of this social modality is to withdraw from or to move underneath order. Again, I am not in any way implying that order is bad, but that it inevitably obscures for us the source of the "stuff" that it orders, and that this *is* limiting. It tends to foreshorten our sight, where we can only see the ordering structures that are to a great degree products of our culture. When we live in a disenchanted culture this can be disastrous for a transcendental ministry.

The effect of moving underneath the ordering structures, however, is to live unprotected from *chaos*. The image of chaos is for many people co-terminous with evil. Paul Riceour states that the identification of chaos with evil is the primary mythic explanation of the origins and ends of evil.[13] Chaos becomes the residence of personified evil: Tiamat in Babylonian mythology, Satan in Christian mythology (Rev. 20:2). The pollution laws of the Hebrews can be seen as a ritual purification which protects man from the disorder of what does not fit, what is chaotic. This notion of chaos seems to lie behind the Priestly writer, who describes the process of creation in Genesis 1:1–2.

My argument would be that this is a one-sided, although not entirely mistaken, notion of chaos.[14] The English word "chaos" goes back to what Hesiod, a Greek author of the eighth century, B.C., called *chasko,* meaning the abyss between heaven and earth. (It will be helpful if the reader keeps the imagery of the abyss *between* man and God in mind. We shall return to it intermittently.) Chaos is related to the *chasma,* the space between Lazarus in the bosom of Abraham and the place of torture, where the rich man suffers (Luke 16:26). Note that *chasma* is not the place of torture. The root meaning of *chasko* is the humble act of "yawning," and a *chasma* is a "yawning space." Chaos is related to the image of the abyss—"the earth was without form and void, with darkness over the face of the abyss" (Gen. 1:2)—and that word comes from the Greek *abussos,* which is related to the Babylonian *Apsu. Apsu* is the good, fresh water of the primordial situation.

Chaos can be appropriately judged to be the primeval matter prior to creation. Water is a symbol of chaos to the Hebrew mind, because it is unstructured and fearful in its lack of order. The Hebrews are a desert and mountain people, for whom water is associated with the murky depths of the unknown. The act of creation is that of "a mighty wind that swept over the surface of the waters" (Gen. 1:2). Water is feminine, the serpent that is the source of temptation lives in the waters (the serpent being a feminine symbol); to go under the water is to die, and to burst from the water is to be born. Obviously this lies behind the Christian meaning of Baptism (Rom. 6:3–4), and it possesses some relationship to the legend of Jonah (Jon. 1:1–2:10). Life comes from the waters of chaos, but for the Hebrew mind the ordered, rational world of defining structures is the appropriate goal of man's religious quest. It is a very masculine view, as the God of the Hebrews is a very masculine God.

The need to pass through chaos or the abyss is well known among the Christian mystics. The author of *The Cloud of Unknowing* speaks of the darkness of that cloud. He goes on to say,

> Do not think that because I call it a "darkness" or a "cloud" it is the sort of cloud you see in the sky, or the kind of darkness you know at home when the light is out. . . . By "darkness" I mean "a lack of knowing"—just as anything that you do not know or may have forgotten may be said to be "dark" to you. . . . For this reason it is called a "cloud," . . . a cloud of unknowing between you and your God.[15]

He adds later, "Nowhere is where I want you."[16] The "cloud" is clearly the abyss. Other writers, such as John of the Cross, confirm the image.

The image I am suggesting in accepting Turner's idea of liminality as a sphere of action, and communitas as a social modality within the antistructure, is of a structured world of status-sets and role-sets within the institutions of a social system set within a penumbrial environment on all sides. As one moves over the *limits* of society into the antistructure, one becomes aware of that which is *without limit,* the boundless. He is confronted by infinite being, which is ultimately the divine itself; but he is confronted with it, not as meaning or something to be known but rather as a *hidden* meaning or something that is not known. He reaches out beyond the horizons of his ordered knowing. It is chaos, or experience not reduced to meaning, not ordered.

To stand before chaos is to encounter nothingness, not in the sense of an empty space but as of a pregnant void. Chaos has no form and no order; it is pure potentiality from which the dynamic of life springs into our consciousness. It is the waters of life. From the abyss of chaos emerges that to which God gives shape through us, and which we call the created order. Chaos is the precondition and the source of power for life in its various degrees of structured existence. God is, of course, prior to chaos and is the "cause" of the abyss, which preserves the notion that he creates *ex nihilo,* "out of nothing" —a point Genesis 1:1–2 does *not* make.

Christianity is a very masculine belief, however, meaning we put a high priority on order (1 Cor. 14:40). This makes us uncomfortable with notions of an antistructure, the experience of liminality and communitas, and the confrontation with chaos. This is to our loss, because the antistructure is the place where the intuitive sense of God's presence and power engages us. It is the locus of the imagination or the fourth vector of ministry, where the primordial and the consequent intersect.

Although he certainly would not speak in these terms, Karl Rahner writes eloquently to my very point.

> The real argument against Christianity is the experience of life, this *experience of darkness . . .* these ultimate experiences of life causing the spirit and the heart to be *sombre, tired and despairing . . .* this very experience is also the argument of Christianity. For what does Christianity say? . . . Nothing else, after all, than that the *the great Mystery remains eternally a mystery,* but that this mystery wishes to communicate Himself in absolute self-communication—as the *infinite, incomprehensible and inexpressible Being* whose name is God, as self-giving nearness—to the human soul in the midst of its *experience of its own finite emptiness. . . .* Man, however, experiences . . . the Christian Faith . . . by his inescapable experience of the fact that *he is grounded in the abyss of insoluble mystery,* and by experiencing and accepting this mystery . . . anyone who courageously accepts life . . . has already accepted God.[17]

My argument is that to be "grounded in the abyss of insoluble mystery" is to exist as a structured being in an environment that is ultimately beyond our structures and which can only be perceived as boundless and chaotic. Yet to accept that is to find, in the mystery that is chaos, the power of being.

John S. Dunne is saying the same thing when he writes that for modern man God is not found in the light of his self-understanding, but in the darkness of his ignorance of what he is before birth and after death.[18] He uses Carl Jung in a very helpful manner to demonstrate the chaos of our personal and collective unconscious, wherein God may undoubtedly be discovered speaking to us. The former Archbishop of Canterbury, Michael Ramsey, once described this notion when I explained it to him, as "some erudite American theology," but he is wrong. This is the common experience of any person or persons who are willing to acknowledge despair as a way into the antistructural reality of their being, and to accept the openness that can come with it. Here man may know himself as spirit in the world now, a being open to God's self-disclosure at this moment, unblinded by the clutter of the social system.

Turner writes, "I have recently been paying attention to the notion that the familiar distinction made in Zen Buddhism between the concepts of *pra jna* (which very approximately means 'intuition') and *vi jhana* (very roughly, 'reason' or 'discursive understanding') are rooted in the contrasting social experiences I have described, respectively as 'communitas' and 'structure.' "[19] This is, of course, precisely my point. The imagination is the posture of man's openness to God's word, and it is outside of the city, in the antistructure, standing before the "stuff" of creation, chaos, that one can most readily "see" the transcendence. As Castaneda quotes Don Juan at the end of his fourth book as saying, "There is the door. Beyond, there is an abyss and beyond that abyss is the unknown."[20]

I owe a concluding illustration to a women's study group at Christ Church, Winnetka, Ill. I was speaking to them of this experience of the antistructure, and one person spoke up and said, "It seems to me that what you are describing tells us why both prisoners of war in Vietnam and astronauts in the space capsules journeying to the moon have reported a profound sense of God's presence in their lives. Both of them are in an antistructural situation. Both of them are very far from the city of their socialization." I think there is truth in that illustration, which only shows how by making idols of our structures —the Bible, dogma, liturgies, moral systems—the Church can avoid chaos and, consequently, avoid a sense of the immediate presence of God.

THE PILGRIMAGE INTO THE WILDERNESS

I hope that the place of imaging is beginning to become clear to the reader. The social system, with its structures of role-sets and status-sets, is essential for human life. Yet these very things close us to the source of life and to a power of being that the ordering process cannot domesticate. Clarity, predictability, and certainty are desirable traits in the general flow of life, but by themselves they make Pharisees of us all. There needs to be a movement outside the structures to a world of imagination if we are going to be open to God and be co-creators with him in bringing in the new city.

Participation in this antistructural existence, denoted in the previous section, may be thought of as a pilgrimage. It is important that we get a feel for the nature of the journey—the movement out and back, away from the city and then in return. A pilgrimage is an occasion for what Turner has called

123

"normative communitas," as opposed to "spontaneous communitas" (the momentary interpersonal encounter) and "ideological communitas" (such as in a utopian notion of history), where the social system provides for the experience of the antistructure as a source of revitalization.[21] Contrary to what some have understood me to mean by the term, "pilgrimage" does not denote a culture-denying escape, but an episodic withdrawal for the sake of a transcendent perspective in the social system.

A pilgrimage is always a journey to "peripherality" or into the wilderness. We move out into the margins of our social system as a search through space for antistructure. The image of the wilderness is a significant one in the Scriptures (Ex. 3:1; 16:26; Num. 3:14; 9:1; Matt. 3:1–3; 4:1; Mark 1:13; Luke 5:16; Acts 7:30–44). It is a place to go and to meet God or, as I shall discuss in the next section, Satan. In his books, Carlos Castaneda describes many journeys into the desert, the wilderness of central Mexico, to meet his "ally." The wilderness is by social definition an *empty* place. It is on the periphery of the city, which is *full*. It is there that God is to be known. Certainly the Founding Fathers of America believed this, as they saw their settlement on these shores as an "errand into the wilderness," akin to the wanderings of the Hebrews after the Exodus in search of the Promised Land.

Barbara Myerhoff, in her account of the pilgrimage of the Huichol Indians in search of peyote, says that the participants became the gods.[22] During this arduous journey into the mountains of central Mexico, the members constituted a communitas which saw itself as returning to that primordial order where men were as the gods. There was no need for the differentiation of role and the structures of the social system, because the liminal act is one in which the sacred will protect you as long as the ritual is properly done.

A pilgrimage is possible because its participants see it as possessing a holy purpose, and those things which they need for their safety in the routine of daily living are not necessary in this journey. Surely the early pilgrims coming to this land so conceived their mission, trusting it to divine protection. As long as the members held to the covenant, they were assured in their minds of success.

In moving under God's protection to the periphery of our existence that we might find divine renewal, a pilgrimage is often directed toward places or shrines that have a very chthonic identification. In this way it is very different from a spirituality rooted in a Neo-Platonic cosmology and the myth of the astral ascent. In pilgrimage we do not shed our earthly nature, but see our material life as the context for discerning the mystery of our source. The word "chthonic" means in or under the earth, and it is related to the Greek notions of the gods of the underworld. This is not "mother nature," but is expressive of the primitive intuition that amid the chaos of raw nature the sacred is to be seen. It is the same intuition that we know in Jacob, who, upon awakening from a dream of the ladder between heaven and earth, spoke of the site of his vision, saying "How fearsome is this place! This is no other than the house of God, this is the gate of heaven" (Gen. 28:16).

Pilgrim shrines are generally places associated with a "theophany" (a manifestation of God), such as that of Jacob, who named the place "Bethel," meaning "house of God." Turner points out that Mexican sacred locales, most frequently identified with the Blessed Virgin, have a relationship to pre-Columbian holy sites.[23] The Mayas, Aztecs, and Tarascans were, of course, dependent upon maize for their economy, and it is therefore no surprise that they were intimately connected with fertility and all this means for a highly earthy ritual. The association between pagan shrines and Christian experience should not, in my mind, bother us.

I discovered the pagan in the Christian for myself when I once took a pilgrimage, quite without knowing that this was what I was doing. While visiting Greece, my wife and I went by bus from Athens to Delphi, a morning's ride high up on Mount Parnassus. Here was the shrine of the Delphic Apollo, whose priests served the god of logic in a most intuitive fashion. The Delphic oracle had functioned here for more than a thousand years, dating perhaps to pre-Apollonian times when she served the goddess of earth, Gē, until the fourth century A.D., when Julian the Apostate was unsuccessful in his attempt to restore the ancient glories of the shrine. Here in the Temple of Apollo, in the midst of this eerie place, the oracle uttered her cryptic, divine messages. I do not know whether it was the mountain scenery, the marvelous play of light on the cliffs, the thousands of years of tradition, the air, or Apollo, but somehow I could still feel the oracle's presence, providing countless suppliants a word from God. Later, my father, who as a devout churchman was a frequent visitor there, confirmed the feeling when he expressed horror at a slide I inadvertently let him see of my wife bathing her feet in the run-off from the sacred Castellian spring, where the ancient worshipers bathed themselves before entering the sacred precincts. It is truly a fearsome place.[24]

The language of pilgrimage is, of course, that of symbol and myth. As we remember from Chaucer's *Canterbury Tales,* it is an occasion for sharing the narrative symbol, our stories (see Chapter Seven). This is not to say that there are no symbols or myths, no stories, within the structures of the city. The point is that the symbolic intrudes itself on our consciousness while on pilgrimage with much less clutter. The fine differentiations of the signs, dividing each of us from his brother and providing a basis for a continuing conflict of interest and goal, are greatly reduced on the pilgrimage experience. The collapse of differentiation in communitas opens us to the symbolic. A true pilgrim is childlike. What he is doing is a form of play.

It follows from this that we expect a pilgrimage to be characterized by imaginative meaning, full of ambiguity. A pilgrimage is a risky thing, for we cannot be sure what will be encountered. I am sure that many of the readers, as they have sped through the prairies and over the great mountains along our transcontinental interstate highways, have shared with me a great admiration for the early settlers of the West. They went across these same prairies and mountains—the chaos of the untamed West—on intuition, not knowing what lay beyond the next hill, death or fulfillment. The wagon trains of the nineteenth century were secular pilgrimages, fraught with ambiguity and risk. Even the most experienced wagon master operated off hunch more than logic, knowing only a few "tricks of the trade"—we could call them rituals—to keep them going. (I will return to the wagon master image in Chapter Nine.)

Pilgrimages require the organization of symbols or rituals, for it is the ritual that carries the pilgrims through the ambiguity and risk of a world of symbol and myth. A pilgrimage is not without structure, therefore, and it is the structure of the people's past experience of God; for we do not enter on such a journey without a tradition, or empty-minded. There is an intentionality to the movement, born of past promise and expectation. The ritual of Sukkoth is an illustration, in which the participants went outside the city, performed the dances, sang the psalms of their tradition, and awaited the promised Messiah. This is the sedimentation—the images inherited from the past and stored in our memory—within our corporate intentionality. (See Chapter Two.)

Somebody has called the movement out of the city the "atavistic journey." An atavism is, of course, a meaning and its action grounded in our ancestral roots beyond our immediate parents. The pilgrim communitas lives off an archaic reality and operates with a childlike imagination, but it expects an altogether new vision of God, that we might know who we are to be. It is as if we move back in history in order that we might move forward to a new freedom to be human. We travel light, but what we carry is very "heavy." We return with new stories, a new clarity, to live the structured life in a new way.

The model for pilgrimage which is offered here is clearly based on anthropo-

126

logical studies. My attention has been called, however, to the work of the Grubb Institute in England, and particularly to a provocative essay by Bruce Reed of that group, which sets out a similar theory concerning the *process of oscillation* rooted in psychological research. The oscillation of which Reed speaks is marked by the individual's necessary regression to extradependence, followed by a contrary development to intradependence. Regression, which is *not* used pejoratively, is demanded by the periodic need to live through the inevitable diffusion or chaos in our life. It is followed by a "getting it all together" and an emergent new sense of individual autonomy (development in intradependence). "Religion," says Reed, "is the social institution which provides a setting in ritual for the process of oscillation."[25]

I find in some ways Reed's thesis a helpful support of my own from a different point of view (psychological as compared to anthropological). He makes the point that this oscillation is constructive when it is, as he says, "controlled," as opposed to "contained," and is part of the intentionality of a theologically informed church.[26] This is well said and is true as well of pilgrimage. What leads me to be somewhat cautious with this theory is the result of its psychological perspective. It is too inclined to deal in the vocabulary of pathology, despite Reed's protestations to the contrary, and it is too intrapersonal rather than interpersonal and transpersonal. Yet there are parallels between the notion of pilgrimage and the theory of oscillation, which will give me reason to draw on Reed's discussion again in later chapters.

In many American Indian tribes there was the custom of the "vision quest." I find it in some ways a very apt illustration of pilgrimage through the antistructure. An Indian youth, male, or in the case of the plateau Indians, female, would at some time be sent out in search of the supernatural. It was an expectation of his tradition. For the Indians there were four times in life which needed the particular aid of the Spirits: birth, youth, maturity, and old age. This quest for a sacred vision characterized the second age of man, although it was not uncommon at other times. The participant went out alone—his was a liminal act and not one of communitas—and he lived in great deprivation in the wilderness. There, with much fasting and sometimes self-inflicted torture, he awaited the Spirits, which came to him and spoke to him through some animal image. He returned to his camp with the message, and its authenticity was tested by the power it carried.

An Indian friend told me of his grandfather, who in his vision was ordered to cut off his little finger. There was no question what the young man would do, and he returned to camp with a bloody stump. This action was not thought peculiar, and he carried with him for the rest of his life this reminder of the power of his vision.

Of course self-mutilation is not normally a part of the Christian's understanding of God's expectations of him (although we must not forget Origen). Self-abnegation or, as ascetical theology has usually called it, mortification, is a necessary part of the pilgrimage. One must leave the luxuries of the city, which no longer hide for us the word of God. The Huichol peyote hunt demanded of its participants a denial of salt, washing, sexual intercourse, full meals, and ample sleep. These are the conditions of the vision quest, which is an integral part of the fourth vector of ministry. Self-denial, such as fasting, has its place for all of us, and if we do not grasp some contemporary expression of mortification we are all the poorer. We end up staying at home, when we should be out on pilgrimage. We end up spiritually deprived.

SYMBOLS AND DIABOLS

In the title of this section I am introducing an expression I have coined that signifies the antonym of symbol: "diabol." As the English word "symbol" is rooted in the Greek, *sum-ballō,* meaning "to throw" or "to put together," so the Greek, *dia-ballō,* means "to slander" or "to mislead." In this sense it indicates fragmentation and pulling apart. It is the root of the English "diabolical" or the synonym for Satan, *Diabolus.* It is essential that we have a sense of diabolical meaning as well as symbolical meaning if we are going to avoid an unrealistic optimism in regard to the imagination.

It is important that the reader not gain the wrong impression. The place of imaging is one fraught with danger, a point which may helpfully be made by beginning with an exegesis of the word *daimon* in the Greek New Testament. The word *daimon* appears in the New Testament one time, as recorded in the best manuscripts. It occurs in the story of the two men possessed by demons and the Gadarene swine. In the New English Bible the word is translated "devils" (Matt. 8:31).

Yet the word, from which comes the English word "demon," originally meant the "power of God." In Plato's *Apology,* Socrates discussed why he did what he did, knowing that it would incur the wrath of the Athenian leaders and bring him to trial and death. His claim was that his *daimon* spoke to him and he followed it. Obviously he did not mean an evil spirit, but something akin to the power of the will of God. It is curious that we take this notion and make out of it something leading us to evil, which evil becomes personified for us in the images of late medieval and early modern art. The reason may well be that we are not prepared to face the dangerous power of chaos unprotected by structures, and find ourselves only destroyed by the daimonic.

Rollo May, the noted existential psychiatrist, has sought to recover the earlier notion of the daimonic, as distinguished from the demonic. What he is describing is the power of creativity, the potentiality, which I have discussed as lying within chaos. The daimonic is beyond good and evil. It is for May the dynamism of nature, which can take over the life of a person. It raises from the ground of being, he says, not from the self. It is the voice of the creative process. The daimonic is not an object in itself, rather it is the inspiration of artistic creativity and stands opposed to technology (the structures of the social systems).[27] It is pure energy, which we all want to realize.

Plato wrote, "Eros is a daimon." Love is a power that lies outside of our control, with all the potential for creativity or for destruction. The experience of passion—a word meaning both love and suffering—identified with the antistructure, although some of the sex manuals are doing their best to reduce it to a structural exercise. One experiences the daimonic within the abyss by a "naked intent," by a blind out-reaching of love, to quote the author of *The Cloud of Unknowing.*[28]

May says that the daimonic is not an object of our experience. It is a power, a dynamic, within nature. While agreeing to the suggestion that the experience of the daimonic is not in the final analysis one of an object, I would prefer to engage the question of the daimon at the point where it enters the *meaning* of man. This is at the point when the cipher becomes the symbol (see Chapter Three), or where the focus of daimonic energy takes on identifiable form. At that point I would say that it does take on a representational objectivity. Furthermore, I would want to locate it not so much within nature, although this is not *per se* wrong, but within the abyss. It is chaotic in its pure state, and consequently is known by us most clearly in the locale of the antistructure.

With this in mind, let me shift the argument momentarily to a different tack, the question of evil *per se;* and then we may return to tie in what I now wish to discuss with this analysis of the daimonic.

Generally speaking, the meaning of evil focuses on one of two sets of images. John Spong, a popular devotional writer, has written, for example, that *evil is not something outside of ourselves* but is our responsibility and the result of our insensitivity to one another.[29] There is great truth in that. Human institutions, man in his self-understanding in role and status, the endless pursuit of selfish goals within the social system generates gross injustice. The "busing" of school children, for example, is an effort to overcome the reality of the *de facto* segregation generated by the system. All ethics are social ethics, all questions of right or wrong involve our being in relation to other beings. They are questions of structure. The city itself generates evil, and man is the city. This is, then, one point of view: Evil is the product of man's ungraceful living.

Writers like Spong rightly reject a false demonology, which involves us in a dualism, where God is fighting against the devil, light against darkness, spirit against matter, and where there is more to being than God's being. This may be the cosmology of some in the charismatic or healing ministries, but it is not the cosmology of the Christian God, who creates all things good. Man's evil, however, is ultimately incredibly banal. As some charismatic writers also rightly point out, and May seems to imply, to consider evil only man's doing is naïve and narcissistic.

John Richards, an English scholar concerned for the ministry of healing, has suggested that the majority of persons today are convinced that the only logical explanation for the full power of evil in their lives is that it has a source outside themselves.[30] He believes that an impartial observer, examining the evidence such persons show, would come to the same conclusion. Much of his argument is rooted in May's discussion of the daimonic, which the reader needs to remember is a force or power, not an object, outside ourselves. Richards describes the evil within the daimonic as demonic, and explicitly states that we must distinguish between the "demonic" and "demons."[31] This is a second point of view: Evil is the result of an other-than-human experience in man's life.

Such evil is more exciting. It is, however, very easy for it to lead us into a denial of the Incarnation. Evil can become identified with man's experience of the body, the spirit can become opposed to the structures of society, and Christ can become a "ghost." Out of this may arise a world-denying gnosticism that will tolerate inhuman injustice in society while supposedly meditating on the things of the spirit.

Somehow it is necessary to combine the strengths of both views of evil—as both the product of man's ungraceful living and as the result of an other-than-human experience—without succumbing to the weaknesses of either. To this end I would call us back to a consideration of the daimonic as a function residing in the abyss that has the power to take over the whole person at the point at which it enters our awareness or meaning. It is also helpful to note that several writers on the subject of the imagination, which is the primary orientation of the person in the antistructure, make the point that it is the intuition which keeps matter and spirit together. The gnostic is liable to be the person lacking in imagination.

It is risky for man to take imagination seriously. The imagination can destroy us, just as it can open new possibilities for our being. Therefore, contemporary man tends to hide in the city. When he ventures forth into the country he takes the city with him. This may be one reason why snowmobiles are so offensive. They are an effort to take the atavistic journey into our wilderness past on the back of technology, without the risk of making it on our own. It is like celebrating Sukkoth in a camper. The same can be said of telephones and televisions in camps by the lake, as well as gasoline generators and propane gas ovens. We are an urban people, so we have both a domesticated God and a contemporary brand of evil best expressed by its sheer banality. What could be more boring than the Watergate transcripts?

If we leave the city our meaning of that experience moves from a high sign/low symbol infrastructure to a content of almost pure symbol *or diabol.* I have discussed symbols, and now diabols need to be introduced. The notion of the diabol as the opposite of the symbol was first introduced to me by May.[32] Symbols draw together, as the word itself indicates. A diabol fragments, disintegrates, and tears apart. A diabol is the supreme enemy of religious meaning. In an earlier article I have discussed the manner in which dead symbols within a social system can become diabols that putrify man's life.[33] Diabols can be as much a part of the structures as symbols. In this chapter, however, I am speaking of them, as for symbols, as part of the risk of the pilgrimage through the antistructure.

J. R. Tolkien provides something of an illustration of the risk of the daimonic on pilgrimage in his fairy tale, *Smith of Wootton Major.* The story centers around the possession of a fay-star, which has the ability to lead its owner into the land of Faery. At one point early in the tale the inept Master Cook of the village, who came to the job largely because he was there when his predecessor left, is about to bake the star (which he found stuck away in a box) into a cake prepared for a children's feast held every twenty-four years. The Master Cook's assistant, who is actually the Faery King, warns his master that a fay-star is not to be treated lightly. It can, as we discover later, bring anyone who is not true of heart into a very frightening and destructive world. There are monsters "out there" beyond the safety of the city walls who can devour us, just as well as good fairies.[34]

This destructive power of the daimonic is identified by us in terms of diabols, just as the creative power of the daimonic is known in terms of symbols. This is why some very imaginative people can be extremely demonic. We identify the symbols with God, because they become the messengers of being: God's solicitation of us into being. We identify the opposite, if we wish, with Satan, who is actually a nonbeing, although the diabols seem so terribly personal in their malevolence. They are the representations of "principalities and powers," not the daimonic, but the daimonic "gone wrong." It has gone wrong because we do not have the inner strength, the faith in ourselves, God, and the supporting community, to appropriate the power of creativity. We cannot trust ourselves enough to give ourselves over to the vision of God.

Throughout all of Castaneda's books Don Juan leads Carlos out into the wilderness to meet his "ally." If you are like me, you find it very difficult to discover whether his ally is good or bad. Clearly the ally is power, although we are never told the source of the power. The power can kill as well as enable. The whole point of Castaneda's long apprenticeship, which is finally fulfilled (I think) in *Tales of Power,* is to become a "warrior," one who is "an impeccable hunter that hunts power."[35] The warrior, we are told, has a predisposition, a "naked intent," for the world as a mysterious and unfathomable place. That is, he dwells in the antistructure, and he *sees,* cutting through all the nonsense of the structured world. His "true art," however, is to balance the terror and the wonder that is grasped in seeing.[36] The warrior's ally can be either a symbol or a diabol, but the impeccability of the warrior thwarts the diabolic possibilities of the ally and appropriates the symbolic power.

I use Castaneda as a fresh illustration of the point. From the Christian perspective, the author of Ephesians reminds us that we fight against the inhabitants of the astral spheres; rulers or first causes *(archas),* powers or reasons for doing things *(exousias),* world-sovereigns or mighty shapers of the cosmos *(kosmokratoras),* and the spiritual things of evil in high places *(pneumatika tes ponerias ev tois epouraviois)* (Eph. 6:12). There is nothing, *per se,* evil about rulers, powers, world sovereigns or spiritual things (Rom. 8:38; 15:27; 1 Cor. 9:11; Eph. 1:21; 3:10; Col. 1:16), and they assume either a symbolic or diabolic function within our lives. They are the "allies," in Castaneda's sense, of the Christian warrior or saint.

St. Paul speaks also of the "impeccability" of the saint. He possesses "the harvest [*karpos*] of the Spirit." The "fruits of the Spirit," which enable the saint to balance the terror and wonder of the pilgrimage through the antistructure, are, as we know: "love, joy, peace, patience, kindness, goodness, fidelity, gentleness, and self-control" (Gal. 5:22). St. Paul in speaking of the "harvest of the Spirit" is thinking of the *evidence* in the life of a person that the power of the Spirit fills his life. Drawing on that, I would say that anyone who engages the daimonic without the strength that comes from an inner coherence derived in God, of which the "fruits of the Spirit" are evidence, will be destroyed.

Charles Williams, in the story of the Grail in *War in Heaven,* relates how even the Grail, the holy cup of the Last Supper, brings down those who are not in the Spirit. It is God "without whom nothing is strong, nothing is holy," and without whom in the face of the daimonic, we will be nothing. Perhaps this is one explanation of why many in the charismatic movement are so fearful of oiuja boards and reading tea leaves.[37] Dabbling in the occult can be a journey into the antistructure, which, without that inner impeccability necessary for the appropriation of the power to be encountered there, can tear us apart. Undoubtedly this is why many would prefer not only to hide in the city, but to suggest that what exists beyond the city walls does not exist at all.

One way of describing the destructive experience of the daimonic is to speak of "possession." One is not possessed by a personified evil that exists apart from God, if that is what we mean by Satan, but by the diabolic, which, like the symbolic, has a very personal presence in our meaning. The most powerful feelings always seem to us as "personal." For example, the patriot personifies his country (John Bull or Uncle Sam) and the pious his Church (our holy Mother, the Church). We can be possessed by a symbol; we can also be possessed by a diabol, which *draws us out of relationship into nonbeing.*

For example, I have suggested that sexual intercourse is a type of antistructural experience. Without the religious intentionality for unity in experience, the encounter with our own erotic needs becomes violent use of the other, which in fact separates us from relationship and, by definition, pulls us into nonbeing. To "lay" and "be laid," or to "fuck" someone is to be caught in a destructive vortex of passion which can only be described as diabolical.

To draw on another illustration of a diabol that is not structural but that engages us in the experience of the abyss, we can think of the very appropriate desire of everyone to know who he is. If he enters this quest with a basic predisposition to think of himself as worthless in the eyes of others, then his self-identity has to be found in opposition to those same others. Self-pity and poor self-esteem breed such diabols as racism, where the anger at the fantasy of not being loved focuses on the purity of our race and is turned outward and asserts itself in violence. My generation has seen this violence give birth to the demonic murder of six million Jews. Racism has roots far deeper than just our system, as does sexism, chauvinism, and religious intolerance.

Another way that self-hatred leaves us open to the diabolic, whereas self-love enables us to love God and our fellow men (Matt. 19:19; Mark 12:33; 1 John 4:20), is in the need to isolate ourselves. Isolation in its various forms —intellectual imperialism, dogmatism, spiritual pride, the penury of the rich —is a diabol. C. S. Lewis in *The Great Divorce* describes hell as an empty city, inhabited only on the edges. The image is of a place where people cannot stand to be neighbors, to be in relation, because they cannot stand to be. To the degree I cannot trust myself to see you, to that degree I am nothing, and in whatever terms I excuse this lack of mutual investment, I have invested by the diabolic.

Of course, power itself can be a diabol. Lord Acton spoke of its corrupting force, and we have seen how even the structures of our country can run dangerously close to not standing in the way of an evil that lay, not in the system, but that came clearly from the abyss of existence. Power has many trappings, but at heart it is the desire to be God. For only when we are God can we be assured that we are somebody and the "bastards" cannot get us. There is always an opposition of "we" and "they" when the diabolic, rather than the symbolic, seizes our souls; for indeed it is the nature of the symbolic to gather together and of the diabolic to scatter and destroy (John 10:12).

What I am saying is that evil is both within us and our structures and outside of us. The social system can destroy people; for example, by generating the widening polarization of educational opportunities that "busing" has sought to overcome in recent years. A putrifying revivalism is, in my mind, a structural diabol. Our many failures to respond to needs are obviously sins of omission, such as in ecological waste, that can be directly attributed to our culture and our social self. Evil has, however, also a power of its own, and we hide from this at our own peril. We cannot conquer the forces that well up in our life to destroy us until we face them head on, and I am suggesting that this requires the risk of the pilgrimage through the antistructure. For it is there that the final battle between being and nonbeing is fought, and we need to come to it knowledgeable and prepared.

SUMMARY

Victor Turner writes:

> It was Calvin . . . who probably did most to foster the modern disapproval of pilgrimages, for he thought they "aided no man's salvation" . . . the Calvinist version of the Protestant ethic seems to have won the day in northern Europe and North America. Pilgrimages, for Calvin and the Puritans, were mere peregri-

nations, wasting time and energy that might be better put to the service of demonstrating, in the place where God called one, that one was personally "saved," by a thrifty, industrious, and "pure" style of life.[38]

I think Turner is right. It is very hard for any of us to go into the antistructure. I once asked a group of priests what would happen to them—how they would feel—if they simply took off for a day in the woods and the next day the chairman of their lay board called and asked, "Where were you yesterday? I tried to reach you all day!" Could they tell the truth? One very red-faced, older cleric stood up, pointed his finger at me and yelled, "My God, what nonsense! Do you want me to be crucified?"

There really is no answer to the question the priest asked me. The antistructure is the place of freedom to imagine. It confronts us with what is at the same time most frightening and potentially creative: the stuff of chaos. No one contemplates the possibility of a pilgrimage without the fear that they will never come back. Perhaps, however, the most deadly diabol is the rationalization we use for never going: the disapproval of the structures to which we have sold our soul.

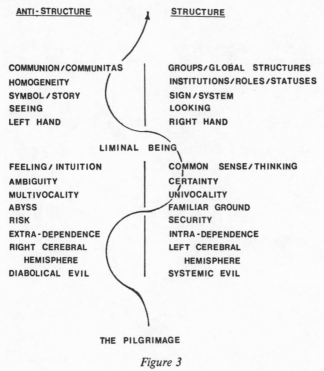

Figure 3

Antistructure, chaos, pilgrimage, symbol, and diabol—these words, strange and alien to our Puritan ears, are the vocabulary of intuitive meaning. In Figure 3 I have depicted what in this chapter is described as the place of imaging, a necessary journey for those who would experience now the word of God. In the next chapter I want to take a look at what happens to the person as he moves into this antistructure, and this will require a new vocabulary. I trust that the reader will perceive that the language is complementary, not contradictory, and it is all in the service of the ministry of the fourth vector.

6

DYING TO IMAGE

The widely known research of Elisabeth Kübler-Ross, a Chicago psychiatrist, into the process of death is both symptomatic and provocative of a new interest among many people these days in dying. Kübler-Ross is concerned with the emotional health of the terminal patient who must face the stark reality of his or her imminent demise. She has pioneered in the identification of the various stages of a person's struggle to live with the final reality, and has developed a pattern of support for such persons in their last weeks and days. It is a new interest, but it is also reminiscent of the concern of such seventeenth-century church divines as Jeremy Taylor (1613–1667), who wrote on the art of holy dying. The difference is that while Kübler-Ross wants to help the patient live with the ultimate bad news (although she has now declared her belief in an existence beyond the grave), Taylor wanted to assist people to pass out of this world in such a manner that they might look forward to the good news of a heavenly reward.

Death is man's final problem, no matter what his period in history. My suspicion is that for a technological age it is, however, a particularly acute problem. Control and predictability are supreme values in such a culture as ours, where we measure our well-being by the Gross National Product. It is very difficult for us, as a result of our continuing socialization, not to limit and to structure our life in such a way that we live in the illusion we are its master. We believe that if we can know ourselves and our environment, then we can so manipulate that world that no evil comes to us.

If nothing else, death is a losing of control. It is a reality over which we have no power. To die is to enter chaos, the abyss of being. Technological society struggles to hide this frightening end behind the hospital walls, with its façade

137

of trust in the power of modern medicine. Yet it cannot succeed in obviating the stark fact that you and I are going to die, and it only succeeds in burdening medical science and those in the healing arts with a sense of failure before the inevitable.

It is common among certain Christians interested in spiritual healing to speak of death as a "failure of faith." Aside from the fact that this conflicts with the history of Christian thought and expresses an ignorance of the theology of the cross, it reveals a curious acceptance of the values of the technological society. Faith is seen as a source of control, even control of the body. If one is dying it would appear, in this pseudo-theology, that he ought to feel guilty for the fact of his approaching demise.

Many of our forebears thought of death as a welcome friend. I once remarked in a sermon that everyone fears death, only to be assured in a kindly fashion by an elderly parishioner—a marvelous woman who had only a third grade education but was wise beyond most of us—that she had no fear of death. The obituary of my great-great-grandmother noted that when, surrounded by her children and grandchildren, she was told the end was near, she gave herself gladly over to her Lord repeating the words, "All is clear; glory be to God forever." Her parting comment was to her grandson (my great-uncle, later alledgedly poisoned by his wife), "Willie, Grandma is going to heaven." She certainly could not have been faulted for a lack of confidence. I doubt that the difference between then and now, a matter of a hundred years, is that we are faithless, but I suspect it is that we are obsessed with a self-image of being in control.

Of course, there are people today who make a fetish out of flirting with death. The race-car driver, the mountain climber, the solitary around-the-world sailor may just have an overactive "death wish," of which someone like Evel Knievel is a classic example. However, Robert Ornstein is probably on to something when he suggests that there is also a "destructuring" of our usual mode of consciousness before the threat of death.[1] As I said in the previous chapter, society inevitably imposes upon its members a structured, univocal mode of thought. The value of a controlled and controlling meaning of experience is a necessary part of the technological society's socialization. The experience or near-experience of death, which involves a surrender of that certain control to a modicum of risk and a trusting of one's self to chance, is a liberation from what is a very banal and stultifying, one-dimensional world.

Death is not necessarily then a loss of being, but it is the loss of the illusion of mastery over our own being. Physical dying, of which we have been speaking

138

here, is primarily a surrender of the self to that which brought it into being. This surrender is undoubtedly typified in the end of bodily life, but the dying to self of which the loss or surrender of control is descriptive (Luke 9:23–25) has much broader implications than mere physical demise. The purpose of this chapter is to argue that death to self is necessary for that destructuring of our perception of the world which opens the individual and his community to the word of God. To image we have to die, if not physically, at least in the sense of surrendering our obsessive need to be in control. In this sense ministry must once again direct itself to the art of holy dying.

This may seem like a strange or even perverted notion. Despite what it may "seem," however, it is much more a truth that we have merely lost. What I am about to argue is based on the theory that secularism is the inevitable result of a passion for control. By secularism I do *not* mean the affirmation of the value of this world as opposed to its denial or some variety of dualism. What I intend by the term is the exclusion from our conception of reality of anything that is not explicable in terms of a materialistic and/or closed temporal world. In order to overcome this rather myopic vision of experience we have to surrender control, to die in order that we may imagine and reunite the world of matter to the world of spirit.

The discussion in this chapter will follow in three sections. First, there is a new interest in meditation, not only among devotees of the Far East, but also in the scientific community. Some of the research in this area opens to us an understanding of meditation as a deautomization of human consciousness and a growing awareness of dimensions of the self that are generally hidden to the socialized citizen of Western culture. Second, while the quest of the self before God is inevitably an inner journey, it evokes a deepening awareness of our being by revealing to us our relationship to the rest of creation. It is crucial that we understand that to go within is to find being in relation to the other, and ultimately to see the world as God sees it. Finally, I believe we all participate as a matter of daily routine in this kind of deautomized thinking. Meditation or contemplation is not for the few, but for everyone. This section will catalogue some ways in which this is true.

We began this part of the book with a discussion of imagination; and in the previous chapter, the place of wonder or the imagination was our subject. What I am saying here is that as we move into the antistructure, into the abyss, where feeling and intuition reign, we will experience within ourselves a death to self.

139

TOWARD A CONTEMPORARY PIETY

THE SURRENDER OF SELF-WILL

In the previous chapter I briefly mentioned John S. Dunne's statement that contemporary man, if he is to experience God, must do so, not in the center of the self's understanding of itself but on the periphery of the self, in the twilight and the darkness of its knowing. Dunne bases his argument on his demonstration that, since Hegel, Western man has been obsessed with the reduction of the mystery of the self in order that through understanding we might gain control of our lives. Another way of saying the same thing is that we have lost what William Blake (1757–1827) called the "second vision." We live by surface appearances. In philosophy, sociology, economics, psychology, and other human sciences, the goal is to illuminate the self for the sake of a better life, but we have become trapped into thinking that the real lies only in appearances.

The effect has been, of course, to narrow the possibility of the self to where understanding becomes congruent with the limits of the self. What we do not understand, or feel that we can understand, we deny as a part of our experience. Yet there are mysteries lurking in the darkness: mysteries of the self before birth, the self after death, the self in history, the self in love, the self in suffering, the self in the evolution of man, the self in failure, and the self in the unconscious—to name some of the more significant mysteries. It is in those mysteries that Dunne says we discover what Schleiermacher suggested is true of man: his dependence upon the unconditioned.

It is only when the self does not demand self-understanding in the name of control and predictability, but is willing to admit the mystery of its own being and surrender itself to this mystery, that God is able to be seen. This is to take a journey within, not in order to reduce the self to univocal categories, but to know the mystery of the self's being. This is certainly not the road to atheism or agnosticism. The author of *The Cloud of Unknowing* sees the inner journey as the way to the knowledge of God. Six hundred years ago he said that if we truly know ourselves we will come to know God, not as he is in himself but as he is for us.

The difference then between this fourteenth-century mystic and B. F. Skinner, for example, is that while both are interested in the self, the former says that there is more to the self than we will ever understand, and the latter says that there is less to the self than we imagine. For myself I have no doubt but that experience supports the mystic and that the business of ministry today is to learn from him how to enter the darkness of the self so as to encounter there the love of God.

140

The issue is one of meaning, our perception of what is real. What is important for an awareness of the experience of God is an open-ended meaning, which does not demand that all data be forced into a procrustean bed of a disenchanted socialization. The mental process by which such an open-ended meaning becomes possible requires what Arthur Deikman has called "deautomization."[2] What Deikman means by this is the shift from a discursive reasoning, conditioned by the prevailing socialization, to a nonanalytical apprehension. Deikman would say that it is the emptying of the man, save for the object of contemplation. I would argue that, as in *The Cloud of Unknowing*, with which Deikman is familiar, it can be, in fact, a total emptying of the mind. The "cloud" is not an object, but a nothingness.

I interpret Deikman's concept of deautomization largely in terms of our socialization and its unconscious limitation of our perceptual filters. Deikman would not stop here. It is not only a breaking down of the structures of our cognition, but it is also related to the automatic motor responses. Reports of the ability of Zen masters to control brain-wave function, as well as Yogis who practice *samadhi* to endure pain intolerable for the average person and to lower the metabolic functions, are generally well known. William Johnson, a Jesuit teaching in Japan, in his recent book, *Silent Music,* offers a good, brief introduction to this research and its findings.[3]

The process of deautomization is, in fact, a surrendering of the will of self, accompanied by an open intentionality of the subject. It is through the will that we choose to act upon the basis of our perception of the real. To will requires a judgment of what is true. It involves the acceptance of the organization of our experience in the sense that to will is to assume certain structures. If one banishes from his mind the structures and their organized construct of the world, he necessarily surrenders his will. He gives it over to something or to nothing, perhaps God. He dies.

Castaneda's shaman tells him "to stop the internal dialogue," which becomes a way of "stopping your view of the world."[4] A friend of mine who does training in meditation tells his disciples to "hold nothing in your mind." This is not to *wrestle* with untold images as some novices think, it is to let them slip through unattended. According to the Authorized Version, the Psalmist says, "Be still and know that I am God" (Ps. 46:10). The New English Bible translation makes the same point, but in a much more subtle manner: "Let be then: learn that I am God." To stop the internal dialogue, to hold nothing in your mind, and to be still is *to let be,* pure and simple. Dying is nondoing. It is intending to intend nothing at all. It is waiting on God, without any presuppositions of what God is or even that he shall speak.

There is a great deal that is paradoxical in all of this. We set ourselves to act so as not to act, to intend so as not to intend, and to hold on to nothing so that we might be filled with the presence of God. This is the constant theme of he who seeks to discover the self in God by denying the self. In his novel, *All Hallow's Eve,* Charles Williams says that Christianity, in order to make man what he is, betrays him into "that state which is—almost adequately—called 'death-in-life.' "[5] In confronting nothingness, the abyss of our surrender of self, we confront the Lord. Again, Williams says—this time in *Taliessin through Logres,* "Catch as catch can; but absence is a catch of the presence."[6]

Here then we have the testimonies of a contemporary Roman Catholic theologian, a secular psychiatrist, a fourteenth-century mystic, an anthropologist apprenticed to a pagan shaman, and an English literary critic and lay theologian—not to mention the Bible—and they all say the same thing. In the surrender of self we will find ourself! The psychiatrist is at pains to say this has nothing necessarily to do with God and is more psychotherapeutic than anything else. However, under his own categories we find in this act of dying the undergirding reality of love.

Love is, of course, perceived as a feeling. Schleiermacher speaks of the feeling of dependence, of being posited. This is a kind of love. The author of *The Cloud of Unknowing* thinks of love meeting love in the abyss. Even Don Juan says to Castaneda, "A warrior is always joyful because his life is unalterable and his beloved, the earth, embraces him and bestows upon him inconceivable gifts."[7] Change the pagan "earth" for the Christian "Lord" and you have a statement made by countless persons who have embraced the cross and died to self.

Love fires the imagination. The world in which that can happen must be one in which there is a minimum of demand or precondition, a world stripped of structures. Above all, it is one where the pilgrim is willing to turn over the self to the very experience of what-he-knows-not. It is the way of the cross, the cross of the deautomized self that surrenders the city of society for the city of community, and beyond to communitas.

THE MOVEMENT TO THE PERIPHERY

As has been noted before, communitas is a modality of being on the periphery of the sociocultural environment. This is to say that the surrender of the control of the self involves a movement from the center of our structured world of status and role to a world in which the self finds its ground in the totality of the created order. It is a breaking out of the *saeculum* of the social system, with its one- or two-dimensional "blinders" of this present age. It is not, however, an escape from this present age.

The attached diagram (Figure 4) gives some indication of what I mean by moving to the periphery of our life, and it also identifies four contexts in which we engage the ground of our being—what John Cobb has called the "subhuman," the interpersonal, the unconscious, and the history of the people.[8]

This movement is a dying to self in the sense of a surrender of our ego boundaries. In my daily contacts in seminary life, one thing that seems so very obvious is the anxiety many students and their spouses feel over themselves as persons. Freedom and individuality are tied up in an almost desperate pursuit of self-identity to a point that the desire to fill the need can become destructive. In the face of this frantic pursuit, the thought occurs that if only we could learn to forget about drawing a circle about ourselves, daring someone or something to invade that inner space, and instead let ourselves flow into the "other" of our experience, we would discover ourselves so much better. This giving over of the self is what I mean by the movement to the periphery.

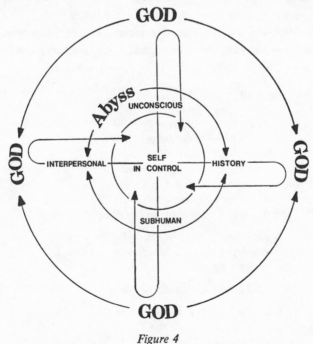

Figure 4

The irony of life is that when we make this surrender we become a self. The autonomy of the individual is not the result of trying hard to be different, but rather the integrity of the person is a function of that which he serves and with which he became one. It is in this oneness, in terms of which we stand before the abyss I described in the previous chapter, and it is this oneness that provides a context and support for coming to see the created order as it is seen by him who speaks to us out of the abyss. It is this notion that is expressed in the diagram.

We might begin to explicate this mystery by looking at the most difficult illustration of the general principle: our dying within the subhuman. A personal reminiscence might be helpful as an introduction. A fellow North Carolinian and I were sitting one winter day in my living room in Wisconsin, where we were teaching and living. It had warmed up to snow, as it does in that part of the world; and after silently pondering the scene outside of falling snow, I commented: "Bob, if I should die here, don't bury me under this snow. Take me back to the red clay of North Carolina." I suppose there was something a bit pagan about this observation. Certainly it is not the kind of comment one shares at a penthouse cocktail party, but it was "shorthand" for what I felt then very deeply—you might say, "in my bones."

My companion was a skilled poet. He said nothing at that moment, but the next day he came into my office and handed me without comment the following poem which he entitled: "Softly Like an Early Snow."

> Say, when the thing is done—
>   my dying—
> that I fell softly like an early snow
> from an undetermined height.
> I would have told you if I could
> that the wind declining is a blow
>   suffered with pleasure,
> that I awoke as a man does—
> O, thankful!—from a dream of falling
>
> Dream-sifted through reveries of other days
> sleep-dropped through darkness of cool sheets,
> and mother-comfort comes to hold you.
>
> I would have told you if I could.
>
> And let it not be said that he was one
> howling like a whipped dog in the tunneled night,
> limping cradling the broken bones he cannot mend,

that he ran off to lick new wounds by old light,
to nurse his raw life—his darkness—that doesn't end.

I would have told you, what I cannot know,
that I feel softly like an early snow.[9]

For me, this poem catches the spirit of contemporary man, who can share for just a moment his sense of death as the experience of oneness with the soil from which he and all of life came, and to which it shall return.

Annie Dillard's book, *Pilgrim at Tinker Creek,* offers an exquisite example of a person whose spiritual life is an ongoing exploration of the subhuman. No "rosy-glassed" romantic is she. Dillard has a clear understanding of the cruelty, as well as the sheer waste, of nature. Yet she sees there also the work of God.

My God, I look at the creek. It is the answer to Merton's prayer, "Give us time!" It never stops. . . . You don't run down the present, pursue it with baited hooks and nets. You wait for it, empty-handed, and you are filled. You'll have fish left over. The creek is the one great river. It is, by definition, Christmas, the incarnation. This old rock planet gets the present for a present on its birthday every day.

Here is the word from a subatomic physicist: "Everything that has already happened is particles, everything in the future is waves." Let me twist his meaning. Here it comes. The particles are broken; the waves are translucent, laving, roiling with beauty like sharks. The present is the wave that explodes over my head, flinging the air with particles at the height of its breathless unroll; it is the live water and light that bears from undisclosed sources the freshest news, renewed and renewing, world without end.[10]

Christian imagery, scientific information, both within the intentionality of a woman who looks at a plain old creek—like the kind I played in as a child —and she sees! That is what I am talking about.

On Ash Wednesday the faithful are reminded, "Remember, O man, from dust you came and to dust you shall return." This is not the morbid thought of some ancient killjoy. It is much more an affirmation of our unity with the totality of nature and the vitality of all matter. Primitive man considered everything to have a spirit, and believed himself to be identified with those spirits. Those spirits, like himself, had a necessary material manifestation. For him it was logical to expect, in the unity with the subhuman, the possibility of an encounter with God. It is probably too simplistic to say that the Judaeo-Christian tradition, culminating in the Manicheanism of the Puritans, removed God from the material world, reduced man to his rational consciousness and a righteous will, and gave license to him to exploit the natural world in the name of progress. It is certainly true, however, that Descartes, since his philosophy militated against seeing the subhuman as real and valuable, was in the Neo-Platonic tradition in which hominisation is a movement away from matter, and which pervades so much of popular as well as speculative Christian thought.

John Cobb argues that ecological survival depends on our believing that the subhuman is worthy of our investment, and this can only come about when we believe in the God who made it so.[11] What I am suggesting moves beyond even that. The "verification" of the belief in God may well come about as we are willing to surrender our rational control to the subhuman. I am sure that it is correct to say that no one comes to believe in the God revealed in Christ by viewing a sunset, climbing a mountain, or walking by the sea. Yet I also think what Teilhard de Chardin says in a footnote in *Le Milieu Divin* is true, "It must surely be obvious that, however transcendent and creative they may be, God's love and ardour could only fall upon the *human* heart, that is to say upon an object prepared (from near or from afar) by means of all the nourishments of the earth."[12] Charles Williams claims that D. H. Lawrence was a Christian heretic who recalled us to the truth of the Incarnation. He goes on to say, "The operations of matter are a means of Christ," for indeed, to quote Julian of Norwich, the fourteenth-century English mystic, we worship a "sensualite God."[13]

In recent years there have been some efforts to recover a sense of man's identification with nature, particularly in the so-called "youth culture" of the late sixties. Robert Bellah identifies the ineptitude of the effort by describing it as the "paleolithic revival." It frequently involved a profound, somewhat naïve fondness for the culture of the American Indians—a fondness which does not take into account the very different reality of American Indian culture. Nonetheless, I have experienced in my personal contacts, with the Dakota people particularly, a new appreciation of the subhuman as a medium of the sacred and I sympathize with what the "youth culture" instinctively believes we have to learn from the American Indian.

It would be well to recall the words of the Cherokee hero, Tsali, who was executed for killing a soldier for assaulting his wife during the barbaric transportation of the Cherokees by the United States government in 1838. While tied to a tree awaiting death, he asked a friend that he might tell his son, should he find him, to remain there also to "die in the land of his birth." For, as he said, "It is sweet to die in one's native land and be buried by the margins of one's native stream."[14] Tsali lived his life close to those lovely mountains, and

146

some say his spirit is still to be seen wandering through its forests. It would make sense for one who was so acutely aware of the transcending value of dying within the subhuman of which we are a part.

Another instance of the surrender of self, or the movement to the periphery as an opening to the fourth vector, which is more readily understood in our culture, is the dying within the context of the interpersonal. For me the paradigmatic expression of the interpersonal experience is the mating bond, in the sense of the unqualified act of will in which we give ourself to another as a fulfillment of the human need to mate.

A couple of years ago I was giving a lecture on this subject in Billings, Montana, and a reporter from the local newspaper was there. Despite my insistence that he carefully listen to what I was saying and not simplify it to the point of idiocy, his write-up came out on the front page of the *Billings Gazette* with the headline: *Father Holmes Says: Sex Is the Gateway to Heaven!* I believe it is true, if we understand by "sex" all the "inward and spiritual grace" that goes with the "outward and visible sign"—but few do. I have the support for this of no less a person than the celibate Jesuit theologian, Pierre Teilhard de Chardin.[15]

There is a theoretical basis for this in the philosophy of Martin Buber (1878–1965). Buber insists throughout his writings that man's most profound encounter with true being is the meeting of two or more persons in the utmost unreserve and openness. This is the "I-thou" relationship, which every student of existentialism in the 1950s recalls well. In his later writings, Buber speaks of this as the interhuman *(zwischenmenschlich)*, a presence which is hardly reducible to what the individuals collectively bring to the meeting. The interhuman, Buber argues, is transparent to the eternal "Thou." "The Thou which goes from man to man is the same as the Thou which descends to us from the divine and raises up from us to the divine."[16]

Paul Tillich speaks of this as the mysticism of Buber, which perceives the extraordinary within the ordinary, where the mystical and the prophetic elements of the religious life find a healthy union. Some would deny that Buber accepted mysticism, but their judgments are based on a very narrow definition of mysticism (as "absorption into the divine," or a special form of knowledge), or on a deep-seated late nineteenth-century prejudice against mysticism, or both. Buber's philosophy precisely describes the sense in which we, as we move into the interpersonal in depth, find ourselves drawn further into the abyss where God meets us and shares with us his vision for his world. There we are made anew.

There is a profound mythic undergirding of this notion of the divine encountered within the interpersonal, of which sexual union and the union of sexuality is the focus. The ancient figure of the hermaphrodite—half male and half female—embodies the notion of human wholeness as possible in the union of masculinity and femininity. Plato was one among a number of representatives of diverse and scattered cultures who spoke of the prototypical human as both male and female. The "fall" was the separation of the sexes, and passion is the dynamic of man's quest for oneness. Certainly passion is an act of surrender and a loss of control; so much so that some of the ancient Church Fathers condemned it as insanity, because it involved our loss of reason.

The fact that "passion" means both suffering and a frenzied release of the libido is not altogether accidental. Sexual intercourse and suffering have long been associated in man's mind. There is the notion that in coitus we die a little. It is also true that we pursue a vision that lies just outside our grasp. Ovid wrote somewhat facetiously *Omne animal post coitum triste* ("Every animal after coitus is sad"), and it is true (even without qualifications). Somehow we can sustain the sexual union, but we should come away with our routine existence more informed by what it might become. This is as true for any deep relationship as it is for mating, and it depends upon our willingness to trust ourselves, to let go of our self-centeredness in that meeting.

That very act of letting go, fueled by the mating urge (eros), renders us vulnerable. Eros is no respecter of the conventions of society, as necessary as they are. Passion draws us into the abyss, with that curious mixture of pain and longing—that strange bittersweet feeling we never outgrow—and we risk that we might find ourselves in the beloved. Our reason tells us we are only foolish, and it is half right. There is only a thin line between "puppy love" and the passion of the mating bond. The proof lies in the return to the world of obligation and role. Have we glimpsed in the mystery of love that which enables us to live out our life with a deeper compassion for ourselves and those whom we serve?

Thomas Hanna, who teaches philosophy at the University of Florida, speaks of a call he once made on Albert Camus. Hanna apparently prides himself upon his liberation from religious superstition, but in actual fact he suffers from the superstitions of the secularist. He was surprised to see that Camus read Karl Barth, but relieved to discover that he "balanced" this with D. H. Lawrence. What does not seem to occur to him is that both are writing about the same thing, the vision of God found within the dying to the presumption of self-control.

A third contextual dimension into which we move when we pass beyond the boundaries of the ego, die to self, and surrender ourselves to the periphery of our experience is that of the unconscious. Whereas the subhuman is a characteristic context for paganism, and the interpersonal has enjoyed a particular popularity in recent generations, the unconscious is a familiar world for the centuries of Christian mysticism. Certainly it has not been so named, but when the contemplative isolates himself in silence and moves into his inner world, there is no question but that it is a journey into his unconscious.

A classic illustration is found in *The Cloud of Unknowing:* "Strain every nerve in every possible way to know and experience yourself as you really are. It will not be long, I suspect, before you have a real knowledge and experience of God as he is."[17] As far as we can tell, this is the opinion of a rather conventional, if talented, priest, writing to a young friend who is making a rather ordinary inquiry about a way of life that, while followed by a few, was widely accepted and sometimes even admired in England six hundred years ago.

Castaneda, who for our time is considered esoteric, is recounting much the same insight in his discussion of the *tonal* and the *nagual,* terms given to us by his Yaqui shaman, Don Juan. The *tonal* "is everything we know about ourselves and our world. . . . The *nagual* is the part of us which we do not deal with at all."[18] The *nagual* is where the power hovers, it is the abyss within each of us (almost like the Freudian *id* and the Jungian "collective unconscious" together). To "see" in Castaneda's sense of the word is to see the *nagual.* Castaneda is very clear. To see the *nagual* one must be ready to die, he must pass through a door beyond which lies the abyss, and beyond the abyss is the unknown (which is as close as he comes to speaking of God).

The author of *The Cloud of Unknowing* also speaks of that which gives its name to the title of his book as the abyss. We must pass into it, he says, forgetting everything we know about ourselves and our world, including our very existence, which act he calls the "cloud of forgetting." Then as we pass with a pure, naked intention through the "cloud of unknowing," or the abyss, we encounter the ineffable God—Castaneda says the *nagual* is "unspeakable" —knowing him as the experience of love.

The abyss of the unconscious must, of course, not be sheer emptiness. If the presence of God there is a hidden presence, we can only realize this in the paradox that at the same time it is a revealed presence, or we would only be aware of emptiness. It is like the "call" Arthur Tommey Porter, a distinguished nineteenth-century priest from Charleston, South Carolina, described.

He returned late one night from a party, and as he entered his darkened room he "knew" a presence was there of which he had no knowledge. God came to him as Rahner's *Vorgriff*—the preapprehended "knowable" only seeable to the open heart, the unconscious self seeking God.

It seems to me that when people say that they "talk with Jesus" or "feel Jesus in their hearts," they are referring in part to a very superficial level of the unconscious, which we would identify by a kind of warm nostalgia they associate with pleasant memories of their parents, probably quite distorted, or of the "good old days." This is not really the content of the unconscious at any level of depth. The *feelings* of the unconscious are more frequently identified with a sense of joy, as described by C. S. Lewis in his autobiography; a strange warmth, such as John Wesley testified to at Aldersgate; a celestial orgasm, as Teresa of Avila relates; a sublime melody, as the fourteenth-century mystic, Richard Rolle, claims; or the oceanic experience such as Castaneda himself records.

Yet this does not get to any kind of perceptual image from which we can build a conceptual notion of that meaning we encounter in the unconscious that can be described as appropriate to the fourth vector of ministry. Carl Jung has probably done as much as anyone to discern this. It is not possible here to explore all that Jung has said, but we can readily surmise that for him the deep content of the unconscious, in which symbolic form man begins to see the vision of God for his creation, lies in the hypothesis of the archetypes. Whether these are archaic images, "pre-existent forms," or a presymbolic constellation of energy (Jasper ciphers)—Jung seems to fluctuate between the two—which are the common inheritance of man, they shape our lives and identify our origins. Theologians who build upon Jung, suggest that the archetypes lead us to the *imago Dei* in man and, therefore, to God himself.

Certainly the God Jung sees within the collective unconscious of man is a heterodox image when it is compared with that of classical Christianity. In the primary archetype of the mandala, the quartered circle, we see the cross; but it is the cross as an expression of conflict, of the coincidence of opposites, which Jung believes is the most profound expression of God's presence among us. This is particularly true since for him God is both good and evil. In "Answer to Job" Jung writes, speaking of the cross, "Why this inevitable product of Christian psychology should signify redemption is difficult to see, except that the conscious recognition of the opposites, painful though it may be at the moment, does bring with it a definite feeling of deliverance.[19] Later in this same monograph, Jung speaks of the "double aspect of God," "the paradoxical idea of God," and the fact that both the dogmatist and the agnostic suffer from the same problem of placing their reason above that which is ultimately numinous. Wholeness is found in transcending these opposites to a new unity in mystery.

The fact is that contemplatives, who make the inward journey into the unconscious, frequently have spoken of the joy and pain, apparent opposites, that confronts them: the symbols and the diabols. Again and again I am reminded also of comments Castaneda makes, or rather quotations he records from his shaman. It is only when one claims to understand, that he is really "in a mess." The task of the "warrior" is to achieve a balance between terror and wonder. The numinous and hidden quality of the vision, combined with the seeming multivocality of its symbols, are a common perception with those who surrender to the unconscious. Marghanita Laski, as we said before, has noted that "ecstasy" has both its fearful and attractive dimensions, just as Otto spoke of the numinous as terrifying and fascinating.

Many who have accepted the late nineteenth-century caricature of Christian mysticism speak of it as an "escape." We can clearly see that this is far from the truth. Their alternative is, however, an equally valid context for the surrender of self and the discovery of God's vision for creation, which is our fourth dimension: history. It is certainly the most *predominant* biblical context, although the other three certainly are in the Scriptures (Isa. 11:6–8; Ezek. 47:1–12; Rom. 2:20; Hos. 1:2–11; Song of Songs; Eph. 5:25–32; Gen. 28:10–17; Ezek. 1–7, 2 Cor. 12:1–5). In a very real sense the Hebrews "invented" history, if we understand by history the recounting of events so as to reveal an inherent purposeful order within them. This can be in a Marxist sense; history is its own purpose. The Judaeo-Christian sense is that history reveals God's purpose.

Robert Bellah has written, "Religious experience of all kinds is almost impossible without some form of group support."[20] This can be interpreted to mean that society is such a pervasive reality in the life of the individual that its life and values may be perceived as having an eternal dimension, which we call "God." It can also mean that society and its history become a context in which, when one surrenders himself to it, purpose is found that can only be attributed to that which transcends the social fact and its history itself. This is what is undeniably true in the history of the Jewish people, who saw in the movement of Abraham and his descendents from Mesopotamia to Canaan to Egypt and back to Canaan, with all the events that followed, the clear story of God's purpose for his people. It was such a powerful image that for centuries the Hebrew was content to believe that when he died he would live on in his descendents. There was no need for a sense of "personal survival."

I was struck the other day by a conversation, in which I was at that moment a passive participant, concerning the liturgy in a church I was visiting. We had been discussing the rather *avant garde* architecture of the parish and moved on to speak of the revised liturgy. There was no particular feeling in the conversation until a layman, who was our host, commented to his rector, "You know, I certainly like that 'flag ceremony' we have." I was amazed to learn in the priest's reply—a man of obvious insight and skill—that he had introduced this "flag ceremony." I have always thought of such ceremonies as the result of the conjunction of wartime patriotic fervor and a poor theology. The priest added, "I stop singing sometimes at that point, because I am so moved by the spirit that fills the church." I was now feeling very uncomfortable, because I generally dislike shows of patriotism in the context of the Eucharist. It has the odor of Auschwitz and the German church of the Nazis. My host pursued the matter, however, and noted, "You know, sometimes I am moved to tears at that moment." There was no thought of being moved to tears at the occasion of communion, nor did the rector note that he stopped singing in the midst of the *Sanctus* in order that he might enjoy the spirit at that point.

On reflection, while there is much that still bothers me in this vignette, I realize there is a power there. They were saying that they were caught out, taken outside themselves, in an act of celebrating God's purpose seen in our country's history. Perhaps I have experienced something of the same ecstatic moment standing on the edge of the woods at Gettysburg and gazing across the one-time cornfield, now planted in grass, where fifteen thousand of my fellow North Carolinians, led by the Virginian Pickett, made their futile charge against the Northern fortifications and only five thousand returned. There I *knew* history as one "knows" his wife, and in knowing history I think one looks at life through God's eyes for a brief instant. It would have been so easy for this to have been a moment of mere Southern chauvinism, blind to the injustice of the "Southern way of life," just as my host and his rector could be professing an insensitivity to current injustice in our land. It is possible, however, that there is much more here, and it is to that I speak when we get caught up in the history of our people.

In the Jewish *seder* great effort is made to remind all the participants of what God has done in the life of the people. It is done that we might become aware of the promises of God. Joshua, when he has led the Israelites across the Jordan river, has the people lift twelve stones out of the midst of the river, where the priests had stood as they crossed, and with them he erects a memorial. The purpose is that when their children shall ask, "What do these stones mean to you?" they shall be told that God has done his work in the history of the people (Josh. 4:1-7). As we have known God's blessings amid tragedy before, so shall we be able to look forward to the future and even to the Messianic Age. From our history we acquire the vision of God, which comes to us out of the future.

America has a tradition of seeing herself in this Old Testament imagery, a people setting out into the wilderness with the faith that God is working in their midst. If some of us experience a certain discomfort—particularly as I write in anticipation of the bicentennial year when we are so ready to boast in God while we dance about the golden calf—it is not because our history is without its memorials to God's guiding hand. We need to be sensitive to those "stones" of our own (the Declaration of Independence, the Gettysburg Address, Lee's Farewell Address), which witness to our experience of God in our history.

In these four contexts of the subhuman, the interpersonal, the unconscious, and the history of the people, I have described possible fields within which the deautomized self finds itself in the presence of the God who moves through the abyss to share with us his vision for creation. I am aware that this is a difficult notion, although I do not believe that it is mere fantasy by any means. It is particularly difficult for us, because we live in an age that has a compelling, stifling fear of death, and to do what I describe means that we must die, in the sense that we must surrender ourselves and move to the periphery of our existence.

In a technological age it is an evil to be out of control. We know what happens to atomic piles that are "out of control." They explode. We know what happens to computers that are "out of control." According to Kubrick in *2001* they take over. We know what happens to an economy that is "out of control." Everything collapses. However, a person is a different thing. Death is a door to the imagination for man. In the next section I will argue that everyone has moments in which he surrenders, dies, or loses control of himself, and that these are among his most creative moments. They are occasions in which he is called into being by God's self-revelation as described in the third chapter.

TOWARD A CONTEMPORARY PIETY

OCCASIONS OF DEATH TO SELF-WILL

We have spoken of the destructuring of our socialized reality, of the deautomization of the conditioned patterns of thought with each of us, and we have seen that to die is to lose control of the self. All of this I have suggested is a way in which we become open to the word of God and share in his vision for the created world as we stand with him on the edge of the abyss and look back at our life. It is a time when we participate in the twilight or periphery of our existence, guided more by the imagination or intuitive meaning than anything else. There is a definite ambiguity and confusion to this moment, for we are not "in possession of ourselves," but the self is possessed by Another. Here the meaning of life is contained in the symbolic and mythic representations, and we stand in the midst of the fourth vector.

A ministry that takes this seriously—and a complete ministry of Christ must —is one that prepares us to die. I am speaking not only of physical death, but also of the process of surrender and "letting go." Surely this appears to many as frightening and to others as a kind of heretical quietism. It *is* frightening. It would be heresy if I intended by this a simple resignation. We need to keep in mind that this is part of a dialogic process: a dying *in order to see how to act on behalf of God in the world.*

My belief is that we do this daily, but we do not identify the event for what it is: a destructuring of our socialized reality and a deautomization of our categories of thought. These events are often the occasion for a creative and innovative insight, which can lead to dramatic change in our lives. They are in a real sense transcendental experiences, when our consciousness is expanded or elevated by the God who makes us more aware of our experience. In this section I will touch upon a number of them under four headings: deautomization as dying to self-will through (1) mental relaxation, (2) eruption into consciousness, (3) willful exploration, and (4) seduction.

First of all, mental relaxation refers to those moments when the ego, or the active, trained consciousness, is lulled into inactivity and the mind is able to come into touch with data that we have been processing but to which we have not been previously attending. These are occasions when "things suddenly come together," which previous mental effort had not been able to resolve. I would list four such occasions: dreaming, the hypnogogic state, routine and repetitive behavior (such as driving along an interstate highway), and defecation.

Maria Mahoney, a Jungian analyst, takes up the theme of Samuel Beckett's

154

play, *Waiting for Godot,* in which three despairing persons are waiting for the God who never comes. She says the problem is that, while all of us can identify with the desperation of the characters in the drama, very few of us know where to look for the answers. She insists that is our real problem. They come in our dreams. Dreams, the Jungian would say, are the way in which normal people consistently come in touch with experience which their routine consciousness filters out.

Certainly there is much precedent in Scripture for dreams as a medium of divine communication (Gen. 40:1–41;45; Matt. 1:18–25; 2:1–15; Acts 12:6–10). Today we tend to dismiss the biblical accounts as pious superstition or to interpret dreams as evidence of pathology (unresolved internal conflict from the past). I am not at all sure that this is satisfactory. The content of dreams may well be the result of our perceptual filters and search for meaning operating at a level, and/or in a realm, which the structured life cannot allow into its conscious awareness for any number of reasons, such as the intolerable demand such meaning would place upon us or the recognition of something which is painful. There is evidence that people who do not dream become ill, unable perhaps to work out at *any* level experience which is very much a part of them.

I counseled on one occasion with someone who reported a dream he had during the last week of his mother's illness, which had stretched into years. She was very frail in those last days, but for months before that she had not known her family. This had been very troubling to him. In the dream, he was standing at the shore of a sea surrounded by mountains, and the waves were crashing against the beach. There in the breakers was his mother's body. He knew that he had to recover it to give it "proper burial," which consisted of getting it into a little wooden shed that stood by the shore. Try as he might, he was not able to do this. According to some interpreters, the sea is our unconscious and, our mother is the feminine principle (the Jungian *anima*) within us. He somehow was still struggling with that feminine image in himself (symbolized by the shed) and was unable to resolve it. His mother's last illness in many ways was a critical moment in that effort. This dream, as reflected now, gives an understanding into a personal dynamic which is part of this person's own pilgrimage.

The hypnogogic state is related to dreaming. The word means literally "lead out of sleep," and it refers to that state of consciousness between sleeping and waking. Wilson Van Dusen, a psychologist, describes the "fragile fringe phenomena" of the hypnogogic state which, with relaxation, a person may pursue with conscious awareness unlike those of a dream. The images of this state are not readily understood, and where the ego intrudes they evaporate.

Recently in my own experience I was on a speaking engagement where I had gone with a touch of the flu. Between each talk I went back to my apartment, not so much because I needed to sleep but because I felt weak. One afternoon I was lying on my bed with my back to the apartment door. I remember thinking, as I entered the hypnogogic state, that a friend might come by to talk. So when I heard the door open and someone walk through the sitting room I was not alarmed. Then I heard them enter the bedroom and I felt the touch of a hand on my right shoulder, which I saw out of the corner of my eye. It was slender, white, without any visible hair. I leapt to my feet—but no one was there. I do not understand what this was about. It could have been enlightening if my ego had not intruded at that moment.

A friend of mine did better, to his own dismay. I was speaking of the hypnogogic state before lunch at a conference some years ago. There was time for a nap after the meal and my friend—let's call him "Jones"—reported that he was lying between sleeping and waking after his nap, when he heard welling up inside of him a voice saying, "Jones, you're no damn good!" He said he asked himself, "What was that?" and the voice repeated, "Jones, you're no damn good!" Usually hypnogogic messages, because they are not explicit, have to be explored; but Van Wilson insists that they can be a source of enlightenment which can change our lives.

I mentioned repetitive behavior. One form of routine behavior that I have found amazingly fruitful is driving the interstate highway. I wrote much of *The Future Shape of Ministry* on I-94, and not a few of the ideas in this book have come to me on I-24. Somehow the mind becomes deautomated as the task is one that requires more habitual response than active, rational decisions. Yet, since a certain degree of attention is necessary, the ego is restrained from excluding the innovative or unexpected idea from emerging into the periphery of our awareness. It can remain there long enough to be "captured" by our consciousness.

A final example of mental relaxation as the occasion for the altered state of consciousness brought on by the destructuring of our socialized categories of thought is defecation. I have often instructed my students in homiletics to keep a pad of paper and a pencil on the back of the toilet. Some of their best ideas for sermons will occur there. Martin Luther reported that it was in the latrine that the full import of justification by grace through faith (Rom. 3:24, 4:16) came to him, despite the fact that he had read, pondered, and lectured on this passage from St. Paul many times before. I know that Erik Erikson, in *The Young Man Luther,* has related this to Luther's pathology—his anal-retentive personality—but I am more sure it was the result of the scholar's logical mind letting go just enough for God to speak to his intuition amid the familiar pleasure of defecation.

Secondly, I think there are times when the structure of our perceptual filters are ruptured by the power of an experience that must find its place in our consciousness. This is the dying to self in spite of oneself. I would cite three instances: rage, obscenity, and psychosis.

Rage is a most difficult problem. Its physiological source is rooted in man's primitive brain and is a tangible connection with his subhuman past. The Greek word is *orgē* or *thumos.* In the Scriptures only the rage or wrath of God has a positive evaluation. Otherwise we are told "a man's anger cannot promote the justice of God" (James 1:20) and "have done with spite and passion, all angry shouting and cursing, and bad feeling of every kind" (Eph. 4:9; cf. 4:26). These are sentiments which have their roots in the Old Testament Wisdom literature (Prov. 12:16; 13:1; 15:18; 19:19; 27:4; Ps. 37:8), which is in turn dependent upon Egyptian wisdom. The New Testament mentions a "holy rage" or "anger" only once. Paul writes to the Corinthians that their anger— the Greek word is *aganaktēsis,* which means more "indignation" than "rage" and does not have the power of *orgē*—has made them more sensitive to God's will for them (2 Cor. 7:11). There is good reason why the New Testament takes this position. Its authors were much under the influence of Middle Platonism and its Stoic elements, including the virtue of *apatheia,* meaning "insensitivity to suffering, absence of passion, emotional indifference." This same notion in early Christian asceticism persisted to curse Christian ethics in regard, not only to the understanding of the passion of anger but of sexual experience.

The Greek tragedians, inasmuch as they came before Plato and Zeno, were more aware of the ambiguity of rage. They saw it as destructive, but perhaps also as the source of creative insight. It has long been debated whether Euripides' *Bacchantes,* with its brutal scene of religious rage, was a tract on behalf of rationalism or a plea for a balanced understanding of human passion. In the *Antigone* of Sophocles, the city and its supporting laws are set over against the rage of winter storms, a metaphor for Antigone's anger. The reader is aware that there is profound ambivalence in this opposition. Aeschylus in *Prometheus Bound* suggests that healing is possible only when rage is expressed. In *Agamemnon,* Aeschylus speaks of the "over-impassioned passion" *(orgai periopgōs),* which is expressive of the insoluble bind of Agamemnon, who cannot but anger the gods, no matter whether he betray his vow or sacrifice his daughter. Rage to the tragedians is not blind, it is more a daimonic power (see the fourth section of Chapter Five), leading to insight, risk, and inevitable fate.

It is only to "fate" that I would object. Rage challenges the complacent acceptance of the unjust structures and impels us to action. That action does not have to end in us being punished by the capricious will of the easily threatened deity as in Greek thought. For example, in William Blake there was a frenzy. He was an angry man, always at war with himself and his world. It was this rage that motivated him not to settle for the single vision of the common-sense man, and opened for him the twofold or imaginative vision which enabled him not to settle for the rationalism of eighteenth-century deists. Blake's anger did not end in his destruction, but in a triumph over his own incoherence. Whether or not one would agree with Thomas Altizer that he is the most original prophet in the history of Christianity, there is no question that Blake's profound mystical vision has enriched contemporary thought. It is equally true, in a very different way, that the anger of Charles Dickens produced a literature which sensitized a generation to the need for creative reform.

Obscenity also presents us with a difficulty which is easily misunderstood. The word literally means the unfavorable, the ominous, and the portentous; that which does not fit. It is related to the sinister, which should give us a clue that there is more to it than mere vulgarity. The obscene pollutes the mind, but if Mary Douglas is right and pollution is the category for contact with that which is incongruous, then we have still a second reason to be careful not to think that obscenity is simple "dirty-mindedness." The same rabbis who were so concerned for pollution and were also, incidentally, given to very closed minds—"hardened hearts" Jesus called them—were the first to tell us that "cleanliness is next to godliness." The Puritans took it up, but then they too were a people who protected themselves from the fearsome and humorous behind an obsessive system in which there was no place for dirt or the earthy.

Legman insists that the dirty jokes we tell reveal our unconscious fears.[21] Obscenity is related to pathology again, which is a ploy we have already seen used to explain Luther's intuitive experience. Luther's table talk, incidentally, is noted for its obscenity. I do not wish to be understood as advocating a kind of "scatological permissiveness," but there is more to obscenity than pathology. The obscene experience can be not only immensely humorous, but also very frightening, which should be something of a clue to the loss of control and the confrontation with mystery that may lie within it. It is an altered state of consciousness.

Rabelais (c. 1490–1553), a contemporary of Luther, is a classical author known for his obscenity. Barbara Bowen has pointed out that Rabelais wrote out of the Renaissance perception of life as ambiguous and paradoxical, and that much of his writing is an attempt to confront the reader with this experience.[22] We need to keep constantly in mind that humor is the experience of that which does not fit. Obscene humor arises out of relating body function, which is related to man's most profound symbols, to the logical structures in a way that challenges our propriety. For example, Rabelais after fifteen hundred words or so of absolute nonsense on "arse-wiping" writes:

> Do not imagine that the felicity of the heroes and demigods in the Elysian Fields arises from their asphodel, their ambrosia, or their nectar, as those ancients say. It comes, in my opinion, from their wiping their arses with the neck of a goose, and this is the opinion of Master Duns Scotus too.[23]

Obscenity is a form of madness—delightful as it may be to some—that ruptures our perceptual filters. The madness of the psychotic break, which can do the same thing, is not so much fun. R. D. Laing, an English psychiatrist, has argued, however, that this too is a violent entrance into a surrender of the ego and an occasion for the awakening of the imagination to a new reality. He writes, "Madness need not be all breakdown. It may also be breakthrough."[24] The breakthrough may be a movement through the cracks in the socialized notion of what is real, what Castaneda calls the "cracks" or "holes in the world," to a new possibility.

Laing is not, of course, classifying all psychotic behavior as transcendental experience. Joseph Campbell writes about the same subject and he makes the distinction between "essential schizophrenia" and "paranoid schizophrenia" as discussed in Chapter Four.[25]

Paul Stern tells the story of how Alan Ginsberg had an ecstatic experience while reading a poem by William Blake, "Ah! Sun-Flower." This followed on a "deconstruction" of Ginsberg's reality, triggered by his having broken with his lover, Neal Cassidy. One could say he was psychotic, a fact which seems apparent, since he then spent eight months in a mental hospital; but the point is the ecstatic experience, which subsequently fed much of Ginsberg's own poetic insights. For in this state, Stern says, Ginsberg illustrated the thesis that, "without falsely romanticizing madness, it is obvious that in many states a deep psychic truth breaks through." "What is tragic," he goes on to add, "is not that the average madman believes in his delusions, but that he does not believe *enough* in them."[26]

Thirdly, there is a willful exploration which many of us engage in that leads to the deautomization of our consciousness. We do not have to spend a great deal of time on this, because examples are more or less obvious: chemically induced deautomization, hypnosis, and meditation.

Sidney Cohen in his work on hallucinogens notes that LSD is associated with a lowering threshold of sensitivity, affects the filters of consciousness, dissolves ego boundaries and a rigid superego, and enables one to accept death.[27] These should be familiar concepts. He relates the phenomenon of the chemical experience to what we have known as religious experience, pointing out that it becomes a way of going beyond the coincidence of opposites. It can be a means, Cohen insists, of producing a "visionary state."[28]

A number of responsible scholars, seeking new ways of perceiving our experience, have made use of drugs. The initial work of Carlos Castaneda is dependent upon drugs. Don Juan tells him much later that he had Castaneda use drugs because Castaneda was so stupid.

There is a relationship between hallucinogens and hypnosis, if no greater than that both enhance the creative act. I have no reason to believe Castaneda was ever involved in hypnosis, perhaps because it is very "Western," but there are similarities in the quest for a "separate reality." Hypnosis, to paraphrase Ronald Shor's definition, is a combination of deautomization of the socialized categories for making sense of our experience (Shor calls this the "generalized reality-orientation") and the building upon the possibility of a new suggested structure of meaning (classically offered by the hypnotist).[29] It is a form of trance in which one works with a new possibility.

Shor suggests that little children are much less captured by the socialized categories and can slip into the imaginative state, akin to hypnosis, easier than can adults. Certainly they are better hypnotic subjects, because they are more willing. They can let go or die to self so much easier. This has been, of course, my persistent theme in what is required in the fourth vector of ministry. We tend to identify hypnosis with drowsiness. ("Now you are going to sleep," says the traditional hypnotist.) A more universal condition for hypnotism is to become as a small child.

Meditation would appear to be related to hypnosis, but it is not really. Meditation is a process of deep, inward reflection, which does not possess the suggestibility of hypnosis. It is a period of intense concentration, which involves the letting go of deautomization. This is not in order to build a new structure suggested from without, but to be open to new possibilities in the form of the symbolic from within. For example, there is no posthypnotic suggestion in meditation.

Castaneda moved from drugs to a curious pagan form of meditation. James Lilly recounts the same experience, coming to meditation through the Far Eastern route, with such persons as Dick Alpert, *alias* Baba Ram Dass, and Oscar Ichazo as mentors. We are more familiar with Lilly's tradition through so-called transcendental meditation (TM), which is a technique of deautomization of East Indian origin based on the mechanical use of mantras. TM is not concerned for the "transcendent," but is a method aiming at effects in the "here and now." It has no theology, but claims good effects, such as reduction in anxiety, lowering of blood pressure, increase in sociability and creativity, cure for drug addiction. Gary Schwartz, in reporting some of the research on the effects of TM, writes:

> TM may enhance the germinal stages of creativity, but if practiced to excess, it may reduce the chance of the meditator's producing a recognizably creative product. The distinction is important. The creative process allows for the novel integrations, or gestalts, and creative ideas often emerge in drowsy or twilight stages of consciousness. But the *expression* of these ideas often requires activity, excitement and a good deal of rational and sequential thought. Creativity in the fullest sense involves both sides of the brain.[30]

We can recognize in this comment the necessity of the pilgrimage in and out of the antistructure.

Classical Christian meditation, rooted in the ancient "prayer of the heart" and evolving into a stringent methodology by the end of the fifteenth and the beginning of the sixteenth centuries, as exemplified in the work of Garcia Ximenes de Cisneros (1436–1517) and Ignatius Loyola (1491(?)–1556), achieves a form of deautomization by a narrowing of mental focus through simplicity and repetition, as in Castaneda, Lilly, and TM. It assumes, however, that this opens the participant to hear the word of God. William Johnson makes the point that the difference between a psychic (one who practices TM) and a mystic is that the former is interested in this world, and the mystic is passionately in love with a reality that lies beyond consciousness.[31] He goes on to say what could be said of any secular meditative technique: "Meditation entails an expansion of mind, a loss of self, an entrance into altered states of consciousness, a thrust into a dimension beyond time and space, in such wise that not only man's spirit but his very psyche and body becomes somehow cosmic." He adds later, however, what can only be said of theistic meditation, "meditation is a love affair" with God.[32]

Fourthly, there are those occasions when we are drawn out or seduced into letting go of our control and a new awareness slips into our consciousness.

Under this category I would place esthetic experience. In Linda Bourque's survey in the mid-sixties of the incidence of transcendental experience among Americans, aside from the fact that a small majority of people did indeed claim such experiences, it is noteworthy that the majority of these placed them in a context of what Bourque calls "aesthetic."[33] This was "triggered" by such contacts as sexual climax or music or a sunset. Yet in a category as large as this there is in common a solicitation of the subject.

The debate over the nature of the aesthetic sense in man, or whether even such a thing exists, cannot occupy us here. It is too complex and vast a subject. I can only point to a certain *sensibility* in man which enables him to associate, from the field of his sensual awareness, certain relationships that form a whole that far exceeds in meaning anything contained within the dissociated parts. Some say that over the last three hundred years we have lost that sensibility, that quality in which our awareness can probe the possible meaning within the objects of our experience to sense the inscape within the phenomena. The suggestion is that we have become so isolated or dissociated from the concrete world of persons, nature, history, and our own interior self that we cannot in fact get behind the appearances to apprehend their reality. If we could we would experience that which transcends the mere data—the divine.

The aesthetic experience possesses at least three general qualities: unity, complexity, and intensity. These are not found each in a discrete form, but are ways of speaking of a total, indivisible experience in three dimensions. In the aesthetic experience we sense the manifold in life drawn together into a oneness, which does justice to the complexity of that manifold and yet defines the unity of the whole in relation to that complexity of the manifold. It does this with such a pervasiveness that the subject is caught up into the experience in a way that is not forced. The object of the aesthetic has an intensity by virtue of the unity it bestows upon the complexity of life that draws us into a broader or higher vision. It is the ability to be aware of this that I mean by "sensibility."

The cross is a particularly helpful example of an object of aesthetic development, which can embody in its treatment that unity, complexity, and intensity of which I speak. The paintings of Giotto in the Scrovegni Chapel in Padua, the Passion of both St. Matthew and St. John, the Divine Liturgy, and the Gospels themselves are all contexts in which the subject experiences the magnetic power of the cross. If one of these does not draw the subject into the compelling power of what it commemorates, the passion, the other will. It is impossible to exhaust the meaning of the Passion of Christ as aesthetic experience.

The English novelist and philosopher, Iris Murdoch, has pointed out that the aesthetic experience is the precondition of the moral sense.[34] Inasmuch as the appreciation of beauty evokes in us a love for that which is beautiful and a care for its integrity, this strikes me as profoundly true. It conforms to my own conviction that the intuition of the purposefulness of creation, of which the aesthetic sense is an expression, is prior to the necessary action to bring into actuality the vision of that purpose.

The aesthetic experience as seduction is then the fourth type of death to self-will, which is common to the average person and provides the possibility of an experience of an altered state of consciousness. The other three types were mental relaxation, eruption into consciousness, and willful exploration. It is important that we do not interpret these four types as somehow "faddish" —they are all clearly recurring dimensions of human existence throughout history—and that we do not lump them with something called the "meditation explosion," which some say is characteristic of the mid-seventies. The heart of my argument is that the periodic loss of controlled or focused consciousness, socially conditioned in a univocal manner, is a desirable characteristic of man. The problem is to recognize it for what it is and build upon it as a possible avenue to an awareness of a transpersonal encounter engaging our imagination.

SUMMARY

The theme of this chapter has been that death to self—the controlled self of the socialized, rational ego—is necessary if we are to know that destructuring of the secular reality and be available to the word of God. Seeing, as opposed to looking, requires dying. Intuition is developed within the fringes of our consciousness, where common sense is no longer master and where all possibilities do not have to have an immediate rational explanation in accordance with the prevailing philosophical system.

In the surrender of the self, the deautomization of the mind, we come to ourselves in terms of God's vision for his creation. "My knowledge now is partial; then it will be whole, like God's knowledge of me" (1 Cor. 13:12). It must be so as we move to the periphery of our existence, which is far richer in the possibilities of knowing God than we ever thought possible: in the subhuman, the interpersonal, the unconscious, and history.

An illustration of this necessity to die in order to imagine and to create with God, is found in the following story one priest told me of his own experience.

His wife is an accomplished painter, now quite successful, who labored for many years without any recognition. Once, while they were visiting an artists' colony in Taos, New Mexico, they stopped to chat with one of the artists, and the wife told of her dismay over so many years of never having her work accepted. "What have you done with your paintings up till now?" the artist inquired. "We keep them in a storage room," the priest's wife replied, "and sometimes we bring them out and look at them." "I'll tell you something," the artist said. "Until you burn them all, you will not achieve any success." This seemingly cruel advice deeply disturbed them both, and they went home and struggled with the idea for several months. Finally, somewhat in despair, they did what the artist suggested and took the paintings out in the back yard and burned them. The wife returned to her easel with a heavy heart. She had nothing left now in which to trust except her own artistic vision. As it happened, that was all she needed. The picture she began that day is now on exhibit at the Riverside Gallery in San Antonio, Texas.

We have to let go if we are to share God's vision.

7

IMAGE AND STORY

The major roles in Peter Shaffer's play, *Equus,* are a late adolescent boy and a psychiatrist. The boy had blinded a number of horses after being seduced by an attractive woman employee of the stables. The psychiatrist's task was to analyze the cause of this psychotic behavior and enable the young man to live a "productive life." What is unveiled through the play is the incredible mental pain the patient feels and the story he has developed to make the pain tolerable. It becomes evident that if one is to endure the pain of just living, a story is necessary. The psychiatrist, echoing his patient, says of himself, "I need a way of seeing in the dark."

On several occasions, after developing the material to be found in the first six chapters of this book at a weekend conference or in a series of lectures, I have had someone come up to me and say, "This is all very nice, but I have found Jesus." And I say, "Yes, I have also, and it is about him, and how we can talk of him who lived in history so long ago with meaning for today, that I have been speaking all these hours (or days)." His face grows puzzled and my stomach develops a tight knot, for he then says, "Why do you make it so difficult, so 'intellectual?' " Several thoughts then go through my mind. The first is something like: we all "need a way of seeing in the dark." This person has found a way. I think it falls very short of the Jesus who, I believe, came to love us and make us free, but who am I to muddle his way? Then it occurs to me, in the second place, that I probably could not get within the concrete certitude of one who believes he understands the mystery of him of whom scholars and saints have pondered for two thousand years. Finally, in the third place, in all humility I remember Jesus' prayer in Matthew's Gospel, "I thank thee, Father, Lord of heaven and earth, for hiding these things from the learned and wise, and revealing them to the simple" (Matt. 11:25). Is all my scholarship only in the way?

Such people have every right to challenge me or, for that matter, you, the reader, with their story, the story of what Jesus means to them. We all must have a story. As Robert Roth has said, "story is reality," and without a story it would appear that we live in an unreal world.[1] Certainly, without it we cannot bear the pain or "see in the dark." The problem comes in the nature of that story, and I want to begin this chapter by making what is in my mind an absolutely essential distinction. It is the difference between an *open* and a *closed* story. No matter how "wise" or how "simple" we may be, the former is true to the Gospel, the latter was characteristic of the Pharisees.

First, however, we need to ask what is a "story"? I have nothing unusual in mind. "In the beginning is the story," to quote Edward Farley.[2] It is the nature of man to order the data in accordance with the story. A story is a narrative account (a constellation of images) of certain events. It usually has a plot, although even a "nonplot" is a plot in the sense that it says something about life's lack of meaning. The story is related to time. History itself is a species of story. There is a *dramatis personae* in a story which we relate to ourselves. A story is by intention a narrative symbol, which makes up the basic meaning that lies within our intentionality or the content of our awareness as we engage the phenomena of our experience. As Sallie TeSelle has written:

> We all love a good story because of the basic narrative quality of human experience: in a sense *any* story is about ourselves, and a story is *good* precisely because somehow it rings true to human life. . . . We recognize our pilgrimage from here to there in a good story.[3]

Stories do not have to be long or complicated. They can be related to "brute past fact," as the Gospel story is, or not, as Adam and Eve are. History is a story. Stories, if they are to have power to make some sense out of the chaos of existence, need to seize us at the level of feeling and intuition. Perhaps an example of what I mean would help. A priest friend of mine tells this account of one of his parishioners. The mother of the parishioner had died very suddenly, and as he drove from the hospital he was trying to get hold of what this turn of events meant for himself. First he said: "I am a forty-one-year-old man, whose mother has just died of a heart attack." That did nothing for him. He tried again: "I am a forty-one-year-old man who has lost his mother." That was only a little better. Finally he said: "I am a little boy who has lost his mama!" And he wept! Obviously this account illustrates one thing more about a story: its difference from a conceptual analysis is its ability to bring our felt meaning into awareness.

Anyone familiar with Chaucer's *The Canterbury Tales* will remember that the pilgrims told stories on the way to the shrine of St. Thomas à Becket. Stories are, in their *inception* at least, an imaginative way of ordering our experience. They require for their birth the free exercise of the right hemisphere of the brain. They are initially antistructural, calling the subject out of his acquired status and role. They are the supportive material for the person who would move to the periphery of his existence, deautomate his mind, and let go.

A story is the possession of the city. "The language of a people is their sense of reality."⁴ If that language is going to be more than the one-dimensional, technological jargon that begets a meaningless, banal existence, then it has to be experienced only in that use of language capable of generating a sense of the graciousness of life, the story. Later on in this chapter I will discuss the culture's story, my story, and God's story. The pivotal story in the effort to relate all three stories is the culture's story, as it interprets God's story for our time, and it provides the context to nurture the story of each person living within it.

To return to the distinction between an *open* and *closed* story, the former is a narrative that *remains* imaginative, developing, and capable of accompanying us into providing that essential ongoing nurture, the abyss. The open story is never finished. The Gospels are open stories. "There is much else that Jesus did," the Fourth Gospel tells us. "If it were all to be recorded in detail, I suppose the whole world could not hold the books that would be written" (John 21:25). There is always more to be said in a narrative that is open, because it lives in ambiguity. This is what gives the story the unique capacity to deal with paradox, which logical systems—scientific or philosophical—find so difficult. This is why the incongruity of Jesus has a better place and more power in the Gospels than in the Chalcedonian formula. In fact, each generation of the church adds and alters the story of Jesus. As St. Paul said of himself, "It is now my happiness to suffer for you. This is my way of helping to complete, in my poor human flesh, the full tale of Christ's afflictions still to be endured, for the sake of his body which is the church" (Col. 1:24).

A closed story is one that in its inception required the act of seeing that is characteristic of intuitive thought, but the result of the original apprehension has been *codified* within the structures. The story has been made into certitude, which absolutely requires that not one word, one image, one concept can be changed. For the Christian with a closed story there is a *lack* of tension between his story and the Gospel story, which means there can be no interplay between the various versions of the Gospel story.

It strikes me that only in a highly literate society could we have closed stories. For as Homer recorded in the *Iliad* and the *Odyssey* tales which had for generations been memorized and passed on to be told, it was not until he committed them to paper that someone could call into question the "orthodoxy" of a given version with any "objectivity."

No one ought to tell a closed story on a pilgrimage, for its very nature is a denial of the antistructure. Closed stories have no humor (ribald humor is particularly open) or terror. They are the lifeless accounts of persons who want to assure themselves and others that they are among the "sheep" rather than the "goats" (Matt. 25:31–33). The story has been drawn back into the structures of the "saved." The tragedy is that when the Christ comes, if he ever does again, it will not be in the images of the old story—which is the error of "bathrobe Christianity"—but in terms of the new; and, like the Pharisees in the New Testament, no matter how good our intentions, if the Christ does not "fit" our categories, we will pass him by.[5]

My hope is that, as persons concerned for the fourth vector of ministry and open to the present word of God, our stories will be those always expanding with the horizons of our knowing. They will not be expressions of our pathological fear of life, but of our hope. We need such stories, and in order that we might better understand them, I will discuss the nature of the open story as the heart of the intentionality of pilgrimage. First we will analyze the nature of story itself. With the growing popularity of this realm of theology there is much confusion. Second, it is necessary to discuss how stories function in persons' lives and in society. Third, in anticipation of the next part, more directly practical, of this book, we will look at some experience in identifying stories in our lives.

The important thing to keep in mind is that no one comes to the experience of anyone else, much less God, with complete emptiness. We hope that we are *relatively* empty of stultifying presuppositions, but at the very least there is the story. If we are to hear or see God it has to be a living story, open to his presence now, which feeds our imagination.

THE NATURE OF STORY

A story is like a ritual, it preserves the memory of past events in a way that those events still have power for us. A story basically lives first in the lives of people. It does not begin as a detached literary imposition, like a pornographic novel ground out to make money. There is a certain restraint proper to a story, much like the ambiguity of the symbol, which makes room for the indescribable. Also, like symbols, stories can be personal—like the one about the artist at the end of the last chapter or the one about the man who suddenly lost his mother in the introduction to this chapter—or they can be cultural, historical, or universal.

Edward Farley argues that no story is *purely* personal, but is "a quasi-existential vehicle of expressing segments of one's own autobiography."[6] The self is necessarily a product of the community; therefore, the story that constitutes our personal vision is, in fact, drawn from our most intimate communities and beyond. I would argue, however, that there is within the nature of story, a discrete quality which can be clearly identified in terms of person, culture, history, and the ultimate; and yet there is a movement through all categories which is characterized by certain common motifs. If we adhere to our definition of story and recall that we are speaking of a level of revelation that lies between sheer interpersonal, nonverbalized subjectivity and systematic analysis (see Chapter Three), we can see that at all levels—personal, cultural, historical, and universal—we are dealing with the stuff of an intermediary or parabolic theology.[7]

The term *anecdote,* as I use it here, indicates the story as the expression of the idiosyncratic process of shaping the individual's vision. I am aware that the recounting of "anecdotes" is considered by some as a waste of time, or at least trivial, but I think this arises from the pattern of performance to which we have become conditioned, not the meaning of the word itself. I am also aware that "anecdote" sometimes is used to describe a type of folk literature that is different from what I have in mind here. Yet it seems true that the personal story is anecdotal, because, like the original Greek root of the word *(anekdoros),* it is "unpublished," "secret," as compared to the common property of the community. Such anecdotes constitute the subjective intentionality, and hence the character, of a given individual.

I owe this last reflection to James William McClendon, Jr., who means by "character" the prevailing yet changing shape of the person. He is speaking of the continuities, the interconnections, and the integrity of a person as his character. He goes on to say, "A man's character is formed by the way he sees things, by his vision or subjective intentionality."[8] McClendon is influenced by the late H. Richard Niebuhr, the distinguished ethicist at Yale University, and therefore, while acknowledging the role of the society in shaping the character of a person, he will not dismiss lightly the individual's responsibility for that self he is and its action. It is this, it seems to me, that leads him to differentiate his approach to story from all others I have read. The story here is not only a corporate narrative imposed upon the individual by his culture, history, religion, or collective unconscious, but it is the life of the person, and it is this he is making the basis of theology in his book, *Biography as Theology.*[9]

What McClendon does, along with his interpretation, is to give four *anecdotal accounts* of distinguished contemporaries or near-contemporaries: Dag Hammarskjöld, Martin Luther King, Clarence Leonard Jordan, and Charles Edward Ives. The argument is that within these lives, and presumably others, there are powerful images that are interrelated to form a life story that constitutes the vision, character, and action of the individual under consideration. Those images and their narrative relationship form in fact a certain level of theology. For Hammarskjöld, the mystical union between God and man, imaged in the cross, was dominant. For King, the beloved promised community effected by love and nonviolence was all powerful. For Jordan, the central vision was the incarnated presence of Jesus here and now. And for Ives, it was the journey to the transcendent expressed in the music of the American revivalist tradition.[10] All of these images are ecclesial to the core, but in each individual they were worked out with a unique insight that takes the form for each of an anecdotal story. Their vision of the world was in terms of their peculiar life story, which is for some the profoundly moving story of the quest for God.

Stories that people tell are very important. Psychotherapists know this and are also aware of the value of getting their clients to unveil for their conscious awareness the story they are living out. This is the basis of those psychological tests which ask the client to "tell a story" about a picture. The person who, in spite of his many talents, always fails may very well be a person who is living out a story of personal failure; just so, the person who sees himself as one called to live the cross can sacrifice his life as a Dag Hammarskjöld. Most of us know the pain of having someone tell a story that is all too revealing about himself. As I have already indicated, Legman, in *The Rationale of the Dirty Joke,* argues that scatological stories are indicative of our personal fears. Carl Jung warns us against the telling of dreams as a means of inappropriately exposing

170

our inner self to others; and you, like myself, certainly must have experienced the sharing of stories as a way of coming very quickly to a realization of someone's commitment or character.

The anecdote is a category of the personal, and therefore focuses on the individual over against society. Consequently, the emphasis is on the process of making a certain interrelationship of images our own, and not on the source of the images as the content of the story. For example, it is important to analyze the life story of Hammarskjöld, King, Jordan, and Ives and what they did with the cross, the beloved, the community of love, the incarnated Lord, and the way of transcendence within American revivalism. Yet none of these images are the invention of any of these men, even though their style within the vision was unique. Farley is right in pointing out that stories, as stories, are communal narratives.

Therefore, in moving from personal to folk stories, our focus changes from the process (the individual appropriation of a series of images) to the content (the nature of the images themselves). We come to the world of folk tales, fables, and fairy tales *(Märchen)*, as well as legends and sagas and, finally, myths. These are categories of stories in terms of the nature of their content. All have the quality of a certain region or ethnic origin, although they also share some universal images (as can be readily discovered by perusing Stith Thompson, *Motif-index of Folk Literature,* in all six volumes). They also have a historical dimension, in that they are handed down and recur in successive generations (for example, the Faust motif). The categories of culture, history, and universality are, therefore, ways of looking at levels of the intent in any of the types (folk tales, fables, fairy tales, sagas, legends, and myths). We naturally know cultural stories which are also historical by virtue of being remembered. Other than the stories of our immediate culture, which are usually of the nature of jokes, all stories beyond the anecdotal are at least historical. The issue is the narrowness of the historical definition; for when pushed, the historical horizons of a story can emerge into universality.

Folk tales, for example, are the general category of oral, cultural stories, which constitute much of the narrative material outside the intentional composition of literate authors writing for a reading public. The story of Ruth and of Jonah are examples from the Old Testament. The parables in the New Testament, inasmuch as biblical critics have pointed out that they are not the actual composition of Jesus, are a form of folk tale. They are extended metaphors, stories told which model a truth that could not be otherwise grasped. The stories told by the pilgrims in Chaucer's *Canterbury Tales* are folk tales, full of the kind of common wisdom and ribald earthiness so frequent in literature that is not self-conscious. The tall tales about Paul Bunyan are clearly another example, as are the stories of Uncle Remus. Folk tales are not rhetoric for its own sake, but require a kind of "spontaneous storytelling."[11]

We know folk tales in their particular cultural expression, and sometimes can trace them in their historical evolution. They can also appear to have a universal level. For example, the story of the Pink Jade Lady—so-called after its ancient Chinese manifestation—is the account of a lovely courtesan who takes her delight in seducing kings. One day, however, she encounters the King of Kings, and instead of seducing him to her ways, he seduces her to his. It is a story that appears in numerous cultures and is known by us, of course, in the account of Mary Magdalene. The simple and yet provocative vistas that such stories open for us are, I suspect, perhaps lost in the morals of a society flooded with the printed word.

If we limit the definition of a folk tale to stories that do not depend upon overt magic for their plot but generally follow the rules of nature, it is customary to think of fables and fairy tales as something different than folk tales. The boundary between them, however, is arbitrary at best. Fables are moralistic stories in which animals are the principal characters. More interesting by far are fairy tales. Like the folk tales and fables, fairy tales are told for pleasure and release from dull routine, but that would only keep the Calvinist from taking them seriously. They take place in a kind of never-never land ("Once upon a time there was a king who had three sons . . ." They follow a strict symbolic imagery—although quite uncontrived—which scholars like Rosemary Haughton and Marie Louise von Franz have analyzed to great effect.[12] Fairy tales conceive of nature as fundamentally harmless, which means they avoid the Manichaean tendencies of the philosophers, and they are eucatastrophic (they turn out well in the end). They teach human decency. They are like the Gospel. The most distinguishing feature of fairy tales are their heavy reliance upon magic, as opposed to myths. By magic I mean a power that does not belong to the person who uses it, and yet over which the character in the story has some control. The power of the witch—for example, in Hansel and Gretel or Rapunzel—is not hers, but yet she has control over it. The same is true of the "little man" in Rumpelstiltskin.

What makes the fairy tale so interesting to us is that it draws upon the intuitive dimensions of human meaning and at the same time gathers its images from a resource which lies beneath the individual culture. I have spoken of fairy tales as a cultural and historical form of story, and in their manifest content they often are, but less so than folk tales. In their latent content they encroach upon the universal. This is what makes them the most significant form of story, aside from myth, in embodying the transcendent.

Marie Louise von Franz insists that fairy tales are the best means of studying the human psyche, which would include the archetypes of the collective unconscious.[13] Haughton sees in the image of the youngest son (the *Dummling*, or God's fool) an image of Christ; in the wise animals, the sensitivity, awareness, and selflessness required of the Christian; in the real princess, a moral insight and a willingness to suffer for the right; in witches and ogres, destructive evil and mindless greed; and in the quest, the Christian's pilgrimage.[14] These are images that make concrete our experience of God, while not reducing that experience to the level of univocal tedium. They evoke themes that transcend our culture, give a context to our deep longings and fears, and assure us that we shall live "happily ever after."

I am sure this bothers some. Magic is not "for real," and certainly not, we think, a part of the Christian Gospel. The characters seem frivolous, and the whole spirit of the fairy tale is playful, even childish. Part of our problem is, of course, our conditioning, which assures us that the Gospel is very grim business indeed, in spite of the fact that Jesus seemed to think rather highly of children and rather poorly of the serious people of his time—the lawyers, politicians, and professional religionists. It is true that most of the blatant magic in the accounts of Jesus has been relegated to the "apocryphal Gospels." Many of the miracle stories, however, have parallel fairy stories. Furthermore, certain scholars see a clear relationship to fairy tales; for example, in the stories of the astrologers (Matt. 2:1–15); Isaac and Rebecca in Gerar (Gen. 26:1–11); Balak and Balaam (Num. 22:1–24:25); and the preparation of the Passover meal (Mark 14:12–16). The Gospel stories are not without fairy tales, although they are more predominantly folk tales, legend, saga, and myth.

Perhaps at this point the reader does not need a reminder that to say this is not a "put down" of the Gospels, much less to imply they are any the less true. We are speaking of the content of the intentionality of the Evangelists at all levels, oral and written, who view the experience of God in Christ and tell us what it means. If the story is reality—the most "real thing" after the intersubjective, unthematized experience of God—then it naturally follows that the heart of the Gospel is the story. As we noted in Chapter Three it is a mentality of revelation second only to the interpersonal.

Fairy tales move us toward the cosmic dimensions of story, but before discussing the cosmic story itself, myth, we need to touch on legend and saga.

In terms of the grand themes of life and death, good and evil, man and the gods, both legend and saga are cultural and historical stories closer to the ultimate mythic story. If we consider their power to evoke the transcendent, they do not touch the far reaches of the horizon of our experience as can the fairy tale. They are not what I mean by the *cosmic* tale.

The legend is a hagiographic story, told for the benefit of the pious, as a *midrash* or embellishment upon the lives of the saints. It is for the most part culturally limited and has a short historical expectancy of plausibility. Its universal dimensions are obscure. How many people today believe St. Peter was crucified "upside down," much less find it edifying to think of him dying in such a manner? At one time the legend was of obvious importance. There is real fun in reading about someone such as St. Cecilia (third century), who was to be executed by suffocation in the baths, but who did not even break out in a sweat. The story goes on to tell us that they tried to cut off her head but failed three times. So for three days she preached and prayed while the faithful gathered her blood in napkins and sponges, and then (mercifully) she died. This amazing tale, like many, may not be particularly informative, but it is fascinating—even more so than hearing of how George Washington never lied or how "Honest Abe" Lincoln walked miles through the snow to return a few pennies, which are also legends of the saints.

Saga has more gusto. It is also cultural, but it is linked to historical events and places and focuses on the tragic hero. Odysseus is such a hero, and the tale of his wanderings is a magnificent Ionian Greek saga. The Old Testament sagas, of which the story of David is the epitome, are well known. The term "saga" itself comes from the Icelandic word *segja,* which is the same as the English "say" or the German *sagen.* Its narrow definition refers to the stories told from the twelfth century on in the Icelandic manor halls during the cold winters as one of the few forms of amusement available. Their subject matter deals with fighting, litigation, and pedigree—hardly "good news." Perhaps we can, as some scholars do, consider them myths, localized and attributed to the heroic figure, but they are rarely overtly "cosmic."

The self-conscious cosmic story is the myth. I spoke at length about myth in Chapter Three. There I said a myth is a true story about God and man; this is what I mean by cosmic. It necessarily has its roots in certain universal motifs —such as death and resurrection, conflict and vindication, expulsion and return, integration and transformation, incorporation and assimilation, opposition and individuation—that appear to occur in almost all cultures and in all ages. There are false myths, of course, but it is not of the *nature* of myth to be false. Edward Farley has argued that myths are not stories, because they have already lifted the sense of the experience to a reflective cosmic level.[15] If we accept Farley's definition of story, his case is well made, but for my purposes I prefer to retain the second meaning of story as revelation and include myth as the cosmic narrative symbol within that category. Myth does not depend upon *thinking* meaning, but still lies within *feeling* and *intuitive* meaning. It is consciously universalized, but it is still a story, not a system. Its primary appeal is to the imagination.

I have discussed at some length the nature of myth in my book, *To Speak of God.*[16] There I describe myths as necessary for ordering the world, as communal (we do not invent them), as the all-inclusive stories that shape our vision and character at the most fundamental level, and as the source of our general action toward the world. They symbolize the encompassing whole and tell the story of the sacred cosmos. Joseph Campbell writes:

> Clearly, mythology is no toy for children. Nor is it a matter of archaic, merely scholarly concern, of no moment to modern men of action. For its symbols (whether in tangible forms of images or in the abstract form of ideas) touch and release the deepest centers of motivation, moving literate or illiterate alike, moving mobs, moving civilizations."[17]

Campbell has a very low opinion of the clergy; he thinks they have no imagination. He writes as a student of Carl Jung but, unlike the master, he does not speak of God. Those who would claim a transcendent referent can, however, still accept his insights into the power of myth as no less true.

For example, the expansion of this country is clearly rooted in the mythic content of the intentionality of its people. The advancing frontier and "manifest destiny," with its rape and pillage, first of the aborigines and in recent years of peoples seven thousand miles away, is based upon the notion that has its theological rationale laid in certain theories of the Passion. These theories of the Passion we see enacted in the stories of the West: conflict and vindication, the "white hat" over the "black hat," *High Noon* and all that. Another example, is the great wave of immigration in the latter half of the nineteenth and early twentieth centuries, which was justified in terms of the American "melting pot of peoples." This is an expression of the myth of integration and transformation—a far worthier sacred vision than conflict and vindication, even if it does not seem to have come to pass.

Myths, of course, have all levels of expression: cultural, historical, and universal. The emphasis shifts from what we find in, say, the folk tale, where

175

the cultural is most dominant, to a clearer attempt to relate to universal motifs in the myth. All three levels, however, are present. Robert Bellah in analyzing America's myth of origin describes the imagery of a paradisiac wilderness, which brought millions to these shores in search of the literal Eden. This seems to be rooted in the *universal* motif of expulsion and return. It had its peculiar *cultural* expression in the life of the Puritans, as beautifully expressed in the sermon of John Winthrop in 1630 before landing in New England to form the Massachusetts Bay Colony.[18] Yet, as Bellah traces it *historically,* we know what happened to this particular mythic vision, as it lost its ambiguity to national hubris. The cosmic dimension of the story died in all but name, and it became more an excuse for greed than anything else.

The story has many forms: folk tales, fables, fairy tales, legends, sagas, and myths. All of these, in their manifest or latent content, engage the levels of culture, history, and universality. Yet they are drawn into the subjective intentionality of the person to make for himself the anecdote, his life story, whose content may possess all these elements of story—and must have some of them—and yet has a substance all its own, constituted from those insights that are peculiarly the individual's.

I know that some theologians who embrace an intermediary theology of story say at the same time that for a story to have theological validity it must be a "classical" story.[19] One wonders how an anecdote can be "classical," perhaps even how a fairy tale or folk tale can be (although I think that is easier to understand). What is a classical story? Man's life is seen by him naturally as a narrative. Is that classical? My belief is that a story has theological validity if the root metaphor—"signposts which help us read [or hear] our way" to the gracious presence of God—within that story is profoundly symbolic; that is, it is classical if it in some way draws us into the experience of God and the biblical themes.[20] In this regard, even the anecdote, if it be neither trivial or closed, is an authentic story.

James Cone has made the point, "White theologians built logical systems; black folks told tales."[21] I think he is right. Look at the sermons and speeches of Martin Luther King, for example; they are not only filled with stories, but with anecdotes from his own personal life. McClendon has shown well how the root metaphor within those anecdotes begets a profound theological insight. Liberating truth, Cone goes on to say, is best told in story, even personal anecdote.[22] These are classical stories.

My belief is that contemporary man, contrary to the thought of scholars like Ernst Cassier and Mircea Eliade, has not abandoned a mythic consciousness, which finds expression in various literary genre. There is a universal truth in the fact that man moves to meaning through inspiration, imagination, *and metaphor,* with the metaphor contained within a story that lies, perhaps, within our subsidiary awareness (to evoke once again Polanyi's category of tacit knowing). The problem for theology is how the stories I am told in this age (your story), the story by which I am living (*my* story), and the biblical story (God's story) can be brought together in one unified intention or, as I shall say from here on out, be *conjoined.* This is the prerequisite of effective living in the Christian community for each of us.

THE FUNCTION OF STORY

Stories that are not closed and are the expression of our fear and the neurotic quest for certitude, are the stuff of self-transcendence. If the conjoining of the vision of man with the vision of God, which is the heart of the fourth vector of ministry, requires the experience of a death to self, the consciousness that emerges in the midst of that journey and the meeting with God is most naturally in the form of a story. For the story is the best instrument to convey the incompleteness, the ambiguity, the power, and the wonderful absurdity of such a pilgrimage. Robert Roth has said that story is essential to theology, because only story can deal with the paradox of speaking of a God who is ultimately ineffable, as well as giving ultimate value to what are temporal appearances.[23]

John Dunne's work provides us with a profound and telling commentary on such a pilgrimage. Beginning with his book on the manner in which varied cultures meet death through their stories, *The City of the Gods,* followed by his analysis of the spiritual quest in *A Search for God in Time and Memory* and in *The Way of All the Earth,* we have a developing understanding of the relationship of the story to two dominant themes in this study: *journey* and *death.* Man's self-transcendence is supremely expressed in his realization that his life leads inevitably to death. Dunne's argument is that man has two choices: to flee from that reality or to live toward his dying in such a way that he becomes a man, and in becoming a man God becomes God to him. There is no clearer New Testament teaching but that in dying we find such life. "I am the way," says Jesus (John 14:6), and calls us to love as he loved, and by dying to rise again.

If this is to have more than epigrammatic power, however, it is essential that this paradox of the journey to death as the way to life be conveyed in the form 'of story. The tale becomes the way in which we grasp the meaning of our life as if we were looking at it through the eyes of another. Life-on-the-way-to-death becomes susceptible to a "seeing in the dark" (to recall the quotation from *Equus*) when in story we can put ourselves *into relation* with the things of life. By putting "into relation" we are saying what those things *mean* in relation to the person. Life becomes memorable.

It is very easy to make this a concept complicated beyond what is necessary. Dunne, in his book, *Time and Myth,* speaks of the things of life as the "fundamental tones" of the life story as melody, and lists a series of polarities such as killing and healing, weeping and laughing, mourning and dancing.[24] I have no argument with this, but the word "thing" conjures for me a memory of my grandmother, who used to talk about her "things" with great enthusiasm. She did this incessantly, to the point where we were tempted to burn up her things: her pictures, her jewelry, her clothes, a few bits of furniture, a book or two, and various *objets d'art.* Yet my father, who suffered more than any of us with the eccentricities of his mother, would say, "But *things* are important. They are the 'pegs' on which we hang the story of our life."

This is illustrated from a story that begins with my other grandmother, which I must credit to my sister, who has published the story in an article, "The Crown Derby Teacup and Other Symbols."[25] My maternal grandparents were married in Glasgow the year of Queen Victoria's jubilee, 1897. My grandmother, who came from a prosperous family, was given a wedding gift of thirteen place settings of Crown Derby china, which had been made to commemorate the jubilee. The gift was splendid, it marked a very happy beginning at a glorious moment in the history of the British Empire, and it carried the promise of years of gracious family living. My grandparents were very proud of their Scottish heritage and very loyal to the British crown as long as they lived. It was their identity.

Yet from very early in my grandfather's career he was troubled with alcoholism. He was a binge-drinker. He lost his job in Scotland with the British Railways as a result, and shortly after my mother's birth in 1900 they emigrated to South Africa, where my grandfather was given an opportunity "in the colonies." He failed there as well in 1905. In order for him and his family, now my grandmother and two children—my mother and my uncle—to return to Scotland, they had to sell everything they had. But because my grandmother had thirteen instead of a dozen place settings of Crown Derby china, she was able to keep one. She carried it back to Scotland, where again my grandfather could not make a go of it. So he emigrated again, this time to Canada where he found work. Later, in 1908, my grandmother and her two small children followed her adored, troubled husband to London, Ontario—quite in opposition to her father's advice—with her one set of Crown Derby china. There they settled and there my mother met my father in 1920.

As the years passed—the death at birth of another uncle, my grandfather's occasional slips, World War I with its slaughter of Canada's youth, my mother's departure to the United States, my grandfather's loss of work during the Depression, and finally his death in 1944—pieces of that one place setting were broken, until all that was left was one cup. My grandmother kept it and it came with her when she moved in with us in North Carolina (a strange place that she never understood). After her death it was a treasure my mother could only speak of with a catch in her voice—and she was herself a dour Scot. When my mother died in 1973 the cup went to my sister and it now resides in her china closet. I only hope that her daughter who inherits it will know the love, the pride, the pain, the faith—the sense of who I am from the past and in hope of the future—that is symbolized in that Crown Derby cup.

The "things" of life can be the common, significant events within every life, and they can be the concrete entities which recall those events. The story of life, however, weaves those things together into a plot in which each one of us as the principal character triumphs over the apparent end of the story: death. Dunne writes, "What makes a man's life worthy of being preserved in memory and story . . . is that there is a transcending of death in his life. . . . He does not merely live and die but has a relationship to his life and death."[26] The transcendence lives in the meaning that arises within the relationship of the man to the things of life. My father's mother was never able to make sense of that relationship and she died a broken woman. My mother's mother did grasp symbolic value and she died in hope.

Not just any story will do, of course. The closed story, as we have already said, falls short. It has also to be a story that, in setting us firmly within the memory of the known, gives us the courage to move into the unknown. We need to be able to face the abyss, to enter chaos (of which death is the supreme symbol), without being destroyed by not knowing who we are. This is what I understand Dunne to mean when he writes: "The story of the world . . . finally becomes the human thing that mediates between man and the unknown in the world, and the one who tells the story becomes the human being who is the mediator."[27] Life is a quest, as I have said over and over, and the story which fires the imagination and opens to us the future makes it possible to keep moving. Dunne goes on to say, "A Yes is required of one . . . at each stage of life. . . . If one does succeed in consenting, then the thing that has emerged into consciousness becomes something human. . . . When that happens, one comes up against God. . . . God becomes God in the moment when man becomes man."[28]

To become a man requires the ability (1) to live for another, (2) to live for value, and (3) to live for the end (the kingdom, eternal life, the consummation, or what-have-you). In all three there is a movement which can only be resolved in God. What is begun in the sexual relationship constitutes the beginning of a pilgrimage in search of fulfillment, which leads inevitably to God. There is no ethical system that satisfies the human need for justice which does not ultimately rest itself in the absolute. Whether man longs for a return to the paradisal garden or for the Messianic banquet, he lives for a better, even a perfect world. At our most human, there is God.

Every story requires an ending. Like little children who ask their mother or father for just one more story, every episode of a genuine story, if it is a good story, demands still another. There is no resolution in our story until it is resolved in God. This certainly is true of the story of Jesus. You cannot leave him abandoned by God on the cross (Matt. 27:46, Mark 15:34), and you cannot leave yourself in that affliction. The story draws you across the abyss and into the presence of God, where the opposites are reconciled into that oneness which gives integrity to our particular story.

My father died very suddenly in a strange city, and my mother was unable to make any of the arrangements. I was called off the golf course, seven hundred miles away, and in six hours was "fathering" her and tending to the final arrangements for one whom I had loved and feared, respected and avoided for forty-two years. All my life this man had done for me, but rarely in a way that enabled me to give to him in return. Now in his death I found that I could do for him, and that realization was a source of strength. My sisters and I lived for seventy-two hours on that strength, and then came the time for me to preside at the Requiem Eucharist as I had promised my father I would. He was a man of profound, simple devotion, and while he was proud that I was a priest, he never talked to me about religion for fear that I would challenge his piety. Amid all that tension and work I was not sure what would happen to me, and yet as the service progressed I felt strangely elated. At the end, suddenly the words came into my mind, "All will be well, all manner of things will be well." I did not know what to make of that "message" then, although I knew myself to be called across the abyss and in the presence of God. It was not until over two years later that I learned these were the words of Dame Julian of Norwich, a fourteenth-century mystic, whom I had not yet read at that time, but whom my father, a medieval scholar, knew well. That is an event in my story which embodies for me a reconciliation of opposites, oneness, integrity, and victory. The contradictions in my father and in our relationship are resolved for me.

Stories are, as I have indicated in the previous section, inevitably social. What I have written in the last few pages has been personal in nature and may appear to set the life story over against folk tales, fairy tales, and myths. This is not possible. The personal story is the individual appropriation of what Stephen Popper calls (and which I have already cited from TeSelle) the "root metaphors" of the social phenomenon.[29] A person who tells his story is saying, "My life is . . ." and he then recounts a series of connected images which give him a "handle" by which to transcend being simply caught in the flow of existence. Those images are metaphors which are available to him in the culture. For example, Americans for many years saw themselves as pioneers, taming the wilderness; individuals, who by courage, ingenuity, and native intelligence solved the problems of their life, and succeeded. My favorite reading as a boy of eleven and twelve was a series of books written by Joseph Alexander Altsheler (1862–1919) about a youth who braved the wilderness during the French and Indian War. I think in some sense I have been that young man ever since, because those images have always lived in my imagination.

An adaptation of a theory of Victor Turner's will make the function of story clearer, including the relationship of the individual to the community. These root metaphors are the heart of the society's story of stories, particularly their myth(s), but also their fairy tales and folk tales. Turner argues that in situations of conflict the root metaphors are evident in those "social dramas" which erupt from beneath the structures and form pivotal events in the human social process.[30] The script of the social drama is, of course, the story, and it is the story that carries a social unit through those breaks in the structured phase of its life and moves the society on to the next plateau. In global structures this would be on the occasion of the assassination or resignation of a President —two events familiar to most of my readers. In families it would be the event of a financial collapse, a divorce, or the arrival of a new baby; and with individuals in times of grief, sickness, or mental breakdown. The story is always there, but is acted out and becomes peculiarly evident when conflict breaks through the routinized, imposed patterns of behavior, as in the sudden death of my father. "Social dramas," Turner says, "are units of aharmonic or disharmonic process, arising in conflict situations."[31]

Turner illustrates the function of the social drama in moments of conflict by drawing on the account of the encounter between Henry II of England and St. Thomas à Becket at the Council of Northampton (1164). It is a long essay, which I cannot reproduce here; but in essence Turner argues that the outcome of this confrontation from Becket's viewpoint was the result of the root metaphor or religious paradigm of the *via crucis* or the way of martyrdom. Becket's actions were in accordance with this story.[32] He went into exile and then returned for certain martyrdom in 1170, all in consciousness of acting out a social drama. It is a very compelling thesis, as is another one of Turner's in a similar vein from Mexican revolutionary history of 1810.

It is of further importance that, as Turner says, such root metaphors are generated in the antistructured experience of communitas or liminality.[33] The story itself is the narrative, as has been mentioned, of the pilgrim. The structures, which obscure the tale by which our lives are lived, are stripped away, and we see where we have been and where we would go in a kind of pristine clarity.

Sallie TeSelle in her important book, *Speaking in Parables,* deepens our understanding of this point. She says that the effective story is one which has parabolic form. It is only through metaphor—root metaphor or nuclear symbol—that we can know God, and a parable is a form of metaphor. All there is is the story or metaphor. It assumes nothing, it explains nothing, but it creates meaning.[34] A true parable is nontranslatable and irreducible, but in the telling "a deep crack breaks the surface realism and we glimpse something through it."[35] What TeSelle describes as the parabolic story I mean by the open story. When she speaks of stories that describe something which structural categories (common sense and thinking meaning) could just as well or better relate, she is referring to closed stories. It is, of course, only within the parabolic or open story that we find the movement from aesthetic appreciation to theological apprehension. This is why the relation of story to the antistructure is so important to understand.

It is the telling of your story that draws me into the antistructure. I said that no one goes into the antistructure with an empty head. It is, however, the culture's story that carries me out on to pilgrimage. It is on the return, however, that your story, conjoined with God's story—or so we hope—is appropriated by me. This is the story that I carry back with me into the structures to be lived out within role and status.

Of course, we can also see why a society may muddle along without any clear intent; for the fragmentation, confliction, or absence of story(ies) may become evident when the supporting, external structures are no longer there or no longer suffice. It does not have a story given to it that can lead it into pilgrimage. Robert Bellah has said that the myths of American origin have died, and we need new myths if we are to recover our purpose. The events of recent years—the black power movement, the Vietnam War, and the ecological crisis—have contributed to expose the impoverishment of root metaphors of American life. Hence life in America is literally without meaning. Bellah calls for a reappropriation of our tradition, which is to recapture the American story; but he adds:

> Any reappropriation of tradition must be made in full consciousness of our present experience of loss. In these ways an authentic reappropriation is the direct opposite of the nostalgic, sentimental, and uncritical presentation of tradition in the mass media. They offer tradition as a palliative. We need tradition as a stimulus to rebirth.[36]

The first tradition is the closed story, the second is the open story. Some people's appropriation of the story of Jesus is nostalgic, sentimental, and uncritical. It is the story celebrated in social dramas that draws us on into the unknown that is open. There in a creative imagination we can join our vision with the vision of God in Christ to work for the kingdom in love for one another and all mankind. It is the human story, and hence God's story.

DISCOVERING THE STORY

Ulrich Simon has written:

> All narratives have one thing in common: they give verbal accounts of events which are alleged to have happened in the past. . . . Only when the hearer assumes that what has happened may, even in changed circumstances, happen again and affect him will he give assent to the story with something amounting to faith. However, in that case his interest shifts from the study of events to the persons who order, or suffer from, them. . . . The reading of the narrative will make available the power which in the past enabled men and women to subdue the world of events to their free action.[37]

I suspect that all stories, inasmuch as they are self-transcendent, have a cosmic dimension. They reveal to us a fragment of the sacred whole. Myths and fairy tales do this explicitly. If we take Simon seriously, they do it by immersing us in the archaic, by which I mean the *hallowed past*. At the same time, they offer the sacred whole as a present possibility for us at least at the level of words.[38]

The fourth vector of ministry is concerned that the story of Jesus, the "good news" proclaimed beginning with Pentecost (Acts 2:1–4), be held in remembrance so that today we see the presence of God within our awareness and evident in our individual stories. The memory of the *ecclesia* is essential. As St. Peter recalled it in a straightforward manner, we remember that Jesus of Nazareth, who had a singular relationship to God that was known in the signs he worked among men, was executed by mankind as a part of God's vision to unite his creatures to himself and not be lost to him in death. The Passion of Jesus was effective, because God also raised him from death as the promise that all mankind would be joined to God in a new order of creation (Acts 2:22–24). That is the story to which the church gives its faith because, as Simon says, while it shows us the hand of God in the hallowed past, we trust it can happen again in us, "even in changed circumstances."

There is a clear paradox in the story of Jesus. It is the paradox of all Christians, who want love and find hate, who desire peace and live in war. The story says that God has a design for his creation, but for those who share in it there is freedom. It is a tale in which the end is anticipated but cannot be described. Everything appears to be the worst, but we are confident it will turn out for the best. The story of Jesus is the story of every man: "a kind of pilgrimage from total loss to total gain."[39]

Obviously everything in the New Testament is not story, just as everything is not *kerygma* (from a Greek word meaning proclamation that is religious in character). Perhaps the balance of Scripture serves to provide us with the concepts that enable us to understand clearly the kerygmatic story. There is a great deal of interpretation and reflection upon the life and person of Jesus and the apostolic church in the New Testament, which is necessary for the kerygma to be made operant and lived. But the heart of the Gospel is the proclamation or kerygma, and its principal content is the story of Jesus. Far too many people in the *ecclesia* have not heard that story so as to have faith that it can happen in their lives, not to mention the countless numbers outside the community. It is the story that engages us at the level of felt meaning and moves toward intuitive meaning, and that is why the Gospel must remain story at its center if it is to be accepted as anything *more* than a philosophical construct.

A few paragraphs back I spoke of Peter's summary of the Gospel story after the event of Pentecost. After this summary he goes on to talk about King David, connecting his story, on which every one of his listeners had been brought up, with Jesus (Acts 2:25–36). Whether or not this was what Peter said or Luke composed, it is a masterful ploy. He ties in the story of Jesus with a root metaphor in the Jewish culture, opening for them the possibility of a conjoint vision and calling them to faith.

There is always in Christian meaning the necessity to take into account these three stories—Jesus', the culture's, and mine—all of which are open to the vision of God; and we have to attempt to join those visions by interrelating the stories.

Simon again writes:

> Faith is made by identification with the conflict [in the Gospel story] and sustained by the hope which lies beyond its resolution. The story provides the link. . . . The Spirit moves men to a faith greater than the story itself, for as the story-teller talks and writes, and as the reader listens and reads, God himself confronts both for the future.[40]

My only disagreement with Simon, if it can be called that, is that the "link" of which he speaks is really *three* stories coming together: the story of Jesus, the story of the teller, and my story. There has to be a translation of Jesus' story, as told within that culture, into my culture, and when that is done, we have the link. This is what Peter was doing in his address after the Pentecost experience.

There is no problem identifying the story of Jesus in the New Testament. It is what we live in the Christian year, beginning with Advent and moving through Christmas, Epiphany, Lent, Holy Week, Easter, Ascension, and Pentecost. It has been told and retold in all kinds of literary forms. Even those who question the reality of the brute fact of Jesus' existence do not deny the story of the man called Jesus.

The problem, which is particularly acute for our times, is the hermeneutical problem. How, once we identify *our* contemporary story and *my* personal story, do we conjoin those stories to the story of Jesus? It begins, then, with making certain of your story and mine. It is not that we lack stories. There are two other reasons for this problem, which are apart from the possibility of the existence of stories themselves.

The first reason we find it difficult to identify our story is that we have not been fed a diet of consistent stories. Stories are basically oral in nature and lead to the written story; but storytellers, even story-readers-out-loud, are not as common as one might hope in American families. Yet it is absolutely essential to the evolution of a story, for as Northrop Frye writes, "Literature can derive its forms only from itself."[41] If there is no literature, or if the literature is banal pap (as on television), or if it is fragmented and distorted, then we suffer from the impoverishment of the stuff of stories. Our vision is distorted because of our limited imagery. In other words, only when I am told your story do I begin to be able to tell mine.

The second problem is that stories—good stories—expose us. As characteristic of a dying to self-control, they require that we reveal our childlike qualities and trust others. Our culture conditions us against this. There are few of us who could, like the Icelandic saga-teller, regale our audience far into the night with stories either read or remembered. What do we do when our young child says, "Tell me a story." The excuse is that stories are trivial, the truth is that our imaginations have become rusty with disuse. Recently in doing a conference on stories, which was attended largely by women, I was impressed with how many wives came to me and said how much wider their lives would be if only their husbands were less child*ish* and more child*like*. If only they did not feel the need to appear so "practical" and to take themselves so seriously, and could get in touch with their story. They are describing a chronic disease of the American male.

It is the task of ministry to enable us to get our stories together! It is a crucial part of opening the fourth vector and enchanting the reality (the story) of man. There are a number of ways of doing this. Those influenced by Jung are going the route of dreams and their interpretation. Spontaneous drama, working backwards from the action to the script, is another possible avenue. The keeping of a reflection journal can be a means of identifying the story of our pilgrimage. Transactional analysis, despite its simplistic anthropological overlay (neatly refuted by the cartoon in which Jesus says from the cross, "If you're okay, and I'm okay, what am I doing hanging here?"), gets at this subject through script analysis. My purpose in this book, if for no other reason than I lack a broad experience in experimental theology, cannot be that of the exhaustive description of methods of getting at individual stories, as well as our corporate stories. I think I have made clear the desperate need to do this in America today.

There is one method in which I have had some experience and it can be a means of opening up the story of the person to identification and analysis, which is a prerequisite of conjoining that story, with others' stories, to the story of Jesus. This can be done by asking a person to "write his own fairy tale." The obvious advantage in asking him to do this instead of "writing his own myth" is, that while you have opened up the possibility for the imagination to run free of the cultural illusions of reality, you have avoided so universaliz-

186

ing the task that it becomes a grim chore or even a heavy piece of theology. My experience is that after the initial expressions of embarrassment all kinds of people can write their fairy tales with a great deal of insight, and consequently identify their story.

Among over fifty "fairy tales" that I have from workshops in theology and the imagination, one of my favorites, entitled "The Girl with the Red Balloon," is as follows (somewhat edited for the sake of brevity). I would note that it is not a true fairy tale, but it gets at the point.

Once upon a time, in a little village by the sea, lived a little girl named Lucinda. None of the people in the village called her Lucinda. They called her: "that girl with the red balloon." Lucinda always carried a bright, red balloon, which was tied to a long silver string clutched tightly in her hand.

Many of the people in the village laughed at Lucinda and her red balloon. Lucinda was just a little girl, however, and it was perfectly acceptable for small children to play with red balloons.

When she was very little Lucinda tried to explain about her red balloon. For instance, the red balloon was good for leading her somewhere—to beautiful fields, to the ocean and crashing waves, to a warm place where Lucinda felt love. But the balloon could also lead the little girl to dark mysterious caves which frightened her, or sad forests of grief which made her cry, or into the midst of quarrels. Then she felt great anger; but it all went together.

The red balloon was also excellent for seeing. If she looked at her village, her friends, or the forest through the red balloon, she saw things that others did not see. In the beginning Lucinda tried to tell others about what she saw. They laughed and Lucinda learned not to explain about her red balloon.

Lucinda was as happy as could be expected until one day someone said, "Lucinda, you are too old for a red balloon. It was okay when you were a little child, but now you are almost a woman. You must let that stupid balloon go and be mature." Lucinda held on tighter and tighter, but life became more and more difficult.

One particularly difficult day, people were saying things like; "You are always overdramatizing with that stupid, red balloon in your hand" and "If you let go that ridiculous, red balloon, you might accomplish something." Lucinda then made a decision. She knew she had to keep the red balloon, but she could hide it. The question was, Where? It had to be close to her, but it had to be well hidden. So she hid the balloon inside her head.

While this hiding place fitted the criteria for closeness and secrecy, it had its disadvantages. It gave her a terrible headache. It was very difficult, as well, to laugh and shake one's head with a red balloon stuffed inside. It was also difficult to cry, to be afraid, or even to get angry. There was danger of the balloon popping out and being lost or discovered. To keep the balloon from doing this, Lucinda had to scrunch up her eyes and seeing became very difficult. So while the balloon was close, it was no longer useful for leading and for seeing.

People did stop laughing and they complimented Lucinda on her new adulthood. She got married and had babies. She even went to work in an important job in the village. Her headache got progressively worse, however, and she almost forgot about flowers, waves, warm places, caves, forests, and seeing things through red balloons.

One day, while watching her children through scrunched up eyes, she thought she saw something familiar in the hand of one of them. She tried and tried to see what it was, but she knew that if she was to really see it she would have to open wide her eyes. She knew what would happen if she did. But being a good mother and not wanting her child to have anything harmful, she did open her eyes. Just as she saw a red balloon on a silver string in the hand of her child, she cried out, and out popped her own red balloon. It looked so beautiful and it felt so good not to have that balloon in her head anymore! She could see again and everything appeared as new. So Lucinda decided to leave the balloon out in the open on its silver string. She laughed and laughed and laughed.

Lucinda did *not* live happily ever after. People now laugh at her and call her "spacy" and "childish," and tell her she has no common sense. The red balloon does not always lead Lucinda to beautiful fields of flowers. Dark caves are also there, as well as sad forests and quarrels. When she looks through the red balloon she does not always see beauty and happiness. But Lucinda did live *truly* ever after.

Aside from the fact that this story is a magnificent argument in fantasy for the approach to piety that I have been exploring these last four chapters, it is also a revealing account of a personal pilgrimage. Marie Louise von Franz has said that if we are to understand a fairy tale there are four steps to follow: (1) the identification of the symbols, (2) the comparison with their appearance in other fairy tales, (3) the construction of the relationship of the several symbols within the fairy tale under consideration, and (4) the translation into psychological or, in our case, theological terms.[42] I would then add, as a fifth step, the enjoining of the story to the story of Jesus. Doing just this, but in a much simplified form and without any kind of step-by-step analysis, it seems to me that this story says at least this much.

The central image of the story is Lucinda holding on to the red balloon. It is easy to get tied up in interpreting the balloon. My own intuition is that it is simply a tag. Aside from unpleasant memories some of us may have of balloons from "pop liturgies" of the sixties, the balloon is a relatively recent image denoting the quality of the child: free-floating, whimsical, imaginative, light. The heart of the matter is Lucinda-as-child. The symbolic function of child as child in folk literature is related to the search for roots, self-identity, a meaningful future, life in the kingdom, and so forth. What we have in this story is a quest for transcendent identity, which the author clearly understands is not something the world can give her. "Peace is my parting gift to you . . . such as the world cannot give" (John 14:27).

The price of her quest is both the joy of the child known in flowers (usually identified with children), crashing waves, and warmth; and the agony and the emotional turmoil found in forests and caves. Both these images are connected with symbols of unconscious sexuality, masculine and feminine, as well as the meaning of maternity. To become oneself in union with the fundamental cosmic reality, one has to be able to struggle with one's most basic self. Yet it is worth the price, and is to be chosen over the oppression of the world. "All I care for is to know Christ, . . . to share his sufferings, in growing conformity with his death, if only I may arrive at the resurrection from the dead" (Phil. 3:10–11).

This way demands sacrifice, however. Earlier, Lucinda had succumbed to the temptation of the "serpent," to assume her expected feminine role. Now the turning point of the story is when Lucinda is confronted by the truth that is in her child—"a little child shall lead them" (Isa. 11:6)—and she is willing to endure the ridicule of her family and friends in search of redemption. Lucinda's balloon is like the story of the young man in *Equus,* cited earlier. She needs it "to see in the dark." She does not say that the suffering inflicted by mankind becomes the context of her resurrection, although I think it is true that it does. Neither does she preach a "realized eschatology." The kingdom has not arrived, but she perceives the quest and the eschatological hope as that which has integrity for her. "She does not *always* see beauty and happiness." In my experience, people who hear this story often avoid the continuing darkness in it, which says a great deal about their problem of enjoining "*my* story" to "*your* story" (in this case, "The Story of the Red Balloon"), much less to "God's story." One would believe that the hope here lies in the fact that "Lucinda did live *truly* ever after."

What we have in this tale is the story of the fall, of one who has gone whoring after false gods, of confrontation with the word of God, of crucifixion and anticipated resurrection. When we see the story in such theological terms, the conjoining of the first and second Adams with the Lucinda-of-the-hidden-balloon and the Lucinda-of-the-balloon-now-free becomes obvious. " 'The first man, Adam, became an animate being,' whereas the last Adam has become a life-giving spirit." (1 Cor. 15:45). The headache is gone, she does not have to scrunch her eyes. She lives "truly ever after."

My purpose, of course, is to suggest a method, not to argue a particular case. It is true that I have thought about "The Girl with the Red Balloon" frequently, discussed the story with friends, and researched it in the catalogues of folk motifs. I think I am correct in my interpretation; but the point is that a conjoining of visions emerges, through which the Spirit can move, as Simon puts it, to confront us with the future. That is what the discovery of Jesus' story, your story, my story, and their relationship under the vision of God is all about.

To close this section it is helpful to call attention to a disarmingly modest proposal of Robert McAfee Brown as to how this conjoining of stories—mine, yours, and God's (although he speaks of two rather than three)—might be done. First, Brown says what we have been saying all along. It begins with hearing a story that is a true symbol or metaphor, open or parabolic. Second, God's story becomes my story by your-story-in-God being told me in various ways. To borrow a term from another context, we "facet" God's story in terms of multiple stories from the culture. Third, we see how the contemporary world relates its story to God's story, as the Third World relates its problems to liberation theology. Finally we reenact the story in liturgy. This is a deceptively simple outline, because in general the Christian community, not to mention society as a whole, fails to do any of the four points.[43]

SUMMARY

At a parish workshop on fairy tales, the following query appeared in the "question box": "Do a number of fairy tales and myths lead to a danger of not knowing what is real and true?" Perhaps this has been your question, not only in this chapter, but in the four chapters that constitute Part Two of this book, "Toward a Contemporary Piety." In the minds of many of us when we speak of the "real" or the "true" we are speaking of something "out there," which, if not completely describable, at least lies at the end of a syllogism. I have been offering an alternative to this notion of *necessary truth*, as do most theologians since Kant. The point is that piety and the truth it serves does not consist of adherence to and acceptance of a set of static, prescribed, eternal structures or formulae; it is a *process*. The absolute in that process is the vision of God, for man and the rest of creation, which lies at the end of our spiritual quest. The character of the quest itself is the search for understanding—*fides quaerens intellectum*—in which faith *(fides)* is an act of love, and understanding *(intellectum)* is a dynamic process characterized by man's intuitive self moving in and out of the primordial existence within the abyss or wilderness. It is a spirituality characterized by a dying to self or a letting go, in which we conjoin our vision with the vision God at the unpredictable and uncontrolled margins of our life. It is not a vision or intentionality that is without substance within our consciousness. We come at least with a story we have been told, for it is the reality of this story that brings us to expect to find within our intentionality the presence of God soliciting us into being. We hope that it will become our story.

Hyemeyohsts Storm has recounted the stories of the Plains Indians. In Chapter Five of this book I spoke of the "vision quest" of this people, who at certain pivotal times in their lives went into the wilderness to be met under some form by the Spirit of the universe. I see the vision quest as a native American illustration of a biblical spirituality. It is an integral part also of the Sun Dance Way, the journey of the plains people in search of harmony with the Creator and his creation. Storm speaks of this journey in relation to stories.

> There are many old Stories . . . used among the people to Teach the meaning of the Sun Dance Way. They were themselves a Way of Understanding among the People, and also among different Peoples . . . *everything in them should be read symbolically.* Every story can be symbolically unfolded for you through your own Medicines [totem animals or places in the created order], Reflections and Seekings. As you do this you will learn to See through the eyes of your Brothers and Sisters and to share their Perceptions. Questioning is one of the most vital paths to understanding these Stories, which will teach you of the Sun Dance Way.[44]

Stories provide the *raison d'etre* of pilgrimage. They encourage us to see while on pilgrimage and, as long as we make no idols of the stories, they keep us moving. Stories are products of the imagination, just as systems are the products of ratiocination. They are symbolic, they carry feeling, but they have direction. They point us along the way. As Christians, in our own stories we live out the one story and the way along which it points. It is the story of Jesus, who came, taught, suffered, died, rose, and went to the Father. "So now, my friends, the blood of Jesus makes us free to enter boldly into the sanctuary by the new, living way which he has opened for us through the curtain, the way of his flesh" (Heb. 10:19–20).

PART THREE

PATTERNS IN MINISTRY

8

THE CONGREGATION

As I travel about, people who are aware of my interests sometime share with me cartoons, clippings, and other bits and pieces of stuff illustrative of our shared concerns. One of my favorites, given to me by a priest two or three years ago, was an envelope for a third-class mailing from a church publishing house. Almost half of the envelope was occupied with a "blurb" in purple, which read: "The key to an effective church ministry—an efficient church office."

This statement seems to me to be a clear clue to the cause of the spiritual bankruptcy of the church. This is not to imply that an "efficient church office" is not highly desirable. It is. It is no more, however, the "key to effective ministry," as I hope is obvious by this point, than a winning football team is the "key" to an effective university. Only someone severely conditioned by the prevailing sociocultural world and utterly devoid of a sense of history, proportion, and purpose, could make either statement.

I have said in the first chapter that the four essential elements or vectors in the Christian community, whose vocation is to be an instrument of God's hominisation of the world, are the past, the environment, the internal life, and the openness to the word of God now. In speaking of dying to self (see Chapter Six) as a movement necessary to the imaginative grasp of God's presence in our world, I referred at length to the conjoining of our vision and God's vision in nature, the interpersonal, the interior self, and history. I see these four arenas of our experience as that to which we desparately need to be sensitive.

This kind of sensitivity or sensibility is something we have progressively lost over the last three hundred years through a process of dissociation. The mind of man has withdrawn from nature, the interpersonal, the interior self, and even history, to "distance" itself in what Barfield calls "beta-thinking" (see

Chapter Four). The very notion of a "person" has become one who possesses an integrity of consciousness, independent of anything else. The result has been the emphasis upon the self-in-control and now the door is open to the hubris of the techno-barbaric world. T. S. Eliot illustrates this by differentiating between the sensibility of John Donne or George Herbert and the sentimentality of Alfred Tennyson or Robert Browning. By "sensibility" Eliot means the ability to "devour any kind of experience" with a combination of feeling and ratiocination that has proportion, clarity, and balance.[1] Robert Bellah comments in a similar vein by distinguishing between the seventeenth-century Puritan's "twofold vision," from whom "nothing could be more illusory than the goal of success," and the "single vision" of the late nineteenth-century Protestant, for whom there is "a single truth in religion and business."[2]

The notion of effective ministry as the result of an efficient office is a logical outcome of this single vision and the disintegration of sensibility. Where in the efficient office is their time for the fourth vector of ministry? We pay lip service to the imagination by hanging a few banners about or maybe a Corita print or two, but otherwise piety is reduced to cynicism or sentimentality. I am speaking of the cynicism, for example, of the so-called "professionals," such as one hospital chaplain who showed his ignorance of the Episcopal parish down the street by his saying he only attended divine worship when he was "up front." My current favorite illustration of sentimentality is a recent graveside prayer, which I had the occasion to hear. Somewhere there was the petition: "Teach us, O God, to know that as we remember the spirit of our dear friend, we are only burying IT which is the body." I would identify the minister as Protestant only because that particular sentiment outdoes the astral ascent of the Orphic-Pythagorean mysteries and Dante's *Purgatorio,* without one bit of their metaphysical insight to support it.

Where is there the ambiguity, the risk, the mystery in the bureacracy of statistics, planning, and evaluation? Where are the symbols and the stories that evoke the constant task of theological reflection and hard thinking amid the file cards, the Xerox, and the smartly dressed secretaries? I am not against efficient offices. I try to run one myself. This is not, however, the heart or even the key of the ministering *ecclesia.* The city of God is not the result of personnel management; it is the result of being called out in faith. It is the pilgrim band on the march to where they are not quite sure.

The Christian congregation, if it is to be the matrix of the kind of ministry I have described in this book, has to be one whose life does not depend upon any office, much less an efficient one. Good managerial procedures are part of *external* structures, which uphold and promote the end of the organization. The ability to exist as a communitas, to move through the wilderness, requires a kind of *internal* structure that has no difficulty with the imprecision of intuitive thought, which is itself the key to the life of sensibility and participation in the spirit.

The thought has occurred to me that the typical American congregation is patterned on those dominant denominations: the Methodist and the Baptist. Both traditions, in a real sense, have no roots in natural communities. Both were predominantly enthusiastic movements amid a mobile people, and they had to institutionalize along bureaucratic lines very rapidly in order to survive. Today they are the most structured of the American denominations; and others, older than they, have had to follow their lead as their own spontaneous community has dissolved. This includes the ethnic traditions of the Roman Catholics and Lutherans, as well as the class-conscious gatherings of the Presbyterians and Episcopalians. The institutionalization, to the degree that it has been a substitute for and not an outgrowth of an ongoing spontaneous group life, has successfully thwarted any community sense of God's presence among us.

I am convinced, however, that the hope for the church in the future lies in its ability to discover for itself a community that possesses an internal cohesion, which is joined together by a shared felt and intuitive meaning *of the experience of God that is part of the expanding horizon of man's consciousness.* There are many microsociological entities which have nothing to do with God: hunting bands, the Mafia, the morning coffee group. There are also communions and communities whose religious commitment is pathological (symptomatic of neurotic need for the assurance of personal esteem), as described by Dean Kelley.[3] In these the religious motivation is *extrinsic* to the authentic growth of the self. It does this without being self-serving, self-congratulatory, and self-consciously "daring."

A sign of such a preinstitutional group—what Farley means by *ecclesia*—is its ability to incorporate certain polarities into its life, without choosing one or the other (without creating *false* exclusive, oppositions).[4] In this chapter I will speak of the city of the church as an instrument of the fourth vector of ministry in terms of certain sets of polarities which are necessary for the congregation. One pole of these polarities moves toward the structuring of groups, and therefore I am speaking, not of the congregation as just a microsociological collectivity but as more than this. There is the necessary tension between the communion, community, and mass and the structured group. My

197

emphasis for the sake of the fourth vector of ministry is on the possibility of the congregation to possess an internal vitality, however, which can survive in the wilderness without structural supports. For it is this from which the heart of the church's ministry arises: the attendance to the transcendent word of God.

The polarities which are desirable or even necessary to the healthy congregation, are, first of all, the conservative and the innovative; secondly, the intimate and the formal are needed; and thirdly, the affective and the cognitive are both vital to a balanced community. In the light of all that has been said about ministry and imagination, no congregation can afford to ignore one side or the other of any of these apparent opposites.

CONSERVATIVE AND INNOVATIVE

I owe this particular set of terms to Margaret Mead, who has said that religion must be both conservative and innovative at the same time.[5] Mead means by the word "conservative" as possessing the ability *to conserve* what carries power out of man's past. It is not a political label, identifying an emphasis upon the value of institutional structures over against individual freedom, or the desire to preserve the *status quo* against change. As a matter of fact, it is the communitas that most clearly embodies the conservative and yet has no external structure. Mead is saying that the religious community needs to affirm those expressions of meaning from the past which carry power, not only because they are still plausible but because they are also potent symbols *by virtue of their age.*

Victor Turner has spoken of his conviction that liturgical revision over the last generation has been insensitive to the archaic symbol.[6] This is because we have been caught in social theories of structural-functionalism, and have failed to see that the soul of liturgy is symbolic interaction. What Turner means by the archaic symbol is an image that has been hallowed by a long history of pious use. His contention is that a form of prayer, an object, or a place takes on a power just by the fact that it has been a central part of the felt meaning of worshipers for centuries. An example would be the Shrine of Our Lady of Guadalupe. The *reverent* iconoclast is one who is sensible of those images and does not destroy them with the rest. As a Roman Catholic, Turner has in mind the Latin Mass. I am not sure I would agree with him there, but the principle abides.

There is a story told of the great Louis Duchesne, an eminent Roman

Catholic liturgical pioneer, who lived early in this century and who was noted for his debunking of popular piety. He was visiting in Rome and attended, with a companion, the services on the occasion of the Exaltation of the Holy Cross (September 14th) in a local church. As the procession wended its way, Monsignor Duchesne bowed profoundly when a reliquary containing a particle of the "true cross" passed. His companion noted this and whispered, "Father, I thought you had proven that to be a hoax!" "Certainly," replied Duchesne, "but it must be at least twelve hundred years old!"

In the time I have spent with the Dakota Indians their resistance to liturgical change was obvious to me. Their devotion to the Dakota translations of the worst of the late nineteenth-century Gospel hymns and the reverence they hold for the 1928 Book of Common Prayer, an ideological expression of a culture utterly alien and recently overtly hostile to them, can appear absurd. I have visited in their churches, where the cast-off stoles of some eastern parish of fifty years ago are treated with a profound reverence that could appear excessive to some. Yet there are no people in the church who better live the principal of sensibility to the archaic.

I came to understand something of what lies behind this when I had the happy opportunity of driving with a Dakota priest across the plains for some five hours. In that time we began to share with one another our several religious intuitions, and something of the "anglo" veneer disappeared as this holy man talked. We spoke of dreams and visions, the sweat lodge, medicine men, women in white buckskins, the sacred buffalo, and the evil snakes; and more and more I appreciated a culture which still preserved, in spite of our banal Western ideology, the ability to see the divine in nature. As the priest said, "Even our *fragmented* culture inspires a deeper sense of the holy *(wakan)* than yours at its best."

I think it depends on where you look for that to be true. Carl Dehne, S.J., in a lecture at a conference on spirituality at the University of Notre Dame in June of 1975, spoke of the need to appreciate the power in popular Roman Catholic devotions (such as the rosary, Benediction of the Blessed Sacrament, Holy Hours, and devotions to the Sacred Heart of Jesus). Dehne is a student of the liturgical movement, a post-Vatican II Roman Catholic with deep ecumenical commitments. The point he was making, however, is very similar to what I discovered in the Episcopalians among the Dakota Indians. This is that there is an integrity and authenticity to *folk piety,* just as there is to folk tales, fairy stories, and myths. They go hand-in-hand: the story and its piety. Both have the ability to convey transcendence with an incredible freshness, not only in spite of their essentially conservative nature but because of it.

Of course we worry about heresy in folk religion—or, at least, we used to worry about it. The Reformation was in part a reaction against the essential paganism of popular Roman Catholic piety, shaped and cherished over centuries in the northern European mind. Protestantism was at heart a conceptual movement, which involved an intellectual revulsion at the pagan practices of the average congregation, despite the healthy earthiness of Martin Luther. While this is understandable, I think it was much overdone. If paganism is a religion of nature, a little of it is in the Incarnation. It was our Platonism and, even worse, our neo-Platonism which led to the sterility of the rational systems of the late sixteenth, seventeenth, and eighteenth centuries. The pietist reaction was a quest for a renewed folk piety, as it is today. Unfortunately, a Pietist has a Puritan conscience.

The conservatism of authentic folk piety is a commitment to the symbols of space. Jesus himself was seen frequently at the Temple, a spatial symbol. Space symbols tend to be feminine. The feminine is the conservative. Any people with a strong sense of the soul are conservative and have a feminine emphasis in their religion. In reading the visions of Black Elk, a Dakota shaman of the turn of the century, the dominant symbols are feminine: the center of the world, which he called "the only mother," the sacred hoop, and the tree that blooms.[7] The fact that the popular piety of English Christians through the centuries, except those who are in intellectual retreat, was strongly Marian should not surprise us. Northern Europeans have an intense commitment to land, sea, the forests, and the earth.

Authentic folk piety engages us at the level of felt and intuitive meaning, just as folk stories. That is where the conservative pole of the congregation should be centered. It is the piety of the communitas, liminality, and the antistructure. The world of symbols and myth, which has a much longer life than systems and signs, exists outside the city walls in the wilderness. It is related to the abyss. The problem comes when we attempt to be equally conservative in terms of common sense and thinking meaning. This is the meaning of the sign and system, which belongs within the structures, and which is far more brittle. Here conservativism lacks power and only stifles action. It can be pathological at this level, whereas innovation can be pastorally insensitive and even destructive at the level of felt and intuitive meaning.

Take, for example, the contrast between a congregation handling snakes in the mountains of East Tennessee and a congregation self-consciously recruiting for the Society for the Preservation of the Book of Common Prayer. *There is more real piety in the snake-handlers. There is more power of the presence of transcendence in one such service than in a year of Cranmer and the modulated tones of the Anglican parson.* It is raw power, misdirected power, unchanneled power; but it is still power to move. It is the same kind of power that moved the blacks of the southern United States out of their churches and into the streets. In this instance, the power was more wisely directed.

In calling for a conservatism in the congregation, I am at the same time expressing my unutterable opposition to a kind of dilletantism which is only precious. This has been very common in my own heritage of Anglo-Catholicism, where sexual power is deflected to a love for "old things." There is an incredible difference between a humble scrub woman kneeling before her plastic statue of St. Jude and a learned professor collecting ecclesiastical *objets d'art.*

I have no doubt that some readers will be greatly puzzled by my location of the conservative pole within the antistructure and the innovative within the structures. To see the whole notion of the antistructure as "innovative" is to miss the point. The "notion" is innovative, but the notion as such is a conceptual structure. This book, for example, only occasionally wanders into the antistructure, as in an illustration. What makes the notion innovative is the refusal to accept, out of fear, the pathological conservatism which clings to structures, and to assert that the true conservative is one who has made the pilgrimage to be discovered by the ancient truths that the structures have hidden. The innovation comes when we decide to make something of that discovery, which requires that we return to the world of planning, logic, and concept and change the old structures.

Conservatism without a spontaneous community possessing internal cohesion becomes a parody. Innovation, which is just as necessary to the congregation, without structure is impossible. This is because innovation is the assertive, masculine, planned life of the community. It requires the clarity and precision of common sense and, especially, thinking. It channels the power of the felt and intuitive into patterns of action.

The balance between the conservative and innovative appears to be expressed in the balance between the Catholic or immanentalist dimension and the Protestant or transcendentalist position. In introducing these distinctions there is a risk that the words themselves carry too much "baggage" for the point to be clear, but it is worth trying to get the sense of the distinction. I am *not* relating Catholic and Protestant to two divisions of Christianity, but thinking of them as necessary polarities within any healthy congregation, just

201

as the feminine and masculine dimensions, to which they correspond respectively, must be held in balance within any healthy person.

The Catholic dimension springs from the folk religion of the people. In this sense it is almost gullible. It really believes that the "burning bush" is just around the corner (Ex. 3:1). There is a naïve expectation, perhaps now of the nature of a *"second* naïvete," that God is present within the ordinary experience of life. It is incarnational. Holy persons, relics, art (some of which seems perhaps lacking in any real merit), feasts, and fast days all carry symbolic power, leading us into the antistructure and confronting us with the mystery of being. Catholicism was born of pagan folk, the people of the earth, who heard the Gospel and responded out of their deep belief that the love of people and the goodness of the earth achieved its crowning glory in the Christ.

The Protestant principle springs from the humanist movement of the sixteenth century, which fed the rationalism of Descartes, Spinoza, Leibniz, and Wolf. The emphasis in Calvin upon the absolute sovereignty of God, a concept to which the love of God necessarily took second place, left the uncontaminated Protestant struggling with the meaning of the Incarnation, even repudiating it (as in Paul Tillich). Man's critical faculties, his suspicion of idolatry, and his concern for logic fed an iconoclasm, which has exhibited a passion over the last four hundred years that some of us find in retrospect incredible in its destructiveness of liturgy, art, and time-hallowed custom. The absolute Protestant utterly divorces beauty and goodness in order to affirm the latter with all the certainty of a university lecturer.

I would argue that the Protestant principle functions most effectively within the structures of thinking meaning, and tends to regress to common sense. When it is most effective it is highly innovative. The rise of modern nationalism, the development of science, the breakthrough of the industrial revolution, and the post-Kantian evolution of modern thought in the West are predominantly Protestant. It is good at crusades, such as the abolitionist movement, prohibition, integration, and women's liberation. (In the case of women's liberation Protestantism works against itself, because when the feminine symbol within ourselves is freed our Catholic sense will greatly deepen.)

The Catholic dimension of our life together emerges at its strongest in the realm of the felt and intuitive meaning. Catholicism is a world of symbols, and when it attempts to reduce itself to a system it becomes tyrannical and absurd. It is my experience that the person who lives close to the earth, even though he calls himself "Protestant," oozes Catholicism from his pores. Protestantism is for university professors. Social progress is not likely to be motivated by the

Catholic mind, but a love of land, family, and history is.

My argument here is that the balanced congregation must be conservative or Catholic, but it also must be innovative or Protestant. We cannot be satisfied to live—even in love—in the midst of things as they are. Jesus said, "Do not suppose that I have come to abolish the Law and the prophets, . . . but to complete" (Matt. 5:17). In order to "complete" the tradition he had to suffer and die. This is why the cross, which is so alien to paganism, is central to Protestantism (1 Cor. 1:18). A Christian community has to be one willing to suffer and die for the kingdom, but it has also to be organized so that it knows why it is doing it and can channel the power that comes from death. It needs the structures of a "community of moral discourse," the institutions of a thoughtful, prophetic community.[8]

I said this to a vestry at a weekend workshop once, and one gentleman took great umbrage. "That's absurd," he said. "It has always been my conviction that the job of the rector was to tell us from the pulpit what we ought to do, and that it was our job in the vestry meetings to tell him why we were *not* going to do it." It is undoubtedly true that innovation comes about by one portion of the church confronting another, but innovation is the task of the whole congregation as microcosm of the church working together, in which there is developed a consensus.

There is an historical dimension to religion, as Eliade has told us, and this finds expression in the utopian vision of our life: that utopia is the property of the entire congregation.[9] It is the vision of the new city toward which we move together. So we cannot be content just to be; we must also do. This aspect of religious activism, so frequently associated with the Social Gospel and today's liberation theology, is an essential part of the congregation's life. It is the living today of our resurrection faith for tomorrow.

Therefore, it is altogether appropriate and necessary that the congregation organize to change the world. When we come back from the wilderness we have a new vision, which must be implemented. After Elijah went out into the desert to Mount Horeb, where Yahweh confronted him, he returned at the Lord's command to annoint Hazael to be king of Aram and Jehu king of Israel, and Elisha as prophet in his place (1 Kings 19:1–21). We are all like Elijah. A congregation that does not innovate either has no vision or is not true to its vision, and the fourth vector of ministry is impotent.

We have to ask ourselves, therefore, what is our congregation doing in response to the issues presented it by society. Perhaps the greatest moral issue today is the one of abortion, not because of all the sentimental rhetoric, but because of what it says about life and humanity. What are we doing about it? The so-called American style of life, based upon individual mobility powered by fossil fuels, is rapidly dying. What alternatives is our community considering? Can anyone seriously think that classical capitalism has a future? Is the only alternative Marxism? The poor get poorer and the rich are less involved. Institutions threaten the truth of freedom. Who is going to challenge this? What are we doing to effect change.

Piety that does not result in innovation is no piety at all, unless somehow the thing of that creation is finished. We have to be both Catholic and Protestant, conservative and innovative, if we are going to be a Christian congregation in the light of the fourth vector.

INTIMATE AND FORMAL

Kurt Back, a professor of sociology and psychiatry at Duke University, has said in an analysis of sensitivity training that the best image for understanding this movement is pilgrimage. Unlike the ancient pilgrim, who traveled out of the walled city, with its accustomed ways, in search of merit in the afterlife, the modern pilgrim within the sensitivity movement seeks as his goal what was in fact the side benefit of the earlier prototype: an encounter in depth with others.[10] It is the satisfaction of discovering oneself, free of the shackles of status and role, that has sent people off over the last decade or so to "marathon weekends," to nude bathing at Esalen, and to weeks of "honest encounter."

The effect upon the church of sensitivity training, coming out of Kurt Lewin's work during World War II, was early and radical. The initial impetus, beginning with persons such as Ted Wedel, Warden at the Washington Cathedral College of Preachers, who participated in the initial labs at Bethel, Maine, in the late forties, has generated a number of models of small-group interaction within the life of the church. They all share the theory that in close relationships, where we are pushed or freed to participate in one another's bodies, feelings, fantasies, and inmost thoughts, the goodness that is our self is uncovered and grows in maturity.

This requires, of course, a willingness to move from behind our defenses, including role and status definition, imposed by the structures. Back speaks of sensitivity training as a kind of pilgrimage. Perhaps he is not aware of how apt his metaphor is indeed. Religious pilgrims, as described by Chaucer in *The Canterbury Tales* or Myerhoff in *The Peyote Hunt,* shed role and status and share in the communitas of human kindness. Of course, if one is depending upon the defenses of role and status to protect a very fragile self—the self within that we do not like—then anything, encounter movement or pilgrimage, that removes those institutional definitions is very frightening. This is why sensitivity training has received a bad name among some, occasionally deserved but more often unmerited.

Intimacy is not just the coming together of persons in joy, happiness, and good feelings about one another. It is the dissolution between persons of the ego boundaries or *persona,* Carl Jung's name for the mask we have been conditioned to hold between us and the world. There is tremendous power in intimacy. While the *persona* is the outward form of an ordering of the chaos that lies within each of us—a necessary ordering, I hasten to add—intimacy is a willingness to let the other enter into that chaos that is ours. There we experience the primal shape and motivation of the other in his personal symbols and stories. Chaos is frightening, but it is also the energetic and visionary center of the self.

As I have said earlier (in Chapter Seven), a primary level of the visionary center of the self is to be found in our personal story. In its early days sensitivity training always insisted that the participants deal with the "here and now," and the past was dismissed as irrelevant. This had the effect of denying us the opportunity "to tell our story." The result was that we could not share our own intentionality: the structure of meaning with which we engaged the "here and now." Contrary to the expectations of the process, we never knew ourselves, much less the other. Now we see that the inner chaos of the self is not empty and in complete disarray, but has a basic pattern or plot which the intimate community shares and relates to the story that lies behind its own existence: the Gospel.

Chaos is not just good, it is both symbolic *and diabolic* (see Chapter Five). Negative feelings churn within us, as well as the good things. Intimacy involves anger, rejection, hatred, lust, greed, and all the other "deadly sins" (or their prior temptations) and more. When we share an intimate relationship, we discover these very things. When I was attending the Anglican Consultative Council in Dublin, Ireland, in the summer of 1973, one of the delegates commented on the floor that "certainly Christians never become angry at one another." If that were true then Christians would never really love one another. For love requires that intimate sharing of the self beyond the *persona,* which inevitably runs the risk of encountering the negative feelings, such as anger, that lie within us all.

The intimate marriage is, of course, the paradigm of what I am describing.

A bonding of two persons that transcends a mere contractual agreement and discovers within itself the vision of God necessarily demands the conflict of feelings. Such a marriage calls on us to discover the *creative use* of anger, envy, lust, and violence. In a good bond we discover our humanity, and in making that discovery we move beyond good and evil to share the vision of the God who made us. As long as we avoid this and live together in the security of two lives that never touch one another, we risk nothing, and we have nothing but the idols of our own socially conditioned, one-dimensional, secular *personae*.

The Christian congregation needs to find the means of being an intimate community. For it is only in the intimate community that we can risk moving into the antistructure where we can discover the infinite richness of life that can make the very banality of everyday living not only tolerable but meaningful. Myerhoff in her beautiful description of the peyote hunt, the trip to Wirikuta, considered by the Huichol as the return to Paradise, speaks of these people as poverty-stricken peasants. They live out a mean, short existence, with few of the benefits of the techno-barbaric world. Yet they all make their pilgrimage in intimate bands, which reinforces for them again and again the singular beauty of life.

> The treasure of Huichol culture is aesthetic and spiritual. These people envy no one, at least that is their ideal. They have in abundance a culture's greatest gift —an utter conviction of the meaningfulness of life.[11]

When you consider this it is neither ironic nor strange that, as Barbara Myerhoff has told me in person, the Huichol have sent her back to the symbols of her own Jewish faith.

It takes the intimate community to make this exploration. Because what we are talking about is a community that can live in an empty space, in a kind of abyss, where only the naked intention of its members to conjoin their vision with that of God sustains the community and keeps it from breaking apart and turning on itself in destructive frenzy. It is a community held together by passion, the passion of *eros,* which is unable to endure the inevitable suffering of chaos in its desperate want for oneness in God.

In all honesty I do not know many congregations like that. My suspicion is that no more than forty to sixty persons can sustain a form of intimacy required for such a journey. Seminaries sometimes make an effort at being this, but because they necessarily seek to teach a discipline, to fulfill measurable— or so we think—expectations, and to meet specific role expectations within the institution, this is not realistic. There are glimpses of this in certain congregations. A priest friend of mine speaks of a weekly gathering of forty or so at 6:00 A.M. for the Eucharist and breakfast as the only "real Christian congregation" he has ever known. Conferences at centers of scenic beauty—I know best Kanuga in western North Carolina—have the intimate community as their ideal, but usually there are too many people in attendence. Some congregations have the vestry weekend in such places, which is the right number, but they are not there long enough for the bank president, the doctor, the architect, the mother, the rector, the father, the mechanic to "get out of role" and to forget their "status" *vis-à-vis* the rest.

The various epochs of the pietistic movement, including our own, is clearly grounded in the intimate community. Although many people committed to Faith Alive or the neo-Pentecostal movement would shudder at the suggestion, they have a common intentionality with the sensitivity movement. They have a need for intimacy, which they express by sharing at some level behind the *persona.* The difference is that sensitivity denies or ignores the possible transcendent source of those deep feelings discovered in encounter, and it is not conditioned to cover up the negative feelings in the name of a stern, puritanical God. The effect of the latter in the pietistic movement is to eviscerate the positive symbols as well as the negative ones and to defeat the transcendental possibilities of the group experience.

Recently I was giving a talk on the possibility of faith in our time and was arguing that a rediscovery of the extraordinary in the ordinary required a sensibility to all of life. At the question period I was asked rhetorically if this included the body. The reply was, of course, in the affirmative; I went on to explain that, while I was not advocating the practice of temple prostitution, I thought we were blind not to recognize the sacred intentionality in the celebration of the *hieros gamos* ("the holy marriage") in the ancient cult of the Great Mother, in which "holy marriage" was thought to have begotten the earth in all its fecundity. As the group broke up I was encountered by an extremely irate gentleman, who identified himself as very active in Faith Alive, and who accused me of speaking at the level of an "X-rated movie." My reply was and is that we cannot have it two ways. If we want a lively faith, we are going to have to move into the abyss where abide, without their usual rationalizations, powerful clusters of symbolic meaning, particularly our sexuality. If we insist on retreating from such symbols to the defenses of our *persona,* rather than moving through them to the God that is their source, then we will exist in an illusion. We will confuse the rigid products of our own anxieties for the will of God. This is the kind of idolatry which sent thousands of Christians to the stake and now keeps thousands of God-fearers out of our churches.

Having said this, it is time to invoke the other side of the polarity: the formal. I am not speaking here of the proper dress for a wedding or a reception. The word "form" here refers to the concern for shape, proportion, and structure, which gives definition and distance to experience and allows us to make some judgment as to the most creative use of that experience. In advocating the intimate community, I also suggest that every congregation needs to have a concern for form. There is no value in "letting it all hang out"; it only bespeaks our pathology. As a matter of fact, a mindless sharing of feeling can be as destructive of humanity and the vision of God as the rigidity of those with "sphincters that could crush diamonds."

The difference between the staying power of many so-called "underground congregations" and the Church of Our Savior, Washington, D.C., or the Church of the Redeemer, Houston, Texas, is form or discipline. No congregation can depend forever on "good feelings" for its life together. Either it institutionalizes or it dies. The congregations I mentioned in Washington and Houston have a clear discipline. They present us with unequivocal choices. If we are one with them, we know where we are and where we are not. This is a great deal more practical than attempting to turn a warm glow on and off, which was true of many "house churches" of the late sixties.

Every congregation needs a discipline. Discipline defines the norms of our life together. For example, we ought not to pray or to attend the worship of the church just when we "feel like it." Such behavior is deceptive and thwarts our growth. Openness to the word of God is an act of will.

Norms of discipline begin with a statement of who is "in" and who is "out." I remember a preacher of latitudinarian bent who once described the Catholic Church as "wide as the world and narrow as God's love." That is a meaningless and, consequently, unhelpful statement. I do not know what something is until I know what it is *not*. If I choose to be a Christian I have to know what I am rejecting. The sacrament of Baptism begins with the renunciations, an entirely commendable *form* which enables me to know that diabolic powers, particularly those present within myself and society, are the enemy. Anger, for example, that destroys myself and others is anger which I cannot cherish, but must identify and hound to its roots in order to tear it out. To give in to lust is not an expression of freedom, but actually can reinforce our slavery to the illusion of omnipotence.

Forms are community norms which serve the purpose of the congregation: the hominisation of the world. As one who lives in the land of the TVA, I am

208

deeply conscious of the difference between the destructive energy of the Tennessee River and its tributaries *before* the dams and the creative energy now present since the forms were placed within the raging waters. Roles are a type of such forms. As a seminary dean I am equally aware that I have to live the role of the dean, even when it provokes the fear, hatred, or animosity of members of the seminary community. It is part of the focus and action of the power of the community.

Congregations which lay no expectations upon their members cheat them of a necessary function of the city. They leave them to be victimized by themselves and one another. Some time ago at a church conference whose membership had a high proportion of recently divorced, neurotic women of approximately thirty years of age, I was witness to a not atypical vignette. One of the group leaders was the object of the seductive overtures of a conference member for the entire week—overtures which he wisely avoided. This only intensified her anguish, however. At the final meal of the conference, before an audience of about two hundred men, women, and children, she raced up to her intended victim, screamed "You bastard!" and fell to the floor. Many would assume that the Christian thing to do would be to rush to her side, assure her that she was loved, and carry her off to console her. But the man in question only leaned over and said calmly, "Do you want to lie there, or shall I give you a hand up?" He later commented to me, "The only thing worse than a basket case is a basket-bearer." His response to this attempt to engulf him in a *diabolic* chaos was to engage the event in an in-*formed* manner, helpful not just to himself, but to the distraught woman as well.

Not all forms are juridical or pastoral. Some are aesthetic. It strikes me that much contemporary religious music and "pop" liturgy is sentimental to the point of being maudlin, or preachy to the point of being utterly tiresome. They lack aesthetic form. Such form requires training, not to mention talent, and yet a congregation needs this. I used to feel rather guilty about the fact that I enjoyed going to St. Paul's Cathedral, London, or the Cathedral of SS. Peter and Paul, Washington, D.C., and *listening* to Evensong. I have now decided that this is nonsense and there is more than one way to participate. We owe a great deal to the folk Masses of the last decade or so, just as we did to the Gospel hymns of the nineteenth century. There is also a place, however, for Bach, Berlioz, and Vaughan Williams—and I can sing very little of that. They have a form which the more popular material does not and which lifts us to a sublime level of feeling that is akin to a transcendental experience.

Liturgy itself needs a sense of aesthetic form, as well as a form of moral obligation to be present. Some liturgy is like some acts of sexual intercourse: we think that good intentions make up for the fact that what we are doing ill befits the situation. When someone is *present* to another he or she inevitably conveys a meaning, and we want to make sure that the *manner of his or her presence* conveys the meaning appropriate to what is being done. Coitus with its inevitable vulnerability is not appropriate affection between two mutually uncommitted persons. Wandering around the sanctuary of a church, looking like a lost, callow youth who does not know what to do with his hands and has outgrown his garments, in which he apparently slept last night, does not bespeak intimacy. It simply repels us.

Perhaps the point of the need to balance intimacy and form has been sufficiently illustrated. It is the movement of the congregation, as between the conservative and innovative, between the antistructure and the structure. Every pastor needs to be sensitive to it, but it is difficult to do.

The crisis within the Episcopal Church, following the ordination of eleven women to the priesthood, contrary to the canon law of that church, in the summer of 1973 in Philadelphia, is an illustration of this polarity. While the ordination could be interpreted as an innovative expression of a schismatic structural system, it can also be seen as an expression of the action of a communitas within the antistructure. There is something very conservative in what they did—probably the feminine symbol of God is more deeply rooted in the Anglican northern European biogrammar than the masculine—and it was the expression of an intimate community. Certainly it was action pointing toward innovative, structural change at the next General Convention, but the experience itself was a social drama, expressive of the breakdown of structure. The reaction of the House of Bishops of the Episcopal Church was to invoke a univocal interpretation of the forms, the canon law. In my conversations with some following that action, I found an inability to see that the Christian community is not synonymous with the forms, just as there was a naïve inability of some of the participants at Philadelphia to see that no good purpose could be served unless the experience of calling have a *bona fide* formal expression. We have to live within the polarity of the two.

AFFECTIVE AND COGNITIVE

Sam Keen, sometime Presbyterian pastor and apostle of a Dionysian life style, writes in the *Apology for Wonder* that we need to balance the Dionysian or the affective life with the Apollonian, or cognitive life.[12] His next book, *To a Dancing God,* did a superb job of holding these in tension. I am told by associates of Keen that his own life has been a pilgrimage, not without much pain, to understand how one must live to do justice to both the affective and the cognitive, and that those who see in Keen *merely* an advocate of indiscriminate pursuit of feelings should look again at the master.

The congregation that embraces the need to express the emotional dimensions of religious experience needs to guard itself against two things. Keen reminds us of both. The first is to keep in mind that America is essentially an anti-intellectual country, perhaps because it has an adolescent culture that hesitates to take an honest look at itself and the world. It likes to live in the illusions of its feelings, which it idealizes in a most dangerous way. Like "teen-agers," its judgments are untempered expressions of affect, which are always in the role of the "good guy." The pain of thinking and the hurt of seeing oneself in a realistic light begets in the American mentality a deep suspicion of cognition, to its great detriment. We will return to this shortly.

The second thing against which we need to guard ourselves is the deception that affective living is always happy living. We need to take another look at Dionysius, the god of vegetation, particularly wine, whose ancient worship was filled with more terror than good times. The willy-nilly joy of some proponents of the charismatic movement, the plastic smile of the narrow-minded missionary, or the sentimentality of the "celebrate life" crowd knows little or nothing of the "dark night of the soul." Its authenticity is suspect. Who is the god it serves? It knows not the God of whom the author of Hebrews speaks. "Let us therefore give thanks to God, and so worship him as he should be worshipped, with reverence and awe; for our God is a devouring fire" (Heb. 12:28–29; cf. Deut. 4:24).

Fire refines and cleanses and heals. It does so as it burns and consumes the dross. To seek God is not to have our prejudices confirmed, our judgments ratified, and our ideology affirmed. It is to have all that we are called in question, shocked, and shaken. The congregation that advocates the affective life in God has to be prepared to endure the depths as well as the heights, and to be offended before God just as much as it is consoled—maybe much more (cf. Mark 14:26–31). Once we embrace the affective dimensions of the religious experience, we cannot expect the conviviality of a church picnic or the warm nostalgia of a familiar hymn. Recently I was reading the original version of Grimm's fairy tales. I was struck by the horror explicit is those stories—a horror which expresses the reality of any authentic story, including the Gospel. We must not become blind to our own diabolic self by hiding from images of horror.

I recall once flying to Winnipeg, Manitoba, seated in front of a Hindu (as

I was to discover), whose chance companion turned out to be a joy-filled organizer for an evangelical college movement. His home base, he announced to the gentle Indian next to him, was Dallas, Texas, and he was going to take the word of the Lord to the University of Manitoba. From Minneapolis to Fargo and from Fargo to Winnipeg he cited biblical passages to his Hindu seatmate in an earnest effort to convert him to Jesus, while feigning a kind of tolerance that was at best condescending. I worried for the quiet Indian, who answered every sally with polite interest; but I did not need to be so concerned. As we were landing in Winnipeg the Hindu commented ever so gently, "Sir, I thought your Jesus lived long ago in Palestine. It strikes me that the man you have been describing to me is more like a civic-minded banker in Dallas." My hope is that both our friend from Texas, who fell suddenly quiet, and persons like myself who were eavesdropping, used the pain in that following silence to see God in the piercing judgment that fell on us who sentimentalize or "ideologize" the Christ.

The affective dimension of the religious experience needs to be a congregational experience because it needs to be shared if it is to be endured. The fire of God strips from us our comfortable presuppositions and exposes us to all kinds of emotions, particularly fear. There is a kind of fugue in the New Testament between injunctions to fear or statements of the fear of God and assurances that we are not to be afraid; a paradox which has a ring of truth in it (Matt. 27:54; Mark 4:41; 11:18; Luke 9:45; 23:40; Acts 10:2; Col. 3:22; 1 Pet. 2:17; Matt. 1:20; 10:31; Luke 5:10; 12:32; John 12:15; Acts 27:24; Rev. 1:17). A clue to the meaning of this paradox and the role of the congregation lies in the work of Charles Williams.

Williams's novels are explorations of the antistructural world of symbol and myth. Perhaps the supreme expression of this is *Descent into Hell,* in many ways a frightening story. There Pauline, the central character in the book, is greatly shaken as the result of a recurring event: the vision of herself, her *Doppelgänger* (ghostly counterpart). She tells us that when she finally meets her *Doppelgänger* she will go mad. Williams argues that the problem in this experience, which is of the antistructure, is not the vision of the *Doppelgänger,* but the need to work through the fear to the truth of the experience. To do this Pauline requires the assistance of her community in the person of another character, Peter Stanhope, who assists by bearing her fear for her. In God and his church he says, "Fear not." Williams calls this the principle of exchange or substituted love.[13]

In the Christian community we live a substituted love and bear one another's burdens, but always as an expression of the paschal reality which is God's act of exchange and the focus of our life together. If we live the cross, we come to the resurrection. If the exchange is authentic, we necessarily experience the emotions of the Passion and of Easter. We enter into the abyss of the cross, with its terror, loneliness, and despair. For it is a letting go, a dying. Such surrender evokes in us real fear (see Chapter Six) which only our dependence and the giving up of our burden to others in the congregation can resolve. The remarkable discovery is that in doing this, as Williams points out, we discover that we have given them to God, who gives us life in return.[14] This is to know and share the joy of the resurrection.

It is most important that this be allowed to happen in the congregation. I say "allowed," since I think there is always a tendency to back off from the communal experience of fear. Clergy are very prone to work against this antistructural experience. I certainly have been.

Some years ago I was the priest of a small congregation, which taught me a great deal about bearing one another's burdens. It happened this way. A great tragedy, which could have been the source of scandal and could have destroyed a number of people, occurred to one of the families of the congregation. Despite my efforts and those of others to keep things "hushed up," word leaked out to members of the congregation. One person phoned me and asked what was going on and what could the people of the parish do. I kept my line, saying that they should "back off" and "cool it." My caller persisted until finally she said, "Father, you have taught us to be a family; now let us be one!" I did from that moment, and those good people went into the abyss with that family. Whether or not there is now a glimpse of the resurrection in the lives of any of them I cannot say. It takes humility to surrender your burden to another and to stand in his debt as we stand in the debt of God. Sometimes the outstretched hand is unwelcome. I do know that in handing over to the whole congregation the pain I experienced in that family's suffering I have shared some intimation of the joy of the resurrection.

Of course, we are speaking of the congregation at a conservative, intimate level. It is the communion or community, stripped of differentiation of role and status, which can participate in the affective life of exchange, as Charles Williams has called it. It is the "pilgrim band" that has the possibility of hearing the pain of the other in story, song, cry of anguish, or look of terror, and that can walk along with the suffering as well as the joyful, and be present as Christ was present. It was he who said, "Come to me, all whose work is hard, whose load is heavy; and I will give you relief" (Matt. 11:28). It was the same Lord who—as the god Dionyius was once reported to have done—changed the water into wine that the joy of the wedding feast might be shared for a longer time (John 2:10). Jesus said that the greatest thing is love, and he came to share love and to ask us to do the same even if it meant dying for one another (John 3:16; 13:34; 15:12–13).

The Gospel is so simple—or so it would seem. We are told that it is all about sharing feelings of love. Theologians can hear this over and over again if they will listen to what people are saying to them. What is more, not only is the Gospel simple, but, it seems, we do not need theologians to make it complicated. I once made a presentation to a group of seminary trustees on the value of involving seminaries in parish life. I remember vividly one trustee who asked me: "What does theology have to do with my congregation?" It was a rhetorical question, just as the question of Tertullian so long ago: "What does Athens have to do with Jerusalem?" The implication is that they have *nothing* to do with one another.

The truth is that Athens and Jerusalem have everything to do with one another. As I have argued throughout the book, but principally in the fourth chapter, the orientation of the congregation to the possibility of seeing God in our midst lies in the intuition, *which is the joining of feeling and thinking.* Affect without cognition, however, gives us no perspective of ourselves and leaves us liable to the grossest kind of seduction. Appeals to the "simple Gospel" so often lie within the intentionality of those same people who think that the Montgomery, Alabama, bus boycott was a needless confusion of the city's traffic flow, or who want to throw juveniles into prison with hardened criminals as a solution to a rising crime rate.

Even when the church is full of good will, or even just a warm piety, a lack of thought gets us in trouble. Theologians, no matter what their denominational label, are Protestant by nature, and we need that. The Church of England in the eighteenth century had faithful pastors, committed Christians, but hardly any theologians. This was because it did not think it could innovate in the face of either the Wesleys or the colonies. We all know the results. Another theological low point, perhaps the result of the inflexibility of late nineteenth-century theology in the face of the new human sciences (as in the Roman Catholic modernist controversy), was the period between the two World Wars. The church was unable to respond with any vigor to the growing secularism of Western culture and, with notable exceptions, the average congregation substituted a middle-class respectability for a prophetic faith. In the last two decades such phenomena as the sensitivity movement, the changing

214

images of God, the role of the church in social change, and the neo-pietistic movement have seemed mere fads rather than contributions to a larger truth, which is the result of a lack of hard thinking in the congregations across the land. They are things in which we have "emotional investment," they are not the products of careful thought. Our commitments are as fickle as "puppy love."

The ability to transcend the self lies not in the emotions but in the intellect. This may appear to some to be a contradiction of everything I have said; but if it is, they have been misreading the cognitive component implicit in every symbol and story. The truth of this statement lies for me in my own intellectual journey in regard to the ordination of women to the priesthood. Ten years ago the idea was repugnant to me and I knew the reasons why. Five years ago the idea was still repugnant to me, but my reasons no longer "held water." I was thinking differently. Now my feelings have followed good reasons for the ordination of women to the priesthood.

You cannot argue with a mad dog or an adolescent in love. You can shoot the dog and hope the adolescent grows up. Congregations that are suffering from madness or infatuation are just as blind and self-destructive as the dog or the teen-ager. They are in no position to exercise ministry of any kind, much less see God. Gabriel Moran has said that there are two kinds of religion: the prelogical, which feeds on pathology, and the postlogical, which stimulates the growth of our horizons.[15] Cognition is necessary to postlogical religion and therefore, following from the first chapter, it is necessary for the salvation or the wholeness of man.

There are encouraging signs in the church that anti-intellectualism is not universal. While some still long for the "simple Gospel," others are demanding theological education for the laity. This needs to be a central structure within the life of every congregation. The ritual and story of the congregation is part of its natural life together. It accompanies us out into the antistructures, but it brings us back into the structure of a disciplined systematic theology as well. This calls for a rigorous program in thoughtful Christianity. If a congregation did only one other thing aside from the representation of those events which called it into being, it should be the training of its membership to think theologically. This ability transcends the immediate situation and has universal application. It enables those so trained to live their life thoughtfully, *sub species eternitatis,* "in terms of the vision of the eternal or God."

I think you can frequently tell when this is going on in a congregation. I remember once attending a city-wide gathering of Episcopalians from four or five parishes, in which we were discussing the reconciliation of the races. It was in the deep South in the late fifties. One group of men from a parish in a less economically privileged neighborhood of the city spoke of their belief that Christians, if they took Christ seriously, had to be at the forefront of racial justice. It was surprising to hear this from a part of the city where there was much violent opposition to integration. Later another priest commented to me: "There is a parish that thinks on its knees." It is a good combination!

Some times people say that if we think too much about our religion we lose our faith. It is true that the more educated a person is the less likely he or she is to frame the transcendental experience (as discussed in Chapter Three) in the traditional, religious language. The reason for this is not so much that they have lost faith, but that the vocabulary of a past age is not able to express with any precision or nuance the kind of experience which draws us into the future. The traditional language is often associated with certitude, whereas the groping for new images corresponds to the sense that we need innovative forms to express them in, which is an expansion of the horizons of our consciousness. People who say thinking destroys faith are confusing faith with "baby talk."

It is an issue of truth. The Fourth Evangelist places in apposition "revelation," "truth," and "freedom." Jesus said: "If you dwell within the revelation I have brought, you are indeed my disciples; you shall know the truth, and the truth will set you free" (John 8:31–32). As we have seen—again in Chapter Three—revelation moves from subject to story to system, and it is at the level of system that we make the decision whether or not the story is *true* and the subject is Christ. That decision comes from the experience of freedom. Is it present or absent? Those congregations who will not think together are those who prefer slavery to freedom rather than risk the thoughtful question: Is it true?

SUMMARY

Fifteen years ago Gibson Winter of the University of Chicago was arguing that Christianity was doomed as long as it consisted of homogeneous congregations in the suburbs.[16] His solution was to *structure* parishes so that they cut across socioeconomic boundaries: "pie slices" of the metropolitan matrix. My admiration for Winter is in no sense lessened by my belief that, had we followed his impossible advice, the visible church would have been greatly diminished. It is the homogeneous, small, natural community from which the *ecclesia*

216

emerges. This is necessary for the life of a community, whose vocation is from God not from the city planning board.

My argument in this chapter is that the conservative, intimate, affective community makes possible the innovative, formal, cognitive community. Certainly the structured congregation is necessary if the church is to lapse into self-satisfaction while the world burns around its ears. I forget who it was that once told me that the Russian Church—a group full of natural communities —met on the eve of the Bolshevik Revolution in a grand synod to discuss, if you would believe it, the appropriate occasion for wearing yellow vestments. Some of our debates on liturgical revisions and the ordination of women to the priesthood, while millions starve to death, may seem to partake of such myopia. Yet structures for action need antistructural vision and *vice versa,* and the leadership of the church needs to pursue both at the same time.

I think clergy have been trained to feel a bit of guilt over the spontaneous communities in their parishes: those who prefer the early Eucharist, the guild of the "little old ladies," the "country club set," the singles with not so certain life styles, and so forth. My plea is that such communities are not made, they arise from the society. It does no good to long for a romanticized English village parish. We need to identify and infiltrate those collectivities that have an internal cohesion of their own, and in our times these will take all kinds of forms and often last only for a period. It is all right, contrary to all the incredible theory from the early sixties, for members of a parish to be friends and for friends to invite friends.

When you look about you and see the congregations that are growing, it appears to me that you will discover that they are built on this principle: the gathering of a homogeneous body of people who like one another and who have a sincere desire to know God. Any parish that loses that loses its life, not just because these people are sinners and self-centered; but because the necessary structures to maintain a congregation that has lost its internal cohesion, which enables it to be a pilgrim band, effectively prevent that congregation living beyond the sociocultural environment.

It is certainly true that the conservative, intimate congregation lives by its feelings, and these feelings embody *resistance* to change, particularly at the price of our own creature comforts. Resistance is not only pathological, it is also normal in everyone. James Dittes some years ago did an excellent job of pointing out that resistance in congregations is like that resistance in persons undergoing psychotherapy as identified in psychoanalytic theory.[17] It is the unconscious building of a defense within the organism, which resists the conscious realization of the conflict within. The treatment of resistance is to identify it for what it is and to push through it. The effect of this in the life of a congregation is, in my mind, that it does not settle for a pleasurable life together, but recognizes such diabols inhabiting the wilderness of its inner life. Another way of putting the same point is to say that congregations cannot just enjoy their story; somebody has to ask, "What does it mean?" and "So what?" It is the same question God asked Elijah: "Why are you here?"

That is the kind of question, if taken seriously and pursued, brings the congregation into the structures of innovation and form, which result from thinking or cognition. The cognitive is necessary for clarity and sharing, but it is also the prerequisite of action. So a living and active congregation has to be a community that lives in the dialogical tension of the conservative and innovative, the intimate and the formal, the affective and the cognitive.

9

THE PRIEST

Over the last few years I have spent a significant amount of time speaking at clergy gatherings. The experience is one for which I am grateful, for there is a great deal to learn from the people who staff the parishes of the church. In spite of Mark Twain's quip about Methodist ministers being like manure— spread around they do a lot of good, but in one pile they stink—clergy can be good company. At the same time, as a priest I have become more and more aware of their profound anxiety over their identity and the intense anger in many priests, which occasionally bubbles up at conferences where the church's leadership makes a readily available target.

It was at one particularly tense diocesan clergy conference that I had recounted to me a very telling dream. We had been going at some of the material in this book the night before, and several priests had told me that they were troubled by it. The next morning I was standing at a wash basin shaving and there was a retired priest standing at the next basin. He said "I have been standing here wondering whether I should tell you about my dream last night." Apparently that was just a rhetorical opener, because I had no chance to say anything before he began. "We were at the parish where so-and-so was rector when we elected him bishop. I don't know why we were there, but a friend came up to me and said, 'You know, there is a great cave deep under this church full of precious stones.'" He paused and I asked, "What did you do?" He replied, "I was very surprised to hear this, but I suggested we dig down and get them." He went on, "We brought in some kind of mechanical gouging tool and went through the floor of the bishop's church. I can see now the round hole, with the marks of the tool on the clay sides of a long, dark tunnel. We dug deeper and deeper until we reached the cave under the altar.

We threw ropes over the edge and let ourselves down to where my friend had told me the precious jewels were to be found! You know what?", he asked me. I said nothing and his voice got a little tight. "There was *nothing* there! It was empty!"

I do not tell this dream as an indictment of a given bishop or bishops in general. I am aware, however, that holes into caves, particularly in the midst of a church, are highly charged symbols of the mother, which gives shape to the feminine or *anima* in all of us. It is possible that jewels are a symbol of the child, the intuitive innocence that we have described as the dimension of the person enabling him to see God.[1] The dream is related, as I see it, to the expectation that the church is our "mother" and should enable us to see God, but does *not* fulfill this function. It is a failing particularly related to its leadership: bishop *or* priest.

There is a great deal being published in theology about the priesthood. In the Episcopal Church this has been precipitated by the conflict over the ordination of women to the priesthood. In much of what is being written two notions are evident. The first is a negative one; namely, the essence or central function of the priesthood is *not reducible* to a definition of the professional. A priest can be a professional something (administrator, educator, musician, counselor, change agent,), but this is only incidently related to being a *priest*. The second notion is more positive. The function of the priest is tied to the function of symbol. The priest, as I said in *The Future Shape of Ministry*, is the sacramental person.[2]

He is the sacramental person and/or symbol-bearer in at least two senses. Paul says, in the first place, that we are "stewards of the secrets of God" (1 Cor. 4:1). The New English Bible translation is accurate but weak. We are "administrators," "managers," even "treasurers" (all possible translations of *oikonomoi*) of the "hidden things," "secret rites," the "mysteries" (the word *mustēria* is what the Greek Church uses for "sacraments") of God. The priest is charged with the responsibility for appropriate presence to the congregation of the symbols of God.

Second, however, the priest is also himself a symbol. Again Paul, who actually knew nothing of the ministerial priesthood, writes: "For the same God who said, 'Out of darkness let light shine,' has caused his light to shine within us, to give the light of revelation. . . . We are no better than pots of earthenware to contain this treasure, and this proves that such transcendent power does not come from us, but is God's alone" (2 Cor. 4:6–7). In both this passage and the preceding one, he appears to be speaking of the apostolate—himself and his associates—evangelizing the Mediterranean world.

The role of the priest is not to control or to produce a predictable result that enables us to function better in the techno-barbaric world. This is the mistake, and it is a fundamental error, made by those who *reduce* the priest to contemporary notions of the professional. The function of the priest is intimately and primarily related to the fourth vector of ministry. He works out of the left hand, as one who incites people to imagine. The priest is essentially an inhabitant of the *limines* (he is a "liminal person") or the threshold *between* the structure and the antistructure. He is someone who has died to the world's notion of controlled success. The priest is an essential focus for life, if it will have more than the *status quo* and the "success" which the current prevailing structures provide.

What my friend's dream of the bishop's church, the cave, and the jewels was saying, as I see it, was that the priesthood he knew—his own as well as that of others—was empty of this imaginal, liminal dying to the world of control. Notice that the cave is a *feminine symbol.* It is the power of the feminine, the left hand, the chthonic and the ambiguous, the creative and the risky that was impotent. What is lacking in the priesthood, the dream says, is the sense of mystery, the catalyst to the seeing of God, and the mediation of the penumbrial power of the transcendent.

A number of people have written about the priest as symbol-bearer and symbol as a means of arguing for the ordination only of men. Their style is excessively masculine, but even more, they miss the whole role of symbol. Theirs is a very logical, aggressive, and univocal approach, which reeks of words like duty, obedience, and authority (by which they mean more *authentein,* a Greek verb used only once in the New Testament and meaning "to domineer," rather than *exousia,* which is common in the New Testament and has the root meaning of "inner power" or "ability"). Duty, obedience, and authority are all words popular to the Puritans and Eastern Orthodoxy, who are culturally hyperpatriarchial to the point of blindness. Symbols are, on the contrary, both masculine and feminine, including those of Christ, who is both masculine and feminine (as any complete person is), and who is the fulfillment of priesthood from whom the Christian priesthood is derivative. Christ is husband, shepherd, king, lord, and president (Eph. 5:21–29; John 10:14–18; John 1:49; Matt. 19:27–28), all of which are masculine symbols. There are also feminine symbols of Christ, such as life-giving bread, the door, water, the vine, the sacrificial lamb, our peace (John 6:41; 10:7; 4:14; 15:1; 1:36; Eph. 2:14).

It strikes me that one of the reasons the priesthood is an empty cave is that so many proponents of the symbolic function of the priest are unwilling to admit that the priesthood is a cave at all, but rather want to make it a syllogism. They are tied up in the denial of the feminine symbolism in God, which robs the priesthood of its strange and wonderful left-handedness!

What I want to do in this chapter is relate the priest to the fourth vector of ministry in terms of certain antistructural images. These images are the priest as mana-person, clown, storyteller, and wagon master.

THE MANA-PERSON

I first heard the term "mana-person" in the tape of a lecture by Robert Francoeur, who was speaking of the role of the priest in the life of little children. His claim was that the priest must be a mana-person to the family of the young. What I heard him to say originally was "manna-person," as in the manna that God gave to feed the Israelites in the wilderness (Ex. 16:15). It was not until I read Jung that it occurred to me that the term refers to "mana," the extraordinary, supernatural power which religions, particularly primitive religions, attribute to persons and things that are related to the divine. It may be that Francoeur meant manna (with two "n's"), and was speaking of the priest as the person who brings the bread of God, as in the Eucharist, but this would not be unrelated to mana and to his function as one who bears in himself an extraordinary sacral power.

The mana-person is related symbolically to the hero, the chief, the magician, the medicine man, the saint, the ruler of the spirits, and the friend of God. He is a person who is able in himself to strike a creative compromise between the conscious world of the ego and the antistructural world of symbol and myth. He is one who travels into chaos and returns to tell of it. In the sixth chapter I spoke of this in terms of the surrender to the margins of our existence: the subhuman, the interpersonal, the unconscious, and history.

Jung explores the role of the mana-person in terms of the unconscious. In the poem by Longfellow, *Hiawatha,* the magician comes to Hiawatha paddling his canoe over some very murky water. Such water symbolizes death (the symbolic gateway to the unconscious), the unconscious *per se,* and the devouring mother hidden within the unconscious. This is the world of the magician or mana-person. Such a world is deeply related to the feminine within each of us, derived from the significant-female-other, our own biology, and from the inherited feminine image, which makes up that constellation within the collective unconscious Jung calls the *anima.*[3] The *anima* is a source of great power or mana. It can fuel our creative self or it can tear us apart. The mana-person is one who appropriates that power for a creative purpose.

THE PRIEST

In the dream I recounted at the beginning of this chapter the cave is a symbol of the *anima*. It is expected that the priest would be one who had appropriated the power of the creative within the penumbria or twilight life, the antistructure. This means that the priest is one who does not deny or assault the feminine within himself, but acknowledges it, brings it to the surface, and uses it. The repression of the feminine in the priest or the priesthood is inevitably destructive, as witness the history of the church. The appropriation of the feminine is risky, but has great creative potential.

For example, there is another dream, which Jung recounts at least three times in his writings, told to an associate of his by a theology student. The student was having some intellectual problems of belief. The dream involved the presence of a white magician clothed in black and a black magician clothed in white. Jung saw these as symbolizing the interaction of good and evil, the coincidence of opposites. To Jung God lies *beyond* good and evil. He is reached as one pierces the abyss, wherein lies the opposing powers. In this dream he saw the need for the theology student to overcome the difficulties of his intellectual struggle by making an intuitive and risky leap through conflict.

I have spoken of Jung illustrating the trip of the mana-person into the antistructure or abyss of the unconscious. In this process, Jung tells us, as one seeks to move through the coincidence of good and evil, one comes in touch with a hint of paganism. The primal roots of folk religion become more evident, and the "logic" of the stories rooted in the earth emerges more clearly. This directs our attention to the mana-person as someone who does not dissociate from the subhuman. His power has a chthonic quality.

A friend of mine speaks of the good priest as an "earthy mystic." It is a good term. The mana-person does not shrink from the realities of nature. In medieval times the directions for the anointing of the sick included the unction of the five senses, which included the genitals. Our puritan minds, so caught up in a neo-Platonic piety, wonder how the priest kept his mind pure from heterosexual or homosexual thoughts, depending on the client's sex. The question is actually inappropriate. Why should the priest keep his mind from sexual thoughts? Sexuality is a very potent symbol that should be well known to the mana-person.

We are all familiar with how the structural world perceives the priest as a very repressed person. The "dirty joke" dies away as he walks up to a group at a cocktail party, there is the apology for the "damn" in his presence, and he is protected from the gross as one would a fragile flower of Southern womanhood. Sometimes priests give in to this image of repression and become

223

righteous, right-handed people. They seem to conceive of their every word as a pronouncement from the Father God, they wear clericals as if they were the first cousin to a chastity belt (there was a pastoral manual a generation or so ago that urged priests to wear cassocks to parish dances so they would not have to dance), and they appear as if honest sweat never touched their brow.

There is all kinds of evidence, however, that repression is met by an equal force from that which is repressed. Jung describes it as the inflation of the ego, which results in *possession* by the *anima*. By possession, I understand a destructive take-over that freezes the self and thwarts any efforts toward an integration of the whole man (the object of salvation). The Puritan is frightfully afraid that if he ever lets go he will become an uncontrollable satyr or nymphomaniac. In fact, it happens. The Victorian age produced more pornography of a gross sort, had more prostitutes, and engendered a deeper life of the shadow than one could imagine. Both its virtue and vice were, however, incredibly boring and banal. The person who avoids the sexuality within his unconscious by adopting a rigid stance is simply exposing himself to an uncontrollable and usually destructive eruption of that dark side which is part of each of us. For example, there is not a priest who cannot cite the example of the very proper colleague, who taught unshakeable standards of conduct, only to be exposed as sleeping with one, two, three, or more of his parishioners—female or male.

In arguing for the image of the mana-person I am saying that a priest is one who understands the obscene, both when it destroys and when it empowers. He is familiar with his own sexuality. For example, he has no difficulty with himself when in counseling a lovely women he gets an erection. He would worry if he did not, but he knows not to make more of it than what it is. A mana-person is no stranger to the temptation of evil. After all, neither was Jesus; who risked going into the wilderness, as all priests must do (Matt. 4:1–10). If the priest does "not keep company with drunkards or those who are greedy for the fleshpots" (Prov. 23:20), it is not because he cannot tell a vintage wine from "ripple" or true passion from a striptease. The mana-person is in touch with that which is beyond the mere opposition of good and evil, as this world defines it. He lives by a power which has not yet been categorized as "bad" or "good" by the structures.

This is not an easy notion to understand. In a society that domesticates God and craves certitude more than truth, it is very difficult to accept an image of the local pastor who lives poised amid darkly discerned potencies, exhibiting at the same time a kinship to both beasts and God, both the earth and the stars.

Yet, I have written elsewhere of the need for the priest to be "creatively weird" and this is the ground for that dimension of personality.[4]

How does one go about achieving this? Certainly he has to know himself. When I have found myself caught in a potentially destructive force within me, I understand it to be the result of living too much on the right hand. In a sense, the good priest is one who has been there before, as Christ has been there. To be an effective pastor we do not have to have done everything everybody else has. We do have to recognize the power that is there, the real possibility of misusing it, as well as appropriately using it, and what the creative use of such power looks like when we do. The mana-person knows the diabols, as well as the symbols. As was Jesus, he is on speaking terms with demons (Mark 1:21–26; Luke 8:26–33). He knows them because he knows himself.

This is why I think seminary training cannot be a purely structural, academic exercise. It has to develop occasions where a person must make the decision either to look within and find God or to go away because he cannot take the risk. Efforts to provide such occasions are often considered "playing at psychology." Whereas that can be true of seminary education, the accusation can also be an avoidance of the inevitable pain of spiritual maturation. Potential priests are paradigms of the growing Christian, for whom the story of the man of the ruling class who came to Jesus and asked "Good Master, what must I do to win eternal life?" is particularly telling. As we recall, he had done everything the law required, but he could not take the risk and let go of his riches (Luke 18:18–23). If we are to be a mana-person, we have to run the danger of being devoured by the diabols and cast ourselves into the unknown.

There is that wonderful concluding passage in Castaneda's *Tales of Power,* which I cited earlier in this book, where Don Juan and Don Genaro take Carlos and Pablito to the top of a mesa. Pointing over the edge, Don Juan says, "There is the door. Beyond, there is an abyss and beyond that abyss is the unknown." Castaneda goes on, "Then a strange urge, a force, made me run with him [Pablito] to the northern edge of the mesa. I felt his arm holding me as we jumped and then I was alone."[5] So ended the making of a mana-person. Theological education cannot be an exercise in social conditioning, any more than it is spoon-feeding of theological theses. It is the equipping of a man to open doors for others through which he has already gone.

An apt summation of the discussion of the mana-person as an image of the priest comes from Jung. It follows one of the recountings of the dream of the theology student concerning the white and the black magicians. The dream,

Jung says, points to a compensation or solution of a personal struggle by confronting . . .

> him with a problem . . . which life is always bringing us up against: namely, the uncertainty of all moral valuation, the bewildering interplay of good and evil, and the remorseless concatenation of guilt, suffering, and redemption. This path to the primordial religious experience is the right one, but how many can recognize it? It is like a still small voice, and it sounds from afar. It is ambiguous, questionable, dark, presaging danger and hazardous adventure; a razor-edged path, to be trodden for God's sake only, without assurance and without sanction.[6]

THE CLOWN

I was very interested to discover a year or so ago that the clown school run by Ringling Brothers was being flooded by applications from priests. This is encouraging news. It constitutes a breakthrough in understanding what it is that a priest is about.

I choose the word "clown" for this image of the priest rather than "fool," because the latter presents additional problems to the reader. Enid Wellsford says the terms are interchangeable. Both refer to that person who "is an amphibian, equally at home in the world of reality and the world of imagination . . . the Fool by his mere presence . . . throws doubt on the finality of fact."[7] There are other words as well, which have a sense of the clown: the harlequin, the jester, the buffoon, and even the trickster.

The last term, "trickster," refers to a kind of pre-Christian clown. Related to the Eskimo shaman, he is a prominent figure in the mythology of the American Indian, although the trickster is certainly found elsewhere. Hyemeyohsts Storm, in telling the story of the flowering tree, a prominent symbol in Indian folk tales, attributes the account to the coyote, whom he calls "the gentle trickster of learning."[8] He goes on to say:

> As the Coyote sings, his song is echoed by many other Coyotes. These songs, the Teachers tell us, are the songs of the many Reflections that live within all of us.

> For example, within every man there is the Reflection of a Woman, and within every woman there is the Reflection of a Man. Within every man and woman there is also the Reflection of an Old Man, an Old Woman, a Little Boy, and a Little Girl.[9]

Storm then tells us how two Indian children, a little boy and a little girl are laughed at by the people of their tribe, because they admit to going down the river to see the "powerful person" who solves all problems. Of course, the people also did this, but kept it hidden. They abandon the two children they have ridiculed, and the "old coyote man" and the "old coyote woman," who are the symbols of the powerful person in the river, come to them and offer a way to the little boy and girl to return to their people and to enable them to "see" the buffalo, on which they depend for life itself. Instead of accepting the children and their message from the coyote, the people attack the children and pursue the man and woman. The little boy and the little girl become a flowering tree, and the two kind people become mountain lions and run away. Exhausted from their pursuit of the lions, the people return to sit around the tree, at the four directions of the wind. But the coyotes have their way. Suddenly they see how foolish they have been, and "they put their Arms Around Each Other and Began to Dance Toward the Flowering Tree Together in a Great Circle. The People were Happy."[10]

The people, of course, were living by the right hand, which only gave them hardened hearts. They were caught in their structures, and they ridiculed both the little children who lived in a play world and the kind people who were so impractical as to adopt such silly children. They were rebuking, needless to say, their own childlike qualities and repressing their own love for others. The trickster, however, the coyote, who is also the "wise old man," persisted in calling them to a new vision, using the symbols of the tree, the child, and the circle. The tree is a feminine symbol, as I have said, related to the mother. The child is the self, particularly the self before birth and after death, the periphery of our knowing, wherein John Dunne has said that we in our childlikeness must find God. The circle represents, among other things, perfect harmony. This story of the coyote, who is the trickster, is related then to the priest's dream about the cave and jewels, except that the coyote eventually makes delivery where the bishop did not!

It is noteworthy that in all the works of Castaneda perhaps the most moving and revealing incident aside from his final leap into the abyss, was the vision of the luminous coyote.[11] It was this experience that convinced Castaneda that there was more to the world than the techno-barbaric society had conditioned him to believe. As Don Juan said to him, "What stopped inside you yesterday was what people have been telling you the world is like."[12] Then Don Juan goes on to warn him, however, that he should not trust talking coyotes, because they are tricksters.

What we can understand this warning to mean is that the trickster is a faithful reflection of an absolutely undifferentiated unconscious. He or she— actually, as in the story of the flowering tree, the trickster is androgynous—

has an evil side, as well as a good side. Like the mana-person, he is in touch with chaos, and he can lead us into both the subhuman world and the super-human world. Like the clown, of which he is the forerunner, he turns every-thing upside down; unlike the clown, he can precipitate an orgy that destroys people. There is then a dark side to the trickster, as well as a light side, which in civilized cultures lies within the unconscious.

This dark side can, however, be made conscious in the art of the grotesque. What I mean by "the art of the grotesque" is what Richard Pearce intends in a superb study he has done of the clown; namely, where "the most terrifying and exhilarating experiences are based—in form and meaning—on comic structures."[13] The grotesque shakes us out of our ordinary way of seeing the ordinary, but by itself it leaves us with no order and peace. It provides an imaginative shock, which often leads into terror as well as humor, because it confronts us with that incongruity in terms of the structured world on which both are based. The grotesque is the world turned upside down with no guarantee that what will confront us will save us. In truth, it may destroy us. We must once again remember Tolkien's warning that he who would move into his fairy tale needs to take care. There is more there than kindly elves and fairy godmothers. There are things there that will eat us up (Jung's "devouring mother").

Pearce argues that the clown overcomes the terror within the upside-down world, the chaos in this first book, and makes something out of it because of "his moral and physical resiliency."[14] This is something quite different from the trickster, who has no morals. Socrates, as portrayed by Plato, is a clown, as is Erasmus's Christian Fool and Saul Bellow's Henderson in *Henderson the Rain King*. Charles Chaplin is a living, rather than fictional, example of the clown, who, as Pearce says, seemed "to be taking an 'eccentric pilgrimage' through a mysterious and hostile world 'toward some shrine of honor and value and belief.'"[15] While full of humor, there is no question but that the clown possesses a commitment to value and the whole life. He only calls into question the *hubris* of man, who somehow thinks in all seriousness that he has found the answer. He is the medieval court jester or fool, whose task is to remind the king or lord that all the pomp and circumstance of the society means nothing in the face of God, who sees the inner man.

"The vitality . . . of the clownish characters, and of the characters who choose the role of clown," says Pearce, "depends upon sheer playfulness."[16] Pearce distinguishes at least four kinds of clowns in whom this playfulness abounds. I am interested in a composite figure, who in his playfulness breaks down the distinction between folly and wisdom (1 Cor. 1:18–24), enters the ensuing chaos only to build upon the truth that lies beneath the chaos, which is God.[17] The fool or clown can accomplish this by play because it is the art of the antistructure, against which all that shuts out the vision of God in our society is defenseless.

One of the great clown-priests I know was James Jefferson Davis Hall, known affectionately as "Daddy Hall," or the "Apostle to Wall Street." He was actually the priest in charge of the Galilee Mission. Hall made a practice of absurd dress—he often wore a sandwich board advertising church services —and enjoyed making outrageous comments. For a number of years he conducted a preaching mission at a small North Carolina church, where some years later I began my ministry. The church was originally what we called a "mill mission," a parish established by the owners of the new Southern cotton mills for the people they brought from the farms to work in the mills. The vicar was one of Hall's converts. On one occasion before a packed congregation the local *grande dame,* the daughter of a one-time owner of the mill, made her entrance ten minutes late. I am told that Daddy Hall raised his hand and stopped the service, waited in silence for the lady in question to find a seat and then said, "Let us all welcome Lady Astor, who is so good as to join us poor folks tonight." There was no reply to that and it did wonders for those long enslaved in spirit by the impervious management of the mill. He was equally capable of saying the same thing to the business tycoons of Wall Street.

Another convert of Daddy Hall's, the Episcopal chaplain at the University of Mississippi in the mid-1920s, invited the evangelist to visit the university during the spring term. In those days the Oxford churches were experimenting with union services on Sunday evenings in the spring, and Daddy Hall was about to preach when it was the Presbyterian Church's turn. Folding chairs had been set up on the broad lawn facing the front door, the church porch serving as the pulpit. In the very first row sat a couple, Presbyterians, whose churchly demeanor was noticeably rigid, even for those times. Their manner was not in disapproval of Daddy Hall, although his antics might have made them uneasy. The fact was that they were both old-school Presbyterians and were behaving quite normally. The wife always sat rigidly erect, her eyes fixed, her hands in her lap, her face firmly set. She was in church.

Daddy Hall's preaching was utterly unpredictable, interrupting himself in mid-sentence to go off on totally unexpected tangents, or suddenly stopping, then bursting into what he had previously taught the congregation to sing with him, "ONLY BELIEVE. ALL THINGS ARE POSSIBLE. ONLY BE-

LIEVE," and then without a break he would take up his theme again. As he said, "You have to shake 'em up to wake 'em up."

In the midst of his sermon that evening, after noticing for some time the immobility of the good woman in the front row, he stopped, walked down the two or three steps from the porch, and stood directly in front of her. He said in a voice everyone could hear, "Madam, have you ever seen a cat carry her kitten?" No flicker of response. "Well, you know, the kitten lets go, he slumps just like this." With that, Daddy humped his shoulders, drooped his arms, and went limp. Then in a stentorian voice he said, "My God, woman, RELAX! That's the only way God can ever get hold of you."

Daddy Hall had very little use for formal theological education, and he delighted in making fun of all seminaries. He shared Richard Rolle's prejudices perhaps. On one occasion when he was visiting a certain parish, one of the parish's seminarians stopped by for a visit and was in the congregation the morning Daddy Hall preached. In the midst of the sermon, he stopped, looked over the congregation, and called out, "Mr. Morgan, quickly now, tell me Gospel and chapter for the story of the Prodigal Son." The poor seminarian was so surprised that he could not gather his wits quickly enough, and Daddy went on to say, "See, folks? Two years in seminary wasted."

His experience at Galilee Mission had intensified his dislike for drink, and this included not only liquor but coffee and tea. Being either his host or a fellow guest at breakfast was an open invitation to hear all he had to say on the subject. Nor did he confine himself to breakfast. I well remember how (when altar vessels were cleansed after the benediction) Daddy would stand at the altar, polishing away on a paten or chalice, and talking about the evils of drinking.[18]

Perhaps the reader senses some anger in the absurdity of Daddy Hall and the whole concept of the fool. There certainly is in Paul's use of the term for himself: "If you must [take me for a fool], then give me the privilege of a fool, and let me have my little boast like others. . . . How gladly you bear with fools, being yourself so wise!" (1 Cor. 11:16,19). It is an anger that is associated with sadness. The happy painted face of the clown hides the broken heart beneath. Most of us are familiar with that seeming contradiction within the role of the clown. Yet, as Robert Roth points out, the clown embodies the tragicomedy, which is the reality of the Christian understanding of redemption.[19] Among the animals, it is only man who can weep and laugh, and it is only man that can sin and be redeemed.

The ministerial priesthood is, of course, patterned on the priesthood of

Christ. Christ is also a clown. The movie, *The Parable,* which was exhibited at the Protestant pavilion of the New York World's Fair of 1964–5, developed this theme, but as Harvey Cox has shown, the image is far more ancient than that.[20] One of the earliest attempts to depict Jesus shows him as a fool, hanging on the cross with the head of an ass. Whereas this may indeed have been the ridicule of the heathen, it still contains the truth that in the years of the right-handed world Christ is a fool—for our sake, as we must be for Christ's sake (1 Cor. 4:10). Medieval drama referred obliquely to Christ as the jester. Recently the musical drama *Godspell* developed this same theme of Christ as fool. The clown is one who affirms by denying, and indeed that is what Christ does, and therein lies our hope. Humor is the perception of the incongruity of a life not yet fulfilled; while the tragic sense is the result of despair over an incomplete life. As Cox says, "Laughter is hope's last weapon."[21]

Leszek Kolakowski, a Marxist philosopher of note, in an essay, "The Priest and the Jester," opposes the philosophy of the priest and of the jester. The priest, he says, thrusts the past on the present as if it were real, demanding that we accept for the future the illusion of reality conveyed within the socio-cultural structures. This is the work of despair. He chooses the jester, and he explains why.

> We declare ourselves in favor of the possibilities contained in the extraintellectual values inherent in this attitude [of the jester], although we also know its dangers and absurdities. Thus we opt for a vision of the world that offers us the burden of reconciling in our social behavior those opposites that are the most difficult to combine: goodness without universal toleration, courage without fanaticism, intelligence without discouragement, and hope without blindness.[22]

I would only differ here with Kolakowski that when the priest truly fulfills his vocation he is the jester or clown. This is essential to his function. The task of the priest is to "soften the certainty"—as illustrated in Chapter Four—to open the hearts of the secularists and the idolators. It is done, not by pompous arguments but by gentle foolishness.

One becomes such a priest by bringing into our awareness the childlike qualities that are in each of us. I mean by "childlike" what transactional analysis means by our "child": the spontaneous, creative, fun-loving, innocent, carefree use of the imagination. I also mean what Jung intends by the child symbol or archetype: the uncontrolled dimensions of the self, particularly those that lie in the twilight of our consciousness. (See Chapter Six and John Dunne's use of this image.) The child symbol is like the mana-person, an

231

androgyne, according to Jung, relating once more to the dream of the cave and the jewels and the feminine quality of the wilderness or antistructural experience, balanced with the masculine of the structural experience.[23] Jung goes on to say, "The 'eternal child' in man is an indescribable experience, an incongruity, a handicap, and a divine prerogative; an imponderable that determines the ultimate worth or worthlessness of a personality."[24]

THE STORYTELLER

As a result of the action of the General Convention of the Episcopal Church meeting in Louisville, Kentucky, in the Fall of 1973, I served on an *ad hoc* committee of that convention for a couple of years called "The Episcopal Study Committee on Preparation for Ministry." Our task was to report to the 1976 General Convention on what we understood the Episcopal Church desired in the training of persons for ministry. As necessary for arriving at our conclusions, we surveyed in one way or another all the dioceses of the Episcopal Church. It was a fascinating task, particularly when we talked to parish search committees, people who had recently looked about for a rector or vicar. Aside from the great candor about what they found in regard to priests in general—they are largely undisciplined and troubled—most interesting was what they told us they were looking for in a priest. While the opinion was not unanimous, it was close to being so. They wanted a *good preacher* and someone with a *spiritual depth* more than anything else.

At several clergy gatherings while this survey was going on I mentioned these findings. Their reply was often to the effect that we, the priests, know better. People really do not want a good preacher. They do not know a good sermon when they hear one. I asked the chairwoman of a committee I later interviewed if they *did* mean this, and her reply was very clear. "You tell those priests [and the word "priests" was more like a bit of profanity] *we mean it!*"

The breakdown in communication comes over the definition of a "good sermon." Clergy tend to think of a sermon as conceptual, the result of clear thinking, which "proves" or illuminates in a univocal way a definable point. Undoubtedly this is what some laity mean. My guess, however, is that what most people in the pew really want is "to see Jesus" (John 12:21)—more than one pulpit has, facing the preacher, those words of the Greeks to Philip: "Sir, we would like to see Jesus"—and that is something different. It requires, not just the ability, as Philips Brooks once suggested, to convey truth through personality, but it demands that the words reveal the spiritual depth of the preacher in such a way that they identify and free the longing of the hearer for God that his vision of life may be conjoined through the preacher's vision to God's vision. The sermon in this sharing is a co-mingling of three visions or intentionalities: God's, the preacher's, and the hearer's. It happens in such a way that we are all preachers and we are all hearers.

The most effective way for this to happen is through storytelling. Every preacher knows that what people remember are the illustrations. As one who has taught homiletics for many years, I have become increasingly aware of the danger of the illustration that is so powerful that it obscures the point of the sermon. The congregation is caught up in the story and forgets what else is being said. Instead of struggling with this truth, it seems best that we recognize it as a fact of life and use it.

If we take the fourth vector of ministry seriously, as I think we must, we have to understand the nature of the imagination and its demand that we move out of the structures and die to self-control. This pilgrimage is made while telling stories. All this was discussed in the second part of this book. It should not surprise us, therefore, to realize that what seizes the imagination of the congregation is the story. This is that part of the sermon which makes the excursion into the antistructure or wilderness, where God addresses us unencumbered by the "smog" of the institutional objectivation of reality. It is revelation at the second level, rather than the third (see Chapter Three).

Stories are one giant step toward the mystery of being, and one great leap away from the reductions—*albeit necessary and good reductions*—of systems. Stories lead to systems, as they should, but systems do not open the eyes of men that they might see as does the story.

Joseph Campbell tells the story of a group of Western visitors to Japan, including himself, at the 1958 International Congress on the History of Religions. They toured some of the notable Shinto shrines and Buddhist temples, and afterwards at a lovely garden party a social philosopher from America asked a Shinto priest, "What is your ideology? What is your theology?" The very polite Japanese pondered that, wanting to reply as best he could; but all he could say finally was, "I think we don't have an ideology. We don't have a theology. We dance."[25]

Campbell makes too much of this story, because clearly the Far Eastern religions do have a theology. They *think* about their religion in a very disciplined way, as they should. But he is right in calling our attention to the other side of the reality. There is an openness and a seductiveness to such religions as we find in Japan and neighboring areas because their self-expression is iconic

—a stylized, pictorial representation—inviting our participation. One does not read so much these days about Marshall McLuhan's terms, "hot" and "cool" media, as we did in the mid-sixties. Yet the terms still apply. The dance of the Shinto priest, as the story which is the sermon, is "cool," by which we mean it invites participation with our own meaning.

The priest occupies the threshold between the structures and the antistructures. He is the liminal person, and for that very reason he is a storyteller. A colleague of mine, Harry Pritchett, has done a great deal of experimental work in the role of the priest as storyteller. He says that two things are very clear. First, stories have the power to attract people into the wilderness and to draw them into pilgrimage. This is what I mean by saying that the story of the preacher frees them. Second, stories also give people the means of getting back into the structures in an effective manner. They become the content of their vision of the ordered world which makes that world something less than simply repugnant. This is what I mean by saying that the story in the sermon assists the hearer to conjoin his vision with that of God's. He can *act* by God's grace (that is, his presence and power).

It is fairly simple to illustrate how stories free people. I have shared the material in this book many times over in many forms. Sometimes I can see that my hearers think that Holmes has, indeed, "slipped a cog" with all this talk of the antistructure and the experience of God. One bishop suggested in a joking manner that maybe I was *on* something. Yet it takes only one story from the audience to change that aura of skepticism. One instance of this was in a seminary classroom. We were discussing the sense of the numinous in Rudolph Otto and the class was resisting the idea that the numinous is a common experience. That is, it resisted until an American Indian student said, almost casually, "Sure, I've had that kind of experience. I was once riding horseback across the plains near my home with some friends when all our horses stopped short. In front of us was a strange, gray 'twister.' I never knew horses to behave like that even in the presence of small 'twisters.' We knew then that we were on 'holy ground.' " What followed in that classroom was a flood of similar personal stories, akin to Moses and the burning bush, from about ten or fifteen in the class. The recounting was in itself a numinous experience! Like the sand designs of the Walbiri women in the Australian bush, which Nancy Munn describes, stories are the media between the "dreaming" (as antistructural experience) of the seeker and the everyday world of the people.[26]

This is a difficult point. A more "local" illustration of Munn's statement is an encounter that comes to my mind so subtly that I cannot recall how it began. I was talking to a friend and his wife over drinks. I had never met her before. She struck me as very much "down" on the church. I told a story, which unfortunately I cannot remember, in response to a cynical remark she had made. Quietly and yet suddenly she related in turn her story, consisting of a series of the most incredible personal experiences. Half believing, clearly frightened of what she was telling, she described years of episodes when she had a sense of self apart from her body, which is called in parapsychology "out-of-the-body experiences" (OBEs). The occult speaks of it as "astral projection." Jung relates it to metempsychosis. Paul is possibly describing the same experience when he writes: "I shall go on to tell of visions and revelations granted by the Lord. I know a Christian man [himself] who fourteen years ago (*whether in the body or out of it,* I do not know—God knows) was caught up as far as the third heaven" (2 Cor. 12:1–2) (emphasis added). Whatever we may make of the phenomenon—the prevailing culture rates it somewhat below UFOs—it was clearly a major element in this woman's self-concept, but as she said, she did not know what *to do* with it.

Our conversation went on for about an hour, in which we exchanged one story after another. I was and remain uncommitted on the subject of OBEs (as does her very right-handed husband), but this was not what was in question. The issue was obviously the very creative and imaginative woman who was sharing something that she said she had only previously told her psychiatrist. He, in a very enlightened way, had called it "a gift to be used." How was she to use it? How would her "dreaming" make a difference in the everyday world of herself and others? We talked about this, but we came to no dramatic conclusions. She ended only by sending me her poetry, written in the light of her vision found in her experiences. Yet in uttering (literally "to out-ter") her story she made it part of my everyday world and gave that world a new dimension.

People are natural storytellers and priests need to build on this almost universal capacity. The problem is that storytelling has to be a respectable pastime of adults. There are always the few for whom it is, and there are the occasions when most of us appropriately might tell a story. Good storytelling has to be a constantly practiced art. Yet, while a local raconteur is enjoyed, few take him seriously. The assumption is that anyone who can remember all that stuff must not work very hard, and hard work is our cultural ideal of success.

This brings me to another problem with being a storyteller. It requires leisure time for all of us. A good story cannot be hurried, and good listening has to be relaxed. The Icelandic tellers of sagas had the long winter's night, when there was nothing else to do but weave their stories. The fairytales of northern Europe are the products of the night, when there was only the light of a fire or a flickering candle to illumine the face of the spokesman. The American Indian stories, such as that of the flowering tree which I related earlier in a very abreviated form, were told by the old people sitting around the council ring. Contrast this lack of concern for the calendar, much less the clock, with our hurried life, and we get some idea of the problem.

Furthermore, storytelling makes storytellers, and therein lies still another problem. Whenever I hear a good joke I can hardly wait until I find an audience who has not heard it. A people reared with storytelling are a people who enjoy sharing stories. The story of the Gospel was, for the most part, told orally for fifteen hundred years. In part, the excitement lies in wanting to share the good news; and if we suspect "they" have already heard it, the thrill is greatly abated. We think of the oral tradition of the Christian good news as lasting only until the writing of the Gospels during the last third of the first century. We forget that the Gospels were written, not as I write this book, but as you and I write a letter. The Gospels were copied by hand at great effort and expense. Most of the Christians never saw a Bible, but instead were *told* the story of Jesus. I am not left with the impression that they greatly suffered as a result.

Storytelling is great fun. It is more than that, however. The priest is one who calls the community to attend to God's word in its midst. It is a summons to grasp an abiding reality, rather than a settling for the current social illusion. Roth has said of the abiding reality of God's word that it "can reach fruition only by entering into the story, living it, letting it happen to you, and giving yourself to it in the creative and imaginative way that you can."[27] This is why to be a priest is to be a storyteller.

THE WAGON MASTER

This next image depends on the reader's awareness that the expansion of the European colonization of the North American continent has always been pervaded by a "wilderness" motif. As the dreamer at the beginning of this chapter sought the jewels in the bowels of the earth, so did those who came to this land looking for the kingdom in the unknown forests and fields. From the very beginning the settlers of New England in the early seventeenth century thought of their journey to this land as something akin to Moses crossing

236

the Red Sea and passing through the Sinai wilderness to establish the holy nation. The Puritan theologians, such as the great Jonathan Edwards, taught that it was very likely that the new Jerusalem, promised in Revelation, would come to pass in the American wilderness. There was a millennial spirit about the movement West, beginning at the Atlantic Ocean, which begot both courage and the self-righteousness that blessed and cursed the American adventure. The new settlers saw themselves in the terms of Revelation, "The woman [identified as the true church] herself fled into the wilds, where she had a place prepared for her by God, there to be sustained for twelve hundred and sixty days (Rev. 12:6)."

Granted, all the motivation for the colonization of the continent, beginning with Massachusetts and Virginia, was not religious. The anticipation of new wealth was always there and, as first the generations and then the centuries moved on, it became more and more obvious. The high point of the migrations from the East to California was in 1849–1850, when gold was discovered on the West Coast. Even so, in the face of calloused greed and a simple inability to cope back home, there was always a kind of religious fervor associated with the trek West. For some, such fervor may have legitimated the murder of the native Americans, the rape of the land, and the decimation of the wildlife. For a few, however, like Cornelius Hedges, the founder of Yellowstone National Park, and John Muir, the father of American conservationism, it gave substance to a deep reverence for the beauty of our land.

It was into this world view in the mid-nineteenth century that there came the wagon train, a kind of organized pilgrimage. The story of wagon trains, familiar in some sense to every American child, is one of the fascinating pieces of American history. In the 1820s regular commerce was carried on with the Mexicans of Santa Fe by means of wagon trains. In 1830 the mountain men crossed the Rockies by wagon, and in 1841 California was opened to wagons. By 1859, the high-water mark of the wagon train was the Oregon-California Trail, whose traffic was dominated by the Russell, Majors, and Waddell Company, who controlled the pilgrimage business. It was they who supplied for each trek westward the twenty-six wagons, each pulled by twelve oxen, and commanded by a group of experienced men on horseback. In May of every year these prairie schooners set out from the marshalling areas along the Missouri River across the wilderness for California and Oregon. Only the completion of the transcontinental railroad in 1870 made them obsolete.

The man in command of the wagon train, as some of us may remember from the late Ward Bond on television, was the wagon master. He was like the captain of a ship, with absolute authority and complete responsibility—only more so. It was his task to lead those twenty-six wagons across the wilderness and bring them safely to their destination. He led a collection of people of varied motivation and questionable ancestry, pulled by animals of notorious disposition in wagons not known for their ease of handling. He faced rugged geography, treacherous weather, and hostile Indians. The thousands of miles of prairies, mountains, and deserts held many surprises, few of them pleasant. The pay was not all that great either. Perhaps there were intangible rewards, as well as some tangible ones with which we are not familiar. I cannot help but believe that the wagon master had to be a man in love with the wilderness.

For me, the image of the wagon master offers a way around a certain linguistic impasse that we are experiencing in ministry studies these days. There is much evidence that people on their spiritual journey need direction. Henri Nouwen has said that there are three unshakeable "rules" in the vocation of prayer: word, silence, and *guidance*. "Word and silence both need guidance."[28] I said that once at a workshop and was informed by a lady that she had found Jesus and guidance was not what she needed. If that is true— which I doubt—most of us still need guidance. It is a need corresponding to the universal experience of the church, not to mention Buddhism, Hinduism, and what have you. Even the practitioners of the LSD "trip" make this point. It is absolutely foolhardy to set out on the antistructural experience without a guide.

The problem, as I suggest, is what to call such a guide in order that we provide a helpful image and not a destructive one. The old term was "spiritual director." I find the model it recalls too individualistic, built on a one-to-one relationship that only the professionally religious can afford. To some people "spiritual director" recalls the imperious tyrant of the confessional, the authoritarianism of pre-Vatican II Roman Catholic seminaries, and the triumphalism of the church in general. It lacks a humility before the mystery of God. Mark Dyer, missioner to the clergy of the Diocese of Massachusetts, suggests the term, "friend of the soul." This is fine, although I find it lacking in vivid imagery. In fact, it seems almost precious.

We are speaking of someone who does not have all the answers, who cannot take away the risk for us, and who shares our hardships. Yet we are also describing someone who knows something about the pilgrimage into the wilderness: the kinds of feelings to expect, the way to travel, the places we are likely to encounter, the "Indians," and the good "water holes." His authority is derived from the fact that he has bet his life on our life. We are talking about the wagon master. He has his own quest, but he has been that way before and is willing for us to travel along with him.

I talked with a number of people recently about their desire for a guide such as I describe, and they all say the same thing: "There are very few wagon masters around." They are right. I have also heard priests say that no one comes to them to ask them how they can pray better. As a consequence, they often go and look for training in how to counsel as a psychiatrist counsels. I am not sure where the fault lies. I do know that no one is going to ask someone to help them in their spiritual quest if all the signals—words, para-language, and body movement—show that the priest has never set one foot in the direction of a pilgrimage. It has to be fairly obvious that you must pray before anyone is going to ask you to help them pray. A law clerk will not be recruited to lead the wagon train across the plains, mountains, and deserts.

I suspect that the good wagon master did not have to advertise his liminal qualities or credentials. He probably literally reeked of them. The way to get good guides into the abyss of our spiritual lives is to find people who have gone into their own and come out more authentic people, reeking of the antistructure. Yet the church has to create a climate where that kind of risk-taking is encouraged. The reason why in the last five or six years young people have looked everywhere for "guru's" other than in the neighborhood parish is because they know no neighborhood parish would hire a "guru." He is too unpredictable. He does not fit well.

I mentioned earlier that parish search committees tell us that they want someone with "spiritual depth." That sounds good, but if we pressed for a further definition of "spiritual" we were generally given banal answers. They spoke of people that made the parishioners feel accepted, people who were good "meeters" and would call, and people who counseled well. It was all toward helping people cope and get ahead in the structures. Certainly the odor of liminality will not look good in the print-out for the Church Deployment Office. Search committees might interpret the "liminal" man as the man who "loafs."

There is more than just a bit of the maverick in the wagon master. Some of that intangible reward of the arduous journey is that he gets away from the expectations laid upon him by the city life. He is not marching to that "drum." He is not in a hurry, and he reads the signs. He is good at creative time-wasting.

One of my favorite questions (which I mentioned in an anecdote earlier in this book) in clergy conferences has been: "If you took Tuesday off to walk in the woods, to sit by the brook, and to lie on your back watching the clouds, what would you tell the Senior Warden on Wednesday when he phoned and asked you where you were yesterday?" That same question has special significance here. I do not think we are going to get the kind of wagon masters we need as priests, starting with myself, until we could say to that Senior Warden: "I was at my Father's business—walking in the woods, sitting by the brook, lying on my back watching the clouds—all day long." For the knowledge one gets doing nothing, but being in and in love with the wilderness, is the kind of understanding that gives us the qualifications to guide others into the wilderness of their own self to find God.

A passage in Thomas Merton's *Asian Journal* sums up the challenge I hope the reader sees in the image of the wagon master as illustrative of the priest, whose task is to lead others to seek their vision as he seeks his on a mutual pilgrimage. Merton is citing Arnaud Desjardins.

> "For the 'seeker after Truth' only meetings with very great masters and very great sages can be really interesting. It is better to seek, seek, and seek again a real sage, a truly liberated sage, and spend perhaps no more than a single day with him, than to dissipate one's efforts in encounters and conversations with less representative persons. . . . It is no longer a matter of talking to Tibetans who have the title lama [or clergy who have the title 'reverend']; it is a matter of meeting masters."[29]

In a similar vein, the distinguished translator of Boris Pasternak (1890–1960), Eugene Kayden, told me recently, "All your seminarians must read the first fifty pages of *The Brothers Karamazov* and learn from Father Zossima how to be a master of the spiritual life." The goal of the priest must be to be a master, a "wagon master" in the wilderness of the antistructure.

SUMMARY

Perhaps the reader has concluded that with these four images I am advocating the church ordain as priests eccentric misfits: mana-persons, childlike clowns, lazy story tellers, and men who could not abide the civilization and spent their lives with dirt and Indians. There is some truth in this, because we have been looking for the opposite type for so long and failing. The professional image seems calculated to encourage us to think of a priest as a doctor, lawyer, or engineer. The more we advocate the professional image, however, the greater seems the gap between our theology and our implied intentions in ministry. Theology talks about salvation by grace through faith, and professionalism talks about salvation by works.

Yet we need to keep in mind that this is a book about one of the four vectors of ministry. I think it would be a grievous mistake to dismiss the professional image from a balanced view of ministry. I have written here of the creatively weird priest, but it does not follow that the priesthood is concerned *only* with the antistructural dimensions of life and the intuitive forms of meaning as opposed to structural experience and thinking meaning. The priest stands at the threshold of the antistructure. In that sense he is a liminal person. In the four images in this chapter we speak of the priestly "style" as one moves into the antistructure. The threshold in question is also an entrance into the structures; and, if it were the purpose of this book, it would be quite appropriate to discuss what is the priestly "style" in terms of the institution. This would lead into images such as theologian, administrator, educator, organizer,—all professional images.

My concern is, therefore, that the reader not conclude that I am against reason and logical thought and people who do this well. Several years ago I spoke on the subject of the priesthood at a seminar sponsored for bishops by the Trinity Institute of New York on the subject of this chapter. As is sometimes my custom, I listed each point by number and then developed it. After the talk one bishop commented to me, "That is the most rational exposition of the irrational I ever heard." I took it as a compliment. The need is for priests who are disciples of both Dionysius and Apollo.

I can also imagine that someone coming upon this chapter, after eight previous chapters on ministry as a community function, will wonder how the ministerial priesthood fits into the priestly community. My answer is a functional one, from which undoubtedly theological conclusions can and will be drawn. All research of which I know into the life of a parish shows that the sacramental person, the priest of the community, must be clearly identifiable and responsible if that congregation is to be healthy or even to survive.[30] As Christ is the head of the church, so must that person who is the priest be head of the community—"head" in the anatomical sense, not necessarily in the administrative sense. "All things are held together in him [Christ]. He is, moreover, the head of the body, the church" (Col. 1:17–18). Paul here seems to have the notion of the head as related to the keystone in an arch. That is what keeps it together and enables all the other parts to fulfill their function.

This is a very subtle kind of role, which is difficult to reduce to a job description. This is particularly true when it does not mean to minister to people's pathology—their quest for a father figure to make their decisions for them. (I once knew a co-ed when I was Episcopal chaplain at Louisiana State

University, who phoned me occasionally to see if I thought she could wash her hair that day.) Being the head in an effective, freeing way depends a great deal upon being a self in an authentic way and living into that self with style. Such a function requires a heavy reliance upon the antistructural image of the priesthood, with a "going easy" on the structural functions.

All of this leads to a conclusion that I have made before. A priest, in order to function as I have outlined in this chapter, cannot hold people out on the perimeter of his defenses. He has to trust himself before God enough to allow himself to be *transparent* to others.[31] The mana-person, the clown, the story-teller, and even the wagon master depends for his power on the inner integrity of his life and the fact that it shows. Integrity is not the same thing as perfection. Integrity itself requires that one confess himself a sinner. By integrity I also mean that we have faced ourselves, that we have accepted ourselves, and that we clearly have faith that God has more than this present self in mind for us. It is in the brokenness and the wholeness of such a person, both together, that God can be seen working when we are willing to share that person, unashamedly and explicitly, as a child of God.

10

THE WORLD

Throughout this study I have from time to time reminded the reader that it is an error to think of the fourth vector of ministry, the attention of God's word present in history today, as somehow in opposition to the city within the world. It is a fallacy of major proportions if one sees the need to make a choice between a life of the Spirit and a concern for social justice. However, this is such a common presupposition and, since sufficient numbers of people have seemed to make this choice, it appears necessary to refute it at some length.

The fourth vector describes the spiritual vocation of the Christian community. This raises the issue of mysticism and all that is associated with that term. There is a very clear tradition in Protestantism against mysticism, almost from the start of the Reformation and shared by the Roman Catholic Jansenists of the seventeenth century. This repudiation of mysticism has been renewed particularly since Albrecht Ritschl (1822–1889). He recognized in the work of Schleiermacher and his followers a blend of mysticism and metaphysical speculation which was most "un-Protestant" and in opposition to some clear principles of his own. Mysticism, as followers of Ritschl would think, at least implies that man can achieve the vision of God by his own efforts. The mystical disciplines, according to its Christian opponents, make sense only if one does *not* believe that man is saved by grace through faith. Mysticism is also, they believe, necessarily world-denying. It is clear, they would say, that persons such as the author of *The Cloud of Unknowing* believe we must reject the world if we are to know God. They would appear to have some justification for this. In a common interpretation of the mystical tradition, for example, the fourteenth-century mystic suggests that Mary was *better* than Martha (Luke 10:38–41) because she chose the contemplative life over the active life.[1] Furthermore, mysticism seems to advocate a denigration of the individual, coupled with an unrealistically high evaluation of man's true end, as the followers of Ritschl see it. For the goal of mysticism would appear to be the absorption of the person in the divinity. We become God and cease to be ourselves.

I have noticed in some recent writings that mysticism is attacked on the grounds that it denies the reality of the cross. Jürgen Moltmann inveighs against what he calls the "Mysticism of the Cross" as a kind of romantic effort to avoid the stark reality of that symbol.[2] Robert Roth says that mysticism does not take into account the concrete immediacy of time and place and consequently does not deal with the tragic vision.[3] This perhaps bears some relation to Ronald Knox's pithy observation that mystics are generally "tone-deaf to theology."[4]

It is not my purpose to defend all mystics. The very definition of the word is so slippery that it is impossible, and surely many mystics have said and done some very unfortunate, even tragic, things in the name of Christ. The mystical vocation of the Christian community, however—meaning its openness to an awareness of God's immediate presence in history—is worth defending, and that has been the purpose of this book. In fact, it does not really need defending. It happens. People, who have an expectation of the transcendent, are found of God, become aware of his presence, and fall in love with him all the time. The Scriptures are rife with such persons and it has been happening ever since. It is my personal conviction that the Parable of the Sower is about the expectation of the word, which is why some people fall in love with God and why others do not (Matt. 13:1–9). The true Christian mystic is one who makes of his life the good soil, ready to receive the presence of God.

Certainly we must recognize that, just as in love, the so-called mystical experience can be pathological. It can be the result of our own unconscious, neurotic need for some "crutch" that enables us to survive emotionally. As I noted in the last chapter, Gabriel Moran speaks of prelogical and postlogical religion. Prelogical religion consists of that reassurance to the crippled ego that it is better than other egos because it has hold of a truth no one else has. Another name for this use of belief is extrinsic religion, or a religious belief that constitutes the rigid defense of a frail ego. Still another term for the same thing, as described by Freud in *The Future of an Illusion,* is "superego religion."

Postlogical religion (intrinsic or ego religion) makes the mystical experience a way of engaging the growing edge or the expanding horizons of the self. This is a very different thing, even though both can go under the name of "religion."

Some of the most frightened people I know are "very religious"; yet, as I said in the third chapter, many of the most innovative persons in our recent history were or are mystics. The prophet is a mystic in action, and no true mystic can help but be a prophet—a prophet in the sense of "speaking forth" to the world the vision of God for his creation.

Therefore, I reject the popular dichotomy of prophet and priest, of word and cult, of action and contemplation, of grace and ascetical practice, of faith and discipline, and of sacramentalism and mysticism. Of course, I also reject the notions of irresistible grace, total depravity, imputed righteousness, and predestination. Those particular doctrines are products of a peculiar cultural climate, which makes it very difficult to live in the ambiguity of a God who is both absolute and yet is served by free men.

I want to pursue now this relationship between the fourth vector of ministry and the world under four headings. I do not claim for this anything more than a brief prolegomenon to the study of social ethics—and all ethics are *social.* First, we need to discuss the options of the Christian relationship to the world. This has been done before in many ways, but a bit of review would be helpful. Second, there is the source of the agenda for the Christian concern in the world. Some people are troubled that "new occasions demand new duties" (to quote John Greenleaf Whittier) and we need to deal with that. Third, the heart of the matter for this book is the issue of the Archimedean point or how we get outside of answers offered by the very structures we want to change. Fourth and finally, we need to say a few things about power—a subject quite popular ten years ago, but suffering from an embarrassing silence now.

THE CHRISTIAN POSTURE TO THE WORLD

A number of years ago, at about the height of the student riots in the sixties, I asked several students representing one of the most radical groups at the University of Wisconsin in Madison to come to Nashotah House and talk with my class in Church and Society. They came and we listened. They talked a great deal about the need to destroy the institutions of the oppressive American society as quickly and as completely as possible so that justice would be restored. Then we asked questions and they answered. "How should this best happen?" we inquired. It did not matter how the structures would be destroyed, they replied, but judging from the attitude of the oppressors it looked like violence was the only possibility. "After the Revolution," we asked further, "what did they envision to be utopia?" "That," they responded, "was a mystery implicit in history itself, which would unfold through the rubble." We pressed the question. "You have no plan for tomorrow?" "No," they insisted, "our task is only to make it possible by destroying what stands in its way."

This is, of course, an expression of the Marxist doctrine of the entelechy of history: utopia is implicit in history and only needs the revolution to make it explicit. It has an Aristotelian base, as well as a Christian counterpart. If we remove all notion of transcendence from Christian thought and retain the anticipation of the Messianic age, we have to acknowledge that the kingdom of God is immanent within history and needs to be "cultivated" or "released." There is something of this in the process thought of Teilhard de Chardin and of Whitehead, although neither man is nearly as naïve as our Marxist friends about the inevitability of justice following a leveling of structures.

Naïve revolutionism, of course, is one possible understanding of how social change takes place and it is an option for the Christian community, considering its moral obligations to the world. There are, however, at least three other options: flight from the world, conformity to the world, and interaction with the world. My discussion in this section focuses on all four.

My reaction, after listening and talking with the Madison Marxists, was that they certainly had far more faith than I. It was about this time that some of their colleagues put a bomb up against a university building, blew it up, and killed a man doing some innocuous research there. Over in Milwaukee at Marquette, thirty-five miles from Nashotah House, they fire-bombed another building with the total result that they destroyed a doctoral dissertation representing someone's work of years. Did they think this was going to bring in the kingdom? Even where the institutions appear to have been destroyed, as in Russia and China, where is the utopia? My decided impression was and is, as I think about it, that there is far more of the old Russia and the old China in what goes on in those countries than some are willing to acknowledge. Social change is slow by nature. Structures, which are more than bricks and mortar, more than muscle and bone, are hard to destroy, even with violence. They tend to live on in the minds of the revolutionaries themselves. What emerges after the revolution, particularly if it is left to chance, has a remarkable resemblance to the same thing as before—with different names.

This first possible stance of the church to the world, as I have indicated, is that of revolution, interpreted through pure romanticism. I agree with George Celestin who defined revolutions as by nature violent. This accords with the definition of the Roman Catholic bishops of the "third world," who said that "Revolution . . is rupture with a system which does not guarantee the common good and the setting up of a new order more apt to procure it."[5] What the Madison Marxists were advocating, however, was a particular approach to revolution which had no plan for the "new order"—revolution as an act of faith *per se.* These are the "romantics of revolution" and their behavior is based on a kind of kitsch "poetry of guerrilla action."[6] It is the illusion of anarchy that institutions, at least *these* institutions that I want to destroy, are simply evil.

Before we dismiss this as just a stupid idea best left in the sixties, it needs to be said that it makes a fundamental common assumption with those who would flee the world, a point of view which has now gained a certain popularity in religious circles in the seventies. It is for this reason that I devote so much space to the first alternative. Both points of view, that of the romantic revolutionary and the romantic encratite (one who practices extreme asceticism), see institutions as evil in themselves. They fail to see that the balanced social reality demands a city that is community, group, and even global structure. For example, not a few neopietists advocate rejecting the "institutional church" as detrimental to the Christian life and are very much in favor of the separation of church and state. It is as if they wish to build a wall around the "true believers." Such sectarianism is not infrequently accompanied by a resurgent apocalypticism. The difference is that the naïve revolutionist does not believe God is "out there." God for him is somewhere inside the organism of the world, the prisoner of oppressors, and we have to destroy their institutions so we can let him loose. The contemporary encratite craves a God who is totally "out there" and seeks to keep himself pure from the pollution of politics, socioeconomics, and theology, so he can get there. The poetry of guerrilla action and the flight of the quietist derive their emotional base from the same source: revulsion at the dehumanizing nature of social structures.

I have no trouble understanding this revulsion. In fact, I am amazed at so many people who do not see the demonic possibilities of institutions. Occasionally I stumble across a television show called S.W.A.T., and a recent episode was an account of how the righteous defenders of the institution—in the person of a special police unit—with the technology and firepower of a small army obliterate the grossly caricatured participants in a revolutionary effort—all in the bicentennial year! I commented to someone recently on what an anomaly this is—holding up for our admiration something very close to Hitler's storm troopers, who overwhelm some people who happen to believe that life, liberty, and the pursuit of happiness take precedence over law and order. His only reply was that times are different. Are freedom and justice two of those "ancient goods" time renders "uncouth"?

My problem with the romantic revolutionary is not his perception of the *status quo,* which seems inevitably to become self-serving. My disagreement is on the grounds of his faith and the belief that violence against social structures *necessarily* cultivates justice. It simply is not true. Jesus had something to say about the man who rids himself of an unclean spirit, which goes out only to return and find the house unoccupied, and so he invites seven more unclean spirits worse than himself to join him (Matt. 12:46–50).

Equally naïve is the second posture of the church to the world: flight from society. Some years ago I gave an address to a group of high-school students on Christian witness. I mentioned that I was very much encouraged by a rising interest in the spiritual life, but that no one could remain on the "mountain" forever. We have to come down and deal with the pain of the world (having in mind, of course, the imagery of Luke 9:28–45). After the talk, a young man who identified himself as a "Christian"—apparently to distinguish himself from me—said that I was very wrong. He had been on the "mountain top" for six months and he planned to stay there if his parents let him.

This flight was, of course, a common attitude of the early church, although Paul and the author of 1 Peter clearly opposed it (Rom. 13:1–7; 1 Pet. 2:11–17). There was an element of encratism that dominated much of church life then and made itself felt in the monastic movement, which was in turn a reaction to the growing worldliness of the church. It was not all bad. This witness of the Christian ascetics has always had the value of calling into question the easy identification of culture and religion. Perhaps it is good that the denial of the world never has died out, although it has tended in many places, particularly in those lacking a theology, to become more sentimental than rigorous, more enthusiastic and excessive than prudent and tempered.

In the ancient church the ascetics lived a life of detachment from the world, grounded in the Stoic notion of *apatheia:* the true man is realized to the degree that he is free of passion. There was a philosophical basis. This obviously has its Far Eastern counterpart in theory and practice. It has a contemporary secular parallel in Philip Rieff's "psychological man."' Rieff argues in a cogent if unconvincing manner, for the value of noninvolvement. Stoicism, Far Eastern philosophy and psychoanalytical "metaphysics" are conceptual systems with which one can argue. Far more difficult are the theologically inept reactions of well-intended persons.

The quietists of the seventeenth century, for example, who were anti-institutional even to the point of abrogating verbal prayer, were the last significant Western body of Christians who attempted to develop a theological rationale for flight from the world. As Knox says, however, they tried to repeat what the great mystics of the sixteenth century said and got it wrong.[8] Things then went from bad to worse.

The quietists were followed, by the pietists, whose spirituality was an overt rejection of theology. This easily degenerated into a religion of feeling, without any cognitive component, which fed a neurotic need. Prelogical religion became the rule. Without a theology, pietism lost its critical faculties. Its denial of the world took on the quality of a sedative against the pain of the world: the oppression of the worker in the industrial revolution, the ignominy of slavery, the rootless existence of the growing cities, and the greed of capitalism. It was this kind of promise of a heavenly reward in the face of the world's suffering that led Marx to call religion the "opiate" of the masses—and to this extent he was right.

Pietism fed American revivalism, beginning with the "Great Awakening" of 1732 (which did profit from the keen theological mind of Jonathan Edwards [1703–1758]) and followed, more particularly, by the second "Great Awakening" in the very early eighteenth century. Its notion of sin had little social component, which is one reason why the heart of American religion was blind to the genocide of the American Indian, the inhumanity of the treatment of the working man, and the hubris of "manifest destiny." There are still heirs of pietism and American revivalism who think that the task of the church is to save souls and not get involved in the dirty business of politics.

Of course, as Richard Niebuhr pointed out in his classic, *Christ and Culture*, speaking of this attitude as "Christ against culture," it is impossible to flee human institutions. No man can go out into the wilderness utterly empty. For one thing, he brings along his language, which is a human institution. It is just as true, although perhaps more subtle, that he carries a vision of the world or the culture's story, an intentionality stamped out by the structures into which he was socialized.[9] There can be no absolute separation between the spiritually minded and the world. Instead, there has to be a constant interplay of choice and rejection.

The third option of the Christian stance to the world is to avoid the question altogether. It is to give up, and let the function of religion be the legitimation of the socially prescribed values within the structures of the society. Durkheim said that this was the purpose—a necessary purpose—of religion. I think it is where most American Christians locate themselves, not as the result of thought, but rather out of convenience. Sometimes it is expressed as a separation of the religious function from the other institutions of the system—as when churchgoers are horrified to learn that their priest has political opinions, which he is quite willing to express in various ways—but the effect is the same. What is good for the American system is good for God.

We have good precedent for this. Thomas Jefferson was a strong exponent of what Richard Niebuhr calls the "Christ of culture." Jefferson seems to imply that Jesus was a republican gentleman, who embodied the best in advocating a peaceful, cooperative society where everything worked together to the moral good, which is implicit if inhibited in the structures of the well-designed society. Ritschl was an exponent of such a "culture religion," although at a more sophisticated level theologically than Jefferson. It should not surprise us, therefore, that he was opposed to mysticism.

This is the posture which identifies Christianity with that civil religion of which Robert Bellah has been the principal discussant over the last decade. For Bellah, of course, civil religion at its best has a transcendent judgment placed upon it. However, it seems to me to be more typically the divinization of those feelings of patriotism common in some sense to most of us. The commitment is to the institutions, which we come to feel are of God. For such Americans it would appear that God was the original democrat, we are his chosen people, and he is with us all the way.

Of course, where the first posture of the revolutionary and the second of the encratite were, like all romanticism, antistructural, this third posture embraces the structures and looks with suspicion on those who move outside of them. The counterculture was never embraced by mainline American Christianity, unless it was sanitized (structurally emasculated). It had to cut its hair, clean up its songs, and embrace monogamy before it was allowed in the sanctuary. The priests of the third stance are particularly given to the professional model of the conservativism of contemporary psychiatry, and have little understanding of the liminal.

The great strength of this third posture is that, unlike the first two, it takes structures seriously and is consequently a good bit wiser in the long run. The church cannot be effective or even survive as an instrument of redemption, if it remains in an adolescent pout over the need to conform. The chronic suspicion some church people have of institutions can take the form of a teen-age "fixation." Either we grow up or we die. As Niebuhr points out, if the church had remained a band of despisers of culture it would have had no effective mission to the world.[10] Richard Neuhaus, the Lutheran scholar and pastor, argues in a recent book that a case can still be made at this late date for the sacramentality of the American value system.[11] If man is the city and the city is more than a communitas, then cultural institutions are a part of the Gospel—institutions in specific, not just in general.

The problem is that the Gospel readily becomes captured when it is identified with the structural dimensions of society. Christ becomes the banker from Dallas, the values of the Gospel are identical to the ideology of middle-class America, and the prophets are stoned or, worse, ignored. Obviously, a witless conformity to the prevailing sociocultural fact violates the New Testament. "Adapt yourselves no longer to the pattern of this present world," writes Paul, "but let your minds be remade and your whole nature thus transformed" (Rom. 12:2). This is clear, and I doubt that many people reading this book would argue the point. In fact, as Neuhaus may suggest, we often overstate the gulf between American institutions and the divine will (see my discussion of history as a context for transcendent exposure in Chapter Six). At the same time, the rank-and-file Christian, whom I suspect does not read books like this one and who has lost the ecstasy of the naïve encratite, has lapsed unthinkingly and perhaps invincibly into the ignorance of the identification of the will of God with the *status quo*. It is difficult to stir a people who think Jesus Christ was a white Anglo-Saxon Protestant wearing a George Wallace button and living in a small Southern town—and I am surrounded by them.

The fourth posture is the one, obviously, that I am advocating in this book. It is the stance of one who is constantly moving between the structures and the antistructures. Niebuhr refers to it as "Christ the transformer of culture." I speak of it as the interaction between the vision of God and the world, with the pilgrim community as the listening worker or the "hands of God." Some of the early Church Fathers (Irenaeus, for example) thought of the "hands" of God as the Son and the Holy Spirit. In a sense it is more appropriate to think of us as the hands of God; as, for example, when the skilled surgeon brings about healing by working with God, or when the thoughtful voter turns out the corrupt political machine.

The rest of this chapter is an exposition of this understanding of the relationship of ministry to the world on the basis of an interaction model. Briefly put, it is a confrontation of the social fact with the intentionality of God in power. This can be by means of education or revolution. It can be a call to love as Christ loved, or it can be a judicious use of power politics. It does involve a judgment and a determination to call society to account on the basis of that judgment. The fourth posture also insists that the church has a prophetic

251

witness, and no appeals to the danger of internal strife, dubious calls to reconciliation, or warnings against the fallibility of its members can excuse its abdication from the vocation of prophet.

THE SOURCE OF THE AGENDA

During the debate over the racism of America in the fifties and sixties, an occasional apologetic was heard from the right to the effect that if segregation were so wrong why did not the church speak out fifty or seventy-five years before. More recently at least one prominent theologian has spoken against the ordination of women to the priesthood—an issue which, while it has theological import, is also an ethical question—on the grounds that it seemed incredible to him that it would take nineteen hundred years for the church to discover the mind of Jesus on this matter. Both of these illustrations are instances of a peculiar epistemology of revelation which is detached from history.

It could just as well be asked that since it took the church seventeen hundred years to condemn torture, and in fact used it for its own purposes for extended periods of time prior to that, why is torture wrong now? (A church synod did condemn torture in 384, but it was not until 1819 that the papacy recommended its practice be abandoned by the Inquisition—a generation after the Bill of Rights outlawed it.) On these grounds, abolitionists also will find their position called in question, since it took another seventeen hundred years or more for Christian conscience to discover the mind of Jesus on that issue. Then there is the matter of masturbation, which historically the church has viewed as worse than fornication until the last generation, when we suddenly found out that God did not punish perpetrators of the act with moral turpitude and a softening of the brain. Of course, torture and slavery still exist rather widely, and there are still mothers who threaten to excise the penises of their small sons for "playing with themselves," but we all know that these are no longer condoned in the face of an evolving ethical awareness.

The nature of this evolution rests in the dialogue between the transcendent, informed conscience of man and the institutional structures themselves. It is essential to see that the awareness of evil (which includes the locus of its reality) arises in this dialogue, *not* within the individual or "out there." There is a tendency among some to locate evil either as a defect in the heart of the individual or in the material world. In the first instance, the solution is to appeal to the heart of the individual. The theory is that individuals make communities, and that the evil within institutions is benign and the result of the sin of the individuals. The latter promotes that self-defeating flight from the material world: do not drink, do not smoke, do not dance, do not look at naked women, and so on.

A great problem, as I see it, in current Christian ethics is that despite a century of social science there are still reputable church people who isolate the issue of justice by describing it as a problem of the human heart. This is particularly true of the pietist movement, with its naïvete about the role of structures in the life of man. What is missed is the result of the truth that man *is* his city. It is the city which in many ways shapes the man. The very point I made in the first chapter concerning the essential political form of the means and ends of hominisation is lost. Cardinal Suenens, a prominent proponent of neo-Pentecostalism in the Roman Catholic Church, is guilty of this very error in his most recent book. He says "The ultimate problem [of evil] from which we suffer lies neither in institutions nor in things; it is within us, in our hearts and souls. The interior evil is the reason why social abuses arise."[12]

It is not that simple. The possibility of sin lies within the human intentionality. It is a part of the make-up of those structures of meaning with which each of us individually and all of us corporately engage our environment. It is the defect in our vision, but that vision itself is, in part at least, a function or product of the structures. The imperfect intentionality of man, on the basis of which he acts is a *reflection* of the intentionality of the generalized other within the institutions. If Suenens means the individual is responsible for this, I agree. But he needs also to recognize the malignant role of the social structures. This means, as Piet Schoonenberg has rightly pointed out, that our personal sin is the result of the "sin in the world" (Rom. 5:12). Original sin is a name for our "situated liberty."[13]

Sin lives, then, in the intentionality of man. *It is also true, however, that the awareness of sin is there.* If man is enslaved by virtue of his very history or situation, so is his response to injustice and the denial of his true end in God a function of the sociocultural world. Every age has to write its own textbook of applied ethics. We cannot lament the moral insensitivities of the past, but it is equally true that we must not blind ourselves by appeals to the past to what the present tells us is wrong.

Margaret Mead once said in my hearing that each age has to face its own particular moral issue or issues. She is quite right. This is because the evolution of society itself extrudes, if you will, certain surds that become peculiarly apparent. How else do we explain the quiesence of woman through twenty-five hundred years of subservience imposed by the Graeco-Roman culture until the last hundred years? How was it that after four hundred years of oppression the fatigue of one brave, black woman, Mrs. Rosa Parks, in Montgomery, Alabama, triggered the beginning of a revolution still going on? Moral questions, just like great ideas, have their time to be born. They emerge from the structures into our intentionality and confront all but the morally blind.

The acknowledgement of the moral surds requires, of course, a *distance* on the structures. If we have no way of achieving distance by moving out of our institutional investments from time to time, we remain their prisoners; we are morally blind. I remember vividly my frustration in talking to members of my family who were career military officers about the Vietnam War. It was not that I had the solution and they did not. It was that they did not even see the issue, the ab*surd*ity of the situation! They were trapped in a self-serving military institution. I recall again sitting in the galleries at a General Convention of the Episcopal Church beside some old and dear friends of mine from Louisiana, a diocese I had left seven or eight years before. They were making fun of a Dakota Indian who was speaking on the convention floor, whom they did not know was a close friend of mine. I remember well my pain and heartache, not just for my Dakota friend, but for my Louisiana friends as well. There was no way for me to break into the system in which they were trapped. There was no way for them to see my pain at "Anglo" insensitivity, which I had learned from the Indian. They had not traveled with me from Louisiana to Wisconsin and on to South Dakota. They were the prisoners of that provincialism which is inevitable to one degree or another in all of us. By my apparent assumption of a role of superior insight in these two accounts—of the Vietnam War and the Dakota Indian—it is as if I imply omniscience.

Yet the pilgrimage of every person is not only a quest for God, it is also an act of self-examination and confession. It is a way of examining our lives by getting distance on them. Myerhoff, in her description of the Huichol peyote hunt, tells how on the third day of the pilgrimage there is a ritual of confession, whose purpose is to make new the participants and to bind them together that they might achieve the vision of the gods.[14] The Huichol do not have, of course, a sense of history, in Eliade's meaning, and therefore they are not concerned so much with change toward the future as they are with return to the past. The point is, however, that continued pilgrimage is accompanied by growing sensitivity to the surds that lie within our structured existence. This is why it is just possible that service in the military in different parts of the country and abroad created a sufficient question in the minds of many Southern whites after World War II that a monolithic opposition to integration was no longer possible.

The Christian is called to be *responsible.* The basic root is the verb "to respond," and it carries the additional sense of responding in an appropriate, humane manner. My argument is that responsibility demands a sensitivity to the issues with which history presents us, in terms of both the awareness of sin and the command of God that arises within the structures of our meaning. We are a part of history, we are conditioned by history, and we cannot be expected to see the surds which our history obscures. We have only to be responsible to our times, but that is no small task. It seems more, sometimes, than most of us can bear; so there is no reason to feel guilty that we have not foreseen and solved all the world's possible problems.

THE ARCHIMEDEAN POINT

Archimedes, who first called attention to the power of the lever, is reputed to have said: "Give me a place upon which to stand and I will move the world." That *place* apart from the world has come to be called, consequently, the Archimedean point. In ethics it is the absolute in terms of which one may make a judgment that is not *simply* a product of history. Unless one succumbs to a complete, unresolved solipsism or historical relativism, one has an implicit or explicit Archimedean point.

This is, of course, what this book is all about. I have been arguing that the ministry of the church is more than a rehashing of its tradition, more than a monitoring of its internal life, and more than an awareness and concern for the world. These things are all important, but they are also immanental. They have to do with this world, even if they consist of records others have made of the experience of transcendence (the Bible). The ministry of the church, however, is incarnational by definition, and therefore fails at the center unless it is the mediation of transcendence. It is necessarily the priestly community, bridging the space between the infinite Archimedean point and the finite issues of history. What Paul said of himself is really what the Church claims for itself in the fullness of its ministry: "And yet I do speak words of wisdom to those who are ripe for it, not wisdom belonging to this passing age, nor to any of its governing powers, which are declining to their end; I speak God's hidden wisdom [*sophian en musterpiō*], his secret purpose framed from the very beginning to bring us to our full glory (1 Cor. 2:6–7).

This wisdom which Paul speaks, he locates in the mystery of God. It lies outside the structures and is related to the antistructural experience. Its source and identifying characteristic cannot be structural, but has to be *more* than this. This suggests the inadequacy of all attempts at ethical positivism, such

255

as appeals to natural law, divine law, papal infallibility, irrefutable logic, the loving thing, and so on. *The Archimedean point is God's vision* for his creation, "framed from the very beginning to bring us to our full glory," as Paul says. The task of the fourth vector of ministry is to inform our vision, our structures of meaning, in terms of this vision, *so that we might act upon it.*

The vision of God has no "divine substance." The belief of the Christian is not that God has a unique language or a singular category, but that he makes himself known in history. We see God in the unique and singular *configuration* of the finite toward the infinite. The extraordinary appears within the ordinary, not even as some kind of special stuff, but in the same way as it appeared in Jesus. He was as we are in every way, except that he did not sin (Heb. 4:15). The absence of sin was the unique configuration. There was nothing that broke the relationship between the absolute and the relative.

In my argument, the Archimedean point is the *progressive ordering* of the community's vision by God's vision. As I have cited, James Gustafson speaks appropriately of the Christian congregation as a "community of moral discourse." What makes this community different, however, from other groups doing the same thing is that its vocation is to do this as Christ to the world. It has to work at the possibility and be conscious of the actuality of a transcendental vision known in the experience of a shaping (an expansion or elevation) of our own vision apart from our control.

This kind of statement pleads for illustration. If I am to attempt such, I have to begin by citing the simple fact that the prophetic role of the church itself is a function of history, and has only been recovered in the last century from a long entrapment, certainly since the decline of the papacy in the fourteenth century, and perhaps since Constantine in the fourth century. One does not see the church of the fourteenth to nineteenth centuries speaking prophetically to the social institutions *per se.* Luther's and Calvin's records on this score are particularly poor, despite their authorship of the "Protestant principle." The whole ethical dimension of the church's vision has seemed captured within the structures of Western sociopolitical institutions. To begin at the beginning in search of the illustration of the Archimedean point at work, the Bible is a revolutionary document. The *Magnificat* of the Blessed Virgin is only one clear case in point.

> He has brought down monarchs from the thrones,
>   but the humble have been lifted high.
> The hungry he has satisfied with good things,
>   the rich sent empty away. (Luke 1:52–53)

Whoever wrote that did so in terms of a vision he did not get from the Roman Empire or its willing accomplices. It was was a prophetic insight, but one that stopped here. The early church generally advocated a nonbelligerent attitude toward the state. Prophecy in the first centuries of Christianity was largely ecstatic and apocalyptic, not revolutionary. It did not address itself to the change within the structures of society itself, as Old Testament prophecy did. It is my hunch—and I realize that this is more an unsupported generalization than anything else—that during the whole extended period from the New Testament to the nineteenth century, the only time when Christians gained enough distance from the structures to listen to God in order to speak to the society was in the eleventh, twelfth, and thirteenth centuries, the so-called High Middle Ages.

The ethics of that period were undoubtedly predominantly "conformist." At the same time, there is a *humanizing* form within the institutions of that period, which is easily missed. The Peace of God and the Truce of God are obvious programs that attempted to soften the barbarity of constant petty strife. Less obvious, but far more effective, was the advocacy of the Blessed Virgin as an ideal into the sociocultural mix of the period. Medieval man was a curious paradox of cruelty and mercy, masculinity and femininity, and it was the church which called him to temper his baser emotions with love, and gave him a "handle" to his femininity. Such an awareness provoked a spirit that promoted the seven corporal works of mercy, which bespoke a concern for human suffering—albeit on an individual level—that the early modern church with its antifeminine theology, never equaled. Could it have been the profound mystical tradition of the High Middle Ages that fed this glimmer of prophetic witness in a cruel age?

It has to be said, however, that the great social prophets did not arise in church history until the nineteenth century, and that the greatest of all come in the present century. We have been privileged to know men and women who have been seized by the vision of God for his world and have seen it as a means to speak for the Lord. Personally, the most moving example, as I indicated at the end of the third chapter, is Martin Luther King. I do not consider the words of his last speech mere rhetoric, but a clear testimony to the reality of the Archimedean point that lies within his pilgrimage.

I've been to the mountain top. . . . I just want to do God's will. And he's allowed me to go up to the mountain. And I've looked over, and I've seen the Promised Land. So I'm happy tonight. I'm not worried about anything. I'm not fearing any man. Mine eyes have seen the glory of the coming of the Lord.[15]

The fact that the imagery is from the story of Moses and a popular hymn does not detract from the fact that the vision of which he speaks provoked a continuing action which has been one of the church's great moments in this century.

Yet there is something of which we must beware, for which King provides still another illustration. The context of his vision, as he describes it in the quotation from his last speech, is the religious experience of the poor black. King's intuitive insights were often gathered from the antistructure of a church rejected by the prevailing white culture. This fact cannot defend the notion, however, that the Archimedean point for Christian ethics is simply folk religion. In fact, it generally is not. King was an educated man, a product of the Atlanta black middle class, and a Ph.D. at twenty-six. He was an intellectual, and his prophecy was the product of careful thought, as must be all movement from the energizing cipher of God's vision to the action of the community of moral discourse.

It was only after that when the discipline of a mind trained in Gandhi, Hegel, Reinhold Niebuhr, Rauschenbusch, and Brightman—a rather unlikely company—gave shape to King's vision so that it became a plan of action. The quest for the vision requires the shedding of the presuppositions of the abstractions of systematic theology. Theology can paralyze our prophetic potential. Yet once our vision conjoins that of God, then there has to be a return out of the antistructure accompanied by a process of judgment and decision, which requires careful thinking and which includes systematic theology. This is the lesson of the Peasant's Revolt (1524–1526) and all its ilk.

My belief is that the church engages the world in terms of a theology that is a product of the experience of God *now*. The theology is not the Archimedean point. The experience, which is known in the radical reordering of our vision, is the point. The theology does, however, separate for us the symbols from the diabols, love from hate, God's service from the service of evil. It saves us from being victimized by the demagogues. Revolution can be oppression by another name or it can be merely stupid. As Celestin has said, "God is not always on the side of the revolutionaries." It is reason that is the clearest safeguard toward knowing when he is on one side or the other, or on both.[16]

ACTION AND REACTION

The issue is not whether to have or not to have power, but how we use power. By power I mean the ability to change things. It is always a potential in man, but is actualized in the face of opposition. The person with no actual power is one without a moral position. The grace of God is the power of the saint, for the person who stands in an open relation to God is an instrument of God's power.

In the first chapter it was argued that the wholeness of man requires the wholeness of the city which man is. This is why the kingdom of God, in which all relationships are just, is a dominant theological and ethical theme in the Christian's belief. In the Lord's Prayer we say, "Thy kingdom come, thy will be done, on earth as in heaven" (Matt. 6:10). That is another revolutionary statement, just as the words of St. Mary in the *Magnificat.* The coming of the kingdom clearly requires *change,* change in the structures of the earthly city. We are faced with the opposition of a sinful city. That change requires God's power if it is to be in accord with his vision (heaven). It also requires us as the "hands" of God!

The implication of the Lord's Prayer is, therefore, that we as followers of Christ need to exercise power to change the earthly city. This is really not debatable if we take the prayer seriously. We are offering ourselves to be instruments to bring in the kingdom, in the earthly city as in the heavenly city. The source of the power is God, for it is God's grace, his presence, in us that makes this possible. The prayer is one for the vision of God, but also it is for the power to act on the basis of that vision in an effective way. I am saying that the mystic vision is always accompanied by the prophetic power.

There is certainly an understandable tendency in the New Testament, influenced as it was by a growing dualism, to oppose the heavenly city and the earthly city (John 18:36; 1 Cor. 15:50; 2 Tim. 4:18), and to place the heavenly city outside time and space. This seems to imply that revolutionary action is a misdirection for the Christian. Yet there is reason for saying that the kingdom for which we strive is both in the future and here, and that we now live in eternity. There is no opposition of heavenly and earthly, but there is an unfolding process of which we are a part and which is fulfilled when the kingdom is realized completely through man's cooperation with God's grace. It is to this that Paul refers when he calls the Roman Christians to task and says of them: "The kingdom of God is not eating and drinking, but justice, peace, and joy, inspired by the Holy Spirit" (Rom. 14:17). Justice, peace, and joy do not come by refusing to encounter the world with power.

What the Christian does, which is different from those revolutionaries who are simply of this world, is that he exercises power in terms of the vision he shares with God. This is why I have said that the prophet is a mystic in action. He "speaks" for God, which is to say that he acts for God, as he hears God speaking to him. This difference is the difference between action and reaction. If we simply react to the issue with which the society confronts us because we are offended, then we are not behaving as a servant of Christ. We are nothing more than a "knee jerk" in response to the hammer of society on the patella of our conscience. However, if we have a vision—a divine configuration of our intentionality—then we can work together in a thoughtful, powerful manner.

It is of something like this that Rollo May writes: "Consciousness is the intervening variable between nature and being. It vastly enlarges the human being's dimensions; it makes possible in him a sense of awareness, responsibility, and a margin of freedom proportionate to this responsibility."[17] The person who is merely reacting is not aware, he is not responsible, and he certainly is not free. Act we must, but the consciousness of God's vision accompanies us.

I suspect some associate the word "power" with "violence." Perhaps the reader is thinking that the difference between power exercised as action and power expressed in reaction is the difference between violence and nonviolence. I do *not* wish to give this impression. Violence can be a form of action consistent with the Christian vision. It is true that violence is often the reaction of those with no power, and I have insisted that the Christian has power. There are two kinds of violence, however: subrational and superrational (not unrelated to prelogical and postlogical religion). Violence itself is not rational; either it flies in the face of reason or follows from reason. Again, Rollo May writes, "The authentic innocence of the nonviolent is his power."[18] I can appreciate what he is saying, but all action cannot be judged as having or not having value on the basis of whether or not it is violent.

The root metaphor in the story of the kingdom of God is not nonviolence. It is justice. "There shall be an end to death, and to mourning and crying and pain; for the old order has passed away. . . . As for the cowardly, the faithless, and the vile, murderers, fornicators, sorcerers, idolaters, and liars of every kind, their lot will be the second death, in the lake that burns with sulphurous flames" (Rev. 21:4, 8). Making allowance for the imagery of the times, it is clear that he is talking about a new order, achieved by a bit of rather gruesome violence, but where people will live with one another as God created them to live. Violence can be apocalyptic, as it is in Revelation.

Karl Rahner says that power is a gift of God—and by power he means not the innocence of the nonviolent, but physical force. Power exists "because it is the condition of the possibility of freedom."[19] The absolute renunciation of force on the part of the Christian, Rahner says, is heresy (that is, erroneous thinking). He goes on to say,

> The real question in a moral theology of freedom is this: in what way, and in what proportions in each concrete case, and with what perpetually revised safeguards, can the right of legitimate power to alter and restrict the freedom of the individual (and of his free fellowship) be reconciled with the higher right of freedom, and with the right of the individual to a real, concrete and permanent sphere of freedom? . . . this reconciliation is not something that can be fixed and formed once and for all: it must be constantly searched for anew.[20]

This constant search requires the movement into the antistructure in order to allow for the possibility of looking at our life from some distance and to see how the configuration of God's vision orders the possibilities inherent within the structures of this present moment. What I mean by the crucial "possibilities inherent within the structures" can be illustrated by Martin Luther King's pragmatic nonviolence as opposed to absolute pacificism. Violence in the South in the mid-fifties would have hardly accomplished King's vision. It would have undoubtedly produced a blood bath, resulting, perhaps, in a genocide of the black people equal to that of the holocaust of Nazi Germany. King's action was the result of a calculated position. It was a possible means to an end. Pacificism is not always that, nor is it always the best means. For example, the attempt to kill Hitler, in which Dietrich Bonhoeffer was involved, was, in my mind, morally right violence.

Therefore, action is the implementation of a vision that is the result of careful calculation. The Christian mystic turns effective prophet by "being wise as a serpent, innocent as a dove." We do not achieve the kingdom by being ingenuous. That is no more a Christian absolute than nonviolence, perhaps less so. People who object to the skepticism of the ethics of Reinhold Niebuhr or the presence in Congress of Fr. Drinan, on the grounds that such opinions or officeholding are contrary to the spirit of Christ, miss the point that there is nothing in the fourth vector of ministry which calls for us to be nonpolitical. The spirit of the child in the antistructure does not gainsay the wisdom of the adult in the same person in the structures. They should interact in an effective way.

It is only possible to set the spirit of the antistructure over against the structures if one conceives of life as a duality of sacred and profane, between which lies an uncrossable gulf. It has been my claim all along that such an understanding violates the very root of my experience and certainly does great violence to the heart of an incarnational belief. The alternative to this duality is the service of the kingdom as that which is to come to pass in the totality of our experience, which leaves no choice but *to act* for justice, for freedom, and for love as people who have *seen* and do *see* the Lord. I do not mean anything by "seeing" except that which I have meant throughout this book: the identification of the extraordinary within the ordinary, the power encountered when we die to self and open our hearts to the presence that is there, and the word of God which moves our souls as we attend to the mystery that lies within the twilight of our existence. All this presupposes a pilgrimage in life, where we move in and out, back and forth, between the structures and the anti-structures. We live in the structures in terms of the sensitivity that is the condition of the antistructure.

A friend of mine speaks of his moral theology as an "ethic of reverence." What I hope to have described here is an introduction to just such an ethic. Furthermore, it is a political ethic. Some people suggest we "demythologize" the biblical term *kingdom* of God for "reign of God." I would resist this. The vision of the kingdom is the image of the perfected political nature of man, which is, as the first chapter argues, of the very being of man. So we come full circle. I began by affirming the man as a city creature and I end by saying that the experience of God must, if it is authentic, lead back into the city, to the end that the earthly city become, indeed, the heavenly city, the new Jerusalem.

SUMMARY

In the Introduction I spoke of this book as something of a sequel to *The Future Shape of Ministry*. That book ended with a call for ministry to exercise its imagination; and in this study I have sought both to be imaginative and to explain the absolute necessity for a ministry that draws upon the intuitive self.

In the first section it was stated that ministry is of the *city*, concerned with *meaning*, and rooted in *mystery*. My purpose was to counter the notions that ministry is something done by a skilled professional to other individuals. I also wanted to make clear that we need to avoid any apologies for having a point of view; but that the ministry of the church is always at heart the transmission of the meaning of a transcendental experience manifest in the ordinary world. The church's value system is rooted in the belief that this very system is an expression of the divine vision for the world now.

In the second section the fourth vector of ministry, the city's openness to the word of God was analyzed in several ways. The imagination, the place of the imagination, the condition of freeing the imagination, and the content of the vision of the person who imagines were all discussed. My purpose has been to show that man is naturally pious. To be whole is to live in the free exercise of both hemispheres of the brain; to see, not just look; to know our story; and, as Christians, to conjoin that with the story of God in Jesus. This is what I mean by a natural piety, converted to Christ, and informed by the Christian community.

Obviously this approach to ministry raises some questions about the practical issues of ministry: the congregation, the priest, and the world. My contention is that a congregation must reflect a productive tension between the characteristics of a structured life together and the possibilities of pilgrimage into the antistructure. This requires a leadership which at its heart is *more* than professional. The priest is a mana-person, a clown, a storyteller, and a wagon master. Yet this is not a ministry in a ghetto. It always leads us back into the world as revolutionaries for the sake of the kingdom.

I have always suspected that good churchmen think that Jesus was crucified by mistake. If the Jews had really understood what a good fellow he was, and if Pilate had seen that his rhetoric about kingship was utterly apolitical, then they would never have nailed him to the cross. It has occurred to me that some may believe that the early persecutions were the result of the lack of insight on the part of the Roman state. There was no threat to them in the church.

My concluding point in this last chapter has been that the Jews, Pilate, and the Roman Empire knew exactly what the threat to them was and acted accordingly. They recognized that when a people listen to God and not to the world, the result is going to be the overthrow of the *status quo*. Structures are going to change, hard-earned privileges are going to be lost, and the poor are going to inherit the earth.

Sometimes those who frown upon any change can be heard accusing others of following after the fads and fashions of the present time. "He who marries the spirit of the times," we are told, "is doomed to become a widower." My argument is that while the mindless pursuit of "relevancy" is indeed an exercise in futility, the alternative is not a tenacious clinging to the glories of the past. There is no meaningful choice between the grief of the widower and the eccentricity of the custodian of the abandoned plantation house. The only thing to do is to take our faith seriously and assume that God is speaking now and that his word can be perceived in the shape of our own history—if we will but move out and see.

I know this is frightening. I am terrified frequently. Yet what is the alternative? The world is in a profound disarray, not because of the chaos that has invaded it from without, but because of the loveless and meaningless hollow men within the structures. There has to be a readiness to turn our backs on all easy solutions, at the same time that we reject injustice; there has to be a willingness to surrender our sin-ridden vision of the world to God's vision. That is what this book has been about: the ministry of a transcendent vision which is given to us and is not of our making.

Castaneda in his last book describes a conversation with Don Juan, in which the latter is telling for the hundredth time what it means to *see*. He says that the man of the antistructures (my term, not his) is both humble and alert. He does not lay upon his experience certain requirements, certain expectations that must be met. He is open. He is willing to lose himself to what it is. Then Don Juan adds, "When you come to see me you should come prepared to die. If you come here ready to die . . . everything should gently fall into place because you are expecting nothing."[21] The Christian can say that this is true, but only to a point. In expecting nothing we are expecting everything.

Victor Turner has rightly said that whereas waiting and silence must be the condition of the contemporary Christian, this is not the answer but the problem.[22] The fourth vector of ministry may begin in silence, it may remain there in the speechless void of the antistructure; but it is, I believe, a pregnant void. We are there that we might *see* those symbols of God's presence and love which, carried back by and in us to the structures, may give a powerful hope to a world in profound disarray.

I can almost hear the reader ask, "Tell us what the symbols are." Of course, the whole point of this book has been to say that they are whatever draws us outside, not only of our genotype, as Luckmann would have it, but of our phenotype to our "pneumatype"—to our true self in God. For the member of the Christian city that is certainly Christ, undoubtedly the Christian person he meets in the way, assuredly Baptism and the Eucharist, the many other sacraments that fill his life, and much more.

The imaginative person, together with his symbols gathered in ritual and story, is the *open* human being. The symbols are not ends in themselves, which may or may not have a transcendent referent—a nothingness which possibly does or does not speak to us. Some students of intuition and symbolic realism see no reason to affirm a faith in God. The symbols are enough. This is not the purpose of this book. If we must sometimes wait in silence, it is not as a counsel of despair, but the necessary condition for moving into the antistructure, the place of imaging, where from across the abyss of our death God speaks to us in love.

NOTES

NOTES TO INTRODUCTION

1. H. Richard Niebuhr, *The Purpose of the Church and Its Ministry, Reflections on the Aims of Theological Education* (New York: Harper & Brothers, 1956), pp. 76–91.
2. Carlos Castaneda, *Tales of Power* (New York: Simon and Schuster, 1974), p. 51.

NOTES TO CHAPTER 1

1. Thomas Luckmann, *The Invisible Religion: The Problem of Religion in Modern Society* (New York: The Macmillan Co., 1967), p. 53.
2. C. B. Moss, *The Christian Faith* (London: SPCK, 1943), p. 135.
3. Robert J. Lifton, M.D., "The Sense of Immortality: On Death and the Continuity of Life," *American Journal of Psychoanalysis,* XXXIII (1973), 3–15.
4. Charles Williams, *The Image of the City and Other Essays,* ed. Anne Ridler (New York: Oxford University Press, 1958), pp. 102–110.
5. *Ibid.,* p. 110.
6. Jacques Ellul, *The Meaning of the City,* trans. Dennis Pardee (Grand Rapids: William B. Eerdmans, 1970).
7. Phillip Bosserman, *Dialectical Sociology: An Analysis of the Sociology of Georges Gurvitch* (Boston: Porter Sargent, 1968).
8. Lawrence S. Cunningham, "Eric Gill and Ditchling," *St. Luke's Journal of Theology,* XVII, 3 (June, 1974), 71–78.
9. Charles A. Reich, *The Greening of America* (New York: Random House, 1970), pp. 305, 306, 342, 350.
10. James E. Sellers, *Warming Fires: The Quest for Community in America* (New York: The Seabury Press, 1975), pp. 158–161.
11. Edward Farley, *Ecclesial Man: A Social Phenomenology of Faith and Reality* (Philadelphia: Fortress Press, 1975), pp. 106–108.

NOTES

12. Dietrich Ritschl, *Memory and Hope: An Inquiry Concerning the Presence of Christ* (New York: The Macmillan Co., 1967), pp. 124–130.
13. Urban T. Holmes, III, *To Speak of God* (New York: The Seabury Press, 1974), pp. 81–93.
14. Ernst Troeltsch, *The Social Teaching of the Christian Church*, trans. Olive Wyon, Harper Torchbooks (New York: Harper & Row, 1960), pp. 1000–1013.
15. T. W. Adorno, *et al., The Authoritarian Personality* (New York: Harper & Row, 1950), provides an exhaustive study of this leadership style.
16. "I tell Thee that man is tormented by no greater anxiety than to find some one quickly to whom he can hand over the gift of freedom with which the ill-fated creature is born." Fyodor Dostoevski, *The Brothers Karamazov*, trans. Constance Garrett (New York: The Modern Library, n.d.), pp. 263–264.
17. Kurt W. Back, *Beyond Words: The Story of Sensitivity Training and the Encounter Movement* (New York: Russell Sage Foundation, 1972), pp. 3–12.
18. Morton Kelsey, *Encounter With God: A Theology of Christian Experience* (Minneapolis: The Bethany Fellowship, 1972); cf. my review of this book, Urban T. Holmes, *"Sic Sed Non,* Fr. Kelsey!" *Anglican Theological Review,* LVI (1974), 482–489.

NOTES TO CHAPTER 2

1. Seward Hiltner, *Preface to Pastoral Theology* (Nashville: Abingdon Press, 1958), p. 59.
2. *Ibid.,* pp. 28, 220.
3. "The Christian Community in the Academic World," *Student World,* LVII (1964), 362.
4. Paul A. Mickey, "Is There a 'Theology' in Seward Hiltner's Pastoral Theology," *Pastoral Theology,* XXI, 207 (October, 1970), 27–32, suggests that Hiltner is a cryto-process theologian. This comes across as an effort, which other students of Hiltner are making as well, to get theology back into ministry. Donald A. Groskreutz, "Modern Pastoral Theology and the Christian Tradition," *The New Shape of Pastoral Theology: Essays in Honor of Seward Hiltner,* ed. William B. Oglesby, Jr. (Nashville: Abingdon Press, 1969), pp. 61–73, makes the same effort by relating personalism to theology. Perhaps the most satisfying (to me) effort to do this is done by a colleague of Hiltner's, James N. Lapsley, *Salvation and Health: The Interlocking Processes of Life* (Philadelphia: Westminster Press, 1972). Lapsley works out of a process theology.
5. Thomas Jackson, *Go Back, You Didn't Say May I* (New York: The Seabury Press, 1974).
6. Don Browning, "New Trends in Pastoral Care: The Search for Method in Religious Living," *The Christian Century,* XC (September 5, 1973), 851.
7. Richard Rolle, *The Fire of Love,* trans. Clifton Wolters (Baltimore: Penguin Books, 1972), p. 61.
8. Max Weber, *The Theory of Social and Economic Organization,* trans. A. M. Henderson and Talcott Parsons (Glencoe, Ill.: The Free Press, 1947), p. 88.

NOTES

9. Leslie H. Farber, *The Ways of the Will: Essays Toward a Psychology and Psychopathology of Will,* Harper Colophon Books (New York: Harper & Row, 1966), pp. 7–25.

10. Alfred Schutz, *The Phenomenology of the Social World,* trans. George Walsh and Frederick Lehnert (Evanston: Northwestern University Press, 1967), p. 63.

11. Thomas S. Kuhn, *The Structure of Scientific Revolutions* (Chicago: University of Chicago Press, 1962), pp. 52–65.

12. Daniel C. Maguire, *Death by Choice* (Garden City: Doubleday and Company, Inc., 1974), p. 77.

13. Holmes, *To Speak of God,* pp. 17–53.

14. Victor W. Turner, "Forms of Symbolic Action: Introduction," *Forms of Symbolic Action,* ed. Robert F. Spencer (Seattle: University of Washington Press, 1969), pp. 9–10. One issue is certainly the relation of symbols to language. It appears that some anthropologists think of symbols as "objects" apart from words. I would prefer to think of words as possibly both symbolic and signative in function, along with other images.

15. Erving Goffman, *Relations in Public: Microstructures of the Public Order,* Harper Colophon Books (New York: Harper & Row, 1972), pp. 188–237. A tie-sign is evidence of the nature of a relationship between people (e.g., the pictures a man carries in his wallet). Such signs carry no message.

16. Raymond Firth, *Symbols: Public and Private* (Ithaca: Cornell University Press, 1973), pp. 74–75.

17. *Ibid.,* p. 75.

18. Philip Wheelwright, *Metaphor and Reality* (Bloomington: Indiana University Press, 1962), pp. 98–128.

19. Holmes, *To Speak of God,* pp. 17–29.

20. Peter L. Berger, *The Sacred Canopy: Elements of a Sociological Theory of Religion* (Garden City: Doubleday and Company, 1967), p. 17.

21. Donald A. Clelland *et al.,* "In the Company of the Convicted: Characteristics of a Billy Graham Crusade Audience," *Sociological Analysis,* XXXV (1974), 54.

22. A. N. Whitehead, *The Aims of Education and Other Essays* (New York: The Macmillan Company, 1929), p. 147.

23. "The principal positive (analogical) attribute of God is mentality." Max Scheler, *On the Eternal in Man,* trans. Bernard Nobel (New York: Harper & Brothers, 1960), p. 182. Alfred Schutz, *Collected Papers: The Problem of Social Reality,* Vol. I (The Hague: Martinus Nyhoff, 1967), pp. 207–259.

24. Luckmann, *The Invisible Religion,* pp. 86–106.

25. Schutz, *The Phenomenology of the Social World,* p. 45.

26. " 'Disenchantment' *(Entzenberung)* is a key concept for Weber." George Lichtheim, "Alienation," *International Encyclopedia of the Social Sciences,* ed. David L. Sills (New York: The Macmillan Company & The Free Press, 1968), Vol. I, p. 167.

27. Karl Rahner, *Spirit in the World,* trans. William Dych (2nd. ed.; London: Sheed & Ward, 1968); *Hearers of the Word,* trans. Michael Richards (New York: Herder and Herder, 1969).

28. Rahner, *Spirit in the World,* pp. 142–145, speaks of the "preapprehension" by the knowing agent of the form, which is possible as a capacity within the form itself. He

calls this the *Vorgriff* or "pre-concept." This notion is one way of grasping the idea that beyond the horizon of our knowing we posit, by virtue of the act of knowing, that which is knowable but not yet known, which is an infinite progression.

29. Dietrich Bonhoeffer, *Ethics,* ed. Eberhard Bethge, trans. Neville H. Smith (New York: The Macmillan Company, 1955), pp. 84–91.

NOTES TO CHAPTER 3

1. "If religion is only a garment of Christianity . . . then what is a religionless Christianity?" Dietrich Bonhoeffer, *Letters and Papers from Prison,* trans. Eberhard Bethge (enlarged ed.; New York: The Macmillan Company, 1971), p. 280.

2. Paul Tillich, in a personal communication to me, spoke of the Incarnation as distinctively "an Anglican heresy."

3. *Confessions,* I, 1 (1).

4. Clifford Geertz, "Religion as a Cultural System," *Anthropological Approaches to the Study of Religion,* ed. Michael Banton (London: Travistock Publications, 1966), pp. 12–24.

5. *De Trinitate* IX, 1 (1).

6. Blaise Paschal, *Pensees,* trans. H. F. Stewart (New York: Random House, 1941), 51.

7. William James, *Varieties of Religious Experience: A Study of Human Nature,* A Mentor Book (New York: The New American Library, 1958), pp. 292–294.

8. Abraham H. Maslow, *Toward a Psychology of Being* (2nd ed.; Princeton: D. Van Nostrand Company, 1968), pp. 71–96.

9. *Ibid.,* p. 96; Paul Ricoeur, *The Symbolism of Evil,* trans. Emerson Buchmann (New York: Harper & Row, 1967), p. 352. "Second naïvete" is a critical, self-conscious pursuit of an immediacy with the objects of our experience, particularly the symbolic objects.

10. Marghanita Laski, *Ecstasy: A Study of Some Secular and Religious Experiences* (London: The Cresset Press, 1961), p. 43.

11. *Ibid.,* pp. 369–370.

12. *Ibid.,* pp. 373–374; Abraham H. Maslow, *Religion, Values, and Peak Experiences* (New York: Viking Press, 1964), p. 20, the author cites Laski.

13. Linda Anne Brookover Bourque, "Social Correlates of Transcendental Experiences," (unpublished Ph.D. dissertation, Duke University, 1967), pp. 58, 71–72.

14. Laski, *Ecstasy,* p. 373.

15. Friedrich Schleiermacher, *On Religion: Speeches to Its Cultured Despisers,* trans. John Oman, Harper Torchbooks (New York: Harper & Row, 1958), p. 39.

16. Friedrich Schleiermacher, *The Christian Faith,* trans. from the second German edition, Harper Torchbooks (New York: Harper & Row, 1963), Vol. I, pp. 13–14. Note that *schlechthinnige* is incorrectly translated "absolute."

17. Ricoeur, *The Symbolism of Evil,* p. 351.

18. Rudolf Otto, *The Idea of the Holy,* trans. John W. Dewey (New York: Oxford University Press, 1958), pp. 5–40.

NOTES

19. Pascal, *Pensees,* 626.

20. Bernard J. F. Lonergan, S.J., *Method in Theology* (New York: Herder and Herder, 1972), p. 115.

21. *The Cloud of Unknowing,* trans. Clifton Wolters (Baltimore: Penguin Books, 1961), p. 55.

22. Robert E. Neale, "Surprise: The Horrible, the Humorous, and the Holy," *New Dimensions in Religious Experience,* ed. George Devine (Staten Island: Alba House, 1971), p. 31.

23. *Ibid.,* p. 35.

24. Søren Kierkegaard, *Journals,* trans. Alexander Dru, Harper Torchbooks (New York: Harper & Row, 1959), n. 1213.

25. Bela Kriger, "The Experience of Self as the Beginning of Systematic Theology," *New Dimensions in Religious Experience,* ed. George Devine (Staten Island: Alba House, 1971), pp. 53–66, argues for the reevaluation of Schleiermacher from the viewpoint of a Roman Catholic theologian.

26. Cited by James D. Boulger, *Coleridge on Religious Thinkers* (New Haven: Yale University Press, 1961), p. 68.

27. Samuel Taylor Coleridge, *The Complete Works,* ed. Shedd (New York: Harper & Brothers, 1853), Vol. I, p. 122.

28. William Porcher DuBose, *The Reason of Life* (New York: Longmans, Green, and Co., 1911), p. 31.

29. Ricoeur, *The Symbolism of Evil,* p. 348.

30. Avery Dulles, S.J., *Revelation Theology: A History* (New York: Herder and Herder, 1969), pp. 177–178.

31. F. Gerald Downing, *Has Christianity a Revelation?* (London: SCM, 1964), pp. 249–255, makes this point in arguing against Christianity possessing a body of revealed truth.

32. Austin Farrar, *The Glass of Vision,* The Bampton Lectures for 1948 (Westminster: Dacre Press, 1948), p. 8.

33. Gabriel Moran, *The Present Revelation: The Search for Religious Foundations* (New York: Herder and Herder, 1972), pp. 34–40.

34. Ray L. Hart, *Unfinished Man and the Imagination: Toward an Ontology and a Rhetoric of Revelation* (New York: Herder and Herder, 1968), p. 122.

35. Karl Jaspers, *Philosophical Faith and Revelation,* trans. E. B. Ashton, (New York: Harper & Row, 1967), pp. 100–101, 108.

36. *Ibid.,* p. 101.

37. Carlos Castaneda, *Journey to Ixtlan* (New York: Simon & Shuster, 1972), pp. 293–298; Dag Hammarskjöld, *Markings,* trans. Leif Soberg and W. H. Auden (New York: Alfred A. Knopf, 1964), pp. 124, 165, 174.

38. Selby Beggiani, "Revelation and Religious Experience," *New Dimensions in Religious Experience,* ed. George Devine (Staten Island: Alba House, 1971), p. 47.

39. As quoted to me in a personal conversation with Louis Weil, who studied with Chenu.

40. *Kierkegaard: The Difficulty of Being a Christian,* ed. Jacques Collete, O.P. (Notre Dame: University of Notre Dame Press, 1969), p. 196.

NOTES

41. Thomas Merton, *The Asian Journal of Thomas Merton,* ed. Naomi Burton *et al.* (New York: New Dimension Books, 1973), p. 333.

42. *Ibid.,* p. 117.

43. Hammarskjöld, *Markings,* p. 122.

44. Martin Luther King, Jr., "I Have a Dream," a pamphlet published by the Southern Christian Leadership Conference.

NOTES TO CHAPTER 4

1. Unknown.

2. Castaneda, *Journey to Ixtlan,* p. 88.

3. Jerome S. Bruner, *On Knowing: Essays for the Left Hand* (New York; Atheneum, 1971).

4. *Ibid.,* p. 4.

5. Robert E. Ornstein, *The Psychology of Consciousness* (New York: The Viking Press, 1972), pp. 57–64.

6. *Ibid.,* p. 67. Tacit knowing is the integration of many parts of our sensation into a coherent whole, which involves the focus on the point of coherence with only a subsidiary awareness of the parts. In drawing together the parts into a higher synthesis, there are a series of cognitive steps of which we are not generally aware. Michael Polanyi, *Knowing and Being,* ed. Marjorie Grene (Chicago: University of Chicago Press, 1969), pp. 138ff.

7. Bruner, *On Knowing,* p. 63.

8. Urban T. Holmes, III, "The Feminine Priestly Symbol and the Meaning of God," *St. Luke's Journal of Theology,* XVII, 4 (September, 1974), pp. 3–22.

9. Urban T. Holmes, III, "Social Life in the Flavian Dynasty as Portrayed by the Moralists of That Period" (an unpublished M.A. thesis, University of North Carolina in Chapel Hill, 1954), p. 88.

10. More documentation is available in G. William Darnoff, "But Why Did They Sit on the King's Right in the First Place?" *The Nature of Human Consciousness: A Book of Readings,* ed. by Robert E. Ornstein (New York: The Viking Press, 1973), pp. 143–147.

11. Robert N. Bellah, "Christianity and Symbolic Realism," *Journal for the Scientific Study of Religion,* IX (1970), p. 94.

12. Mary Douglas, *Purity and Danger: An Analysis of Concepts of Pollution and Taboo* (Baltimore: Penguin Press. 1971), *passim.*

13. Carlos Castaneda, *A Separate Reality: Further Conversations with Don Juan* (New York: Simon & Schuster, 1971), p. 186.

14. E. L. Mascall, *The Openness of Being: Natural Theology Today,* The Gifford Lectures, 1970–71 (Philadelphia: Westminster Press, 1971), p. 115.

15. James F. Cotter, *Inscape: The Christology and Poetry of Gerard Manley Hopkins* (Pittsburgh: University of Pittsburgh Press, 1972), p. 20.

16. Gerard Manley Hopkins, *The Journals and Papers,* ed. Humphrey House (London: Oxford University Press, 1959), p. 207.

17. *Ibid.*, p. 230.

18. Theodore Thass-Thienemann, *Symbolic Behavior* (New York: Washington Square Press, 1968).

19. Owen Barfield, *Saving the Appearances: A Study in Idolatry* (New York: Harcourt, Brace and World, n.d.), p. 42.

20. Rubem Alves, *Tomorrow's Child: Imagination, Creativity, and the Rebirth of Culture* (New York: Harper & Row, 1972), p. 55.

21. Barfield, *Saving the Appearances,* p. 137.

22. *Ibid.*, p. 147.

23. Hart, *Unfinished Man and the Imagination,* pp. 90, 114, 184, 200. A. N. Whitehead, *The Aims of Education and Other Essays* (New York: Macmillan Co., 1929), p. 139, says that imagination is the image of the lighted torch of learning, illuminating our experience.

24. Hart, *Unfinished Man and the Imagination,* p. 216.

25. Amos Wilder, *The Language of the Gospel: Early Christian Rhetoric* (New York: Harper & Row, 1964), p. 80.

26. Carlos Castaneda, "A Tale of Power," *Harper's Magazine,* CCXIL, 1492 (September, 1974), 44.

27. Castaneda, *Journey to Ixtlan,* p. 133.

28. Castaneda, *A Separate Reality,* p. 271.

29. Thomas S. Szasz, "The Myth of Mental Illness," *Morality and Mental Health,* ed. O. Hobart Mower (Chicago: Rand McNally, 1967), pp. 69–76.

30. Joseph Campbell, *Myths to Live By* (New York: The Viking Press, 1972), pp. 201–232.

31. William T. Lynch, S.J., *Images of Hope: Imagination as the Healer of the Hopeless* (Baltimore: Helicon, 1965), *passim.*

32. *Ibid.*, pp. 195ff.

33. Whitehead, *The Aims of Education,* p. 139.

34. *Ibid.*, p. 140.

35. Owen Barfield, "Matter, Imagination, and Spirit," *Journal of the American Academy of Religion,* XLII (1974), 625.

36. Polanyi, *Knowing and Being,* pp. 141–144.

37. Mary McDermott Shideler, *The Theology of Romantic Love: A Study in the Writings of Charles Williams* (Grand Rapids: Eerdmans, 1962), pp. 20ff.

38. Whitehead, *The Aims of Education,* p. 141.

39. Castaneda, *Journey to Ixtlan,* p. 301.

40. Northrop Frye, *The Educated Imagination* (Bloomington: University of Indiana Press, 1964), p. 29.

41. *Ibid.*, p. 140.

42. Sam Keen, *Apology for Wonder* (New York: Harper & Row, 1969), pp. 51–56.

43. I am indebted to John A. Lee of East Montana State College, Billings, Montana, for this scheme.

44. Castaneda, *Journey to Ixtlan,* p. 234.

45. Farley, *Ecclesial Man,* pp. 64–65.

NOTES

NOTES TO CHAPTER 5

1. George Herbert Mead, *Mind, Self, and Society: From the Standpoint of a Social Behaviorist,* ed. Charles W. Morris (Chicago: University of Chicago Press, 1934), p. 164.

2. *Ibid.,* p. 196.

3. Robert K. Merton, *Social Theory and Social Structure* (rev. ed.; New York: The Free Press, 1968), p. 41.

4. *Ibid.,* p. 41.

5. Tilden H. Edwards *et al., Spiritual Growth: An Empirical Exploration of Its Meaning, Sources, and Interpretations* (Washington: Metropolitan Ecumenical Training Center, 1974), pp. 25–28.

6. Castaneda, *A Separate Reality,* p. 313. Don Juan is speaking here of "reason" as a socially conditioned perception.

7. Turner first begins to develop the term "anti-structure" in Victor W. Turner, *The Forest of Symbols: Aspects of Ndembu Ritual* (Ithaca: Cornell University Press, 1967), pp. 93–101. The term does not appear as such. "I have spoken," says Turner in this book, "of the interstructural character of the liminal" (p. 99). The category does appear in a developed form in Victor W. Turner, *The Ritual Process: Structure and Anti-Structure* (Chicago: Aldine Publishing Co., 1969). The anti-structure is the locus of the communitas (the equivalent of Gurvitch's communion) (p. 96). The concept is then developed further in Victor Turner, *Dramas, Fields, and Metaphors: Symbolic Action in Human Society* (Ithaca: Cornell University Press, 1974). The term is not an altogether happy one, as Turner has admitted to me in private. It connotes an opposition of some kind to structure, which is not what he intended—and not what I intend.

8. Turner, *The Ritual Process,* pp. 96–97. The term is originally Paul Goodman's.

9. Holmes, *The Future Shape of Ministry,* pp. 219–221; see also Urban T. Holmes, "Liminality and Liturgy," *Worship,* XLVI (1973), 386–392.

10. Turner, *Dramas, Fields, and Metaphors,* p. 237.

11. Henri J. M. Nouwen, *Reaching Out: The Three Movements of the Spiritual Life* (Garden City: Doubleday & Co., 1975), pp. 14–33.

12. *Ibid.,* pp. 46–47, 52–53.

13. Ricoeur, *The Symbolism of Evil,* pp. 172–174.

14. I am endebted for the discussion here to David R. Breed, *A Theology of Chaos* (an unpublished D.Min. thesis, Lutheran School of Theology at Chicago, 1972).

15. *The Cloud of Unknowing,* p. 55.

16. *Ibid.,* p. 134.

17. Karl Rahner, *Theological Investigations,* Vol. V: *Later Writings,* trans. Karl-H. Kruger (Baltimore: Helicon Press, 1965), pp. 6–7 (emphasis added).

18. John S. Dunne, *A Search for God in Time and Memory* (New York: Macmillan Co., 1969), pp. 173–174.

19. Turner, *Dramas, Fields, and Metaphors,* p. 46.

20. Castaneda, *Tales of Power,* p. 286.

NOTES

21. Turner, *Dramas, Fields, and Metaphors,* pp. 169–170.
22. Barbara G. Myerhoff, *Peyote Hunt: The Sacred Journey of the Huichol Indians* (Ithaca: Cornell University Press, 1974), p. 241.
23. Turner, *Dramas, Fields, and Metaphors,* pp. 189–190.
24. I have a friend who had a similar experience at Delphi. In fact, he became so excited —one might say "intoxicated"—that while spending the night in the hotel at the village of Delphi (a remarkable structure, which one enters at the top floor and "goes down" to one's room) his wife found it necessary to tie the balcony doors shut that he might not try to fly with the shining eagles of Mt. Parnassus.
25. Bruce Reed, "The Task of the Church and the Role of Its Members," An Alban Project Reprint (London: The Grubb Institute, 1975), pp. 3–5.
26. *Ibid.,* pp. 14–15.
27. Rollo May, *Love and Will* (New York: W. W. Norton & Co., 1969), pp. 122–129.
28. *The Cloud of Unknowing,* p. 84.
29. John S. Spong, *Honest Prayer* (New York: The Seabury Press, 1973), pp. 99–100.
30. John Richards, *But Deliver Us From Evil: An Introduction to the Demonic Dimension in Pastoral Care* (New York: The Seabury Press, 1974), p. 32.
31. *Ibid.,* p. 134; see references to Rollo May pp. 65, 110.
32. May, *Love and Will,* p. 138.
33. Urban T. Holmes, III, "Revivals are UnAmerican: A Recalling of America to Pilgrimage," *Anglican Theological Review,* Supplementary Series No. 1 (1973), 65–70.
34. J. R. R. Tolkien, *Smith of Wootton Major* (New York: Ballantine Books, 1969).
35. Castaneda, *Tales of Power,* p. 95.
36. Castaneda, *Journey to Ixtlan,* p. 136.
37. Richards, *But Deliver Us From Evil,* pp. 59–66.
38. Turner, *Dramas, Fields, and Metaphors,* p. 188.

NOTE TO CHAPTER 6

1. Ornstein, *The Psychology of Consciousness,* p. 1.
2. Arthur J. Deikman, "Deautomization and the Mystic Experience," *Altered States of Consciousness: A Book of Readings,* ed. Charles T. Tart (New York: John Wiley & Sons, 1969), p. 24.
3. William Johnston, *Silent Music: The Science of Meditation* (New York: Harper & Row, 1974), pp. 22–44.
4. Castaneda, *Tales of Power,* p. 238.
5. Charles Williams, *All Hallow's Eve* (Grand Rapids: Eerdmans, 1970), p. 13.
6. Charles Williams, *Taliessin through Logres* (London: Oxford University Press, 1938), p. 67.
7. Castaneda, *Tales of Power,* p. 285.
8. John B. Cobb, "The Population Explosion and the Rights of the Subhuman World," *IDOC: North America,* 9 (September 12, 1970), 40–62.
9. Quoted with permission of the author, Robert M. Cooper.

NOTES

10. Annie Dillard, *Pilgrim at Tinker Creek: A Mystical Excursion into the Natural World* (New York: Bantam Books, Inc., 1975), pp. 104–105.

11. Cobb, *IDOC: North America,* 9, 61–62.

12. Pierre Teilhard de Chardin, *Le Milieu Divin: An Essay on the Interior Life* (London: Collins, 1960), p. 95.

13. Williams, *The Image of the City,* p. 68.

14. Virginia I. Armstrong, ed., *I Have Spoken: American History Through the Voices of Indians* (New York: Pocket Books, 1972), p. 84.

15. Johnston, *The Silent Music,* pp. 157–159.

16. Cited by Ronald Gregor Smith in *Martin Buber* (Richmond: John Knox Press, 1967), p. 33.

17. *The Cloud of Unknowning,* p. 71.

18. Castaneda, *Tales of Power,* p. 126.

19. *The Portable Jung,* ed. Joseph Campbell, trans. R. F. C. Hull (New York: Viking Press, 1971), p. 587.

20. Herbert Richardson and Donald Cutler, eds., *Transcendence* (Boston: Beacon Press, 1969), p. 90.

21. G. Legman, *Rationale of the Dirty Joke: An Analysis of Sexual Humor* (New York: Grove Press, 1968), pp. 12–17.

22. Barbara C. Bowen, *The Age of Bluff: Paradox and Ambiguity in Rabelais and Montaigne* (Urbana: University of Illinois Press, 1972), *passim.*

23. Francois Rabelais, *Gargantua and Pantagruel,* trans. Thomas Urquhart and Peter Motteux (Chicago: Encyclopedia Britannica, 1955), I, 13.

24. R. D. Laing, *The Politics of Experience* (New York: Ballantine Books, 1968), p. 137.

25. Campbell, *Myths to Live By,* pp. 206, 209.

26. Paul F. Stern, *In Praise of Madness* (New York: W. W. Norton Co., 1972), p. 37.

27. Sidney Cohen, *The Beyond Within: The LSD Story* (rev. ed.; New York: Atheneum, 1972), pp. 34–43.

28. *Ibid.,* p. 102.

29. Ronald E. Shor, "Hypnosis and the Concept of Reality-Orientation," *Altered States of Consciousness: A Book of Readings,* ed. Charles T. Tart (New York: John Wiley and Sons, 1969), pp. 248–249.

30. Gary E. Schwartz, "The Facts on Transcendental Meditation: Part II," *Psychology Today,* VII, 11 (April, 1974), 43.

31. Johnston, *Silent Music,* p. 93.

32. *Ibid.,* pp. 132, 174.

33. Bourque, "Social Correlates of Transcendental Experiences," p. 15.

34. Iris Murdoch, *The Sovereignty of the Good* (New York: Schocken Books, 1971), p. 41.

NOTES

NOTES TO CHAPTER 7

1. Robert Roth, "Reality and Metaphor," *St. Luke's Journal of Theology,* XVIII (1975), 233.
2. Farley, *Ecclesial Man,* p. 117.
3. Sallie M. TeSelle, "Parable, Metaphor, and Theology," *Journal of the American Academy of Religion,* XLII, (1974), 640.
4. Sallie M. TeSelle, *Speaking In Parables: A Study in Metaphor and Theology* (Philadelphia: Fortress Press, 1975), p. 22.
5. The term "bathrobe Christianity," which I owe to a friend, the Rt. Rev. Willis R. Henton, is half of a metaphor which aptly describes for me that approach to Christianity based on the impossible effort to get back to the first century and be like the historical Jesus. The image comes from those ubiquitous Christmas pageants, where we commemorate the Incarnation by dressing up little boys in their fathers' bathrobes to play shepherds at the manger scene.
6. Farley, *Ecclesial Man,* p. 117.
7. TeSelle, *Journal of the American Academy of Religion,* XLII, 635.
8. James William McClendon, Jr., *Biography as Theology: How Life Stories Can Remake Today's Theology* (Nashville: Abingdon Press, 1974), pp. 30–31.
9. *Ibid.,* p. 40.
10. *Ibid.,* pp. 61–62, 79–80, 138, 167–169.
11. Ulrich Simon, *Story and Faith in the Biblical Narrative* (London: SPCK, 1975), p. 35.
12. Rosemary Haughton, *Tales From Eternity* (New York: The Seabury Press, 1973); and Marie Louise von Franz, *Interpretation of Fairy Tales* (New York: Spring Publications, 1970).
13. von Franz, *Interpretation of Fairy Tales,* p. I, 11.
14. Haughton, *Tales From Eternity,* pp. 366ff, 65ff, 80ff, 89ff, 105ff, and 129.
15. Farley, *Ecclesial Man,* pp. 120–124.
16. Holmes, *To Speak of God,* pp. 54–64.
17. Campbell, *Myths to Live By,* p. 215.
18. Robert N. Bellah, *The Broken Covenant: American Civil Religion in Times of Trial* (New York: The Seabury Press, 1975), pp. 1–60.
19. *E.g.,* David Tracy of the Divinity School at the University of Chicago speaking at Vanderbilt University, September 26, 1975.
20. TeSelle, *Speaking in Parables,* p. 97.
21. James H. Cone, "The Story Content of Black Theology," *Theology Today,* XXXII (1975), 145.
22. *Ibid.,* XXXII, 150.
23. Robert P. Roth, *Story and Reality: An Essay on Truth* (Grand Rapids: Eerdmans, 1973), p. 23.
24. John S. Dunne, *Time and Myth* (Garden City: Doubleday & Company, 1973), p. 22.
25. This article by Mary H. Bernard is scheduled to appear early in 1976 in *The Religion Teacher's Journal.*

26. Dunne, *Time and Myth,* p. 24.

27. *Ibid.,* p. 37.

28. *Ibid.,* p. 81.

29. Cited by Turner in *Dramas, Fields, and Metaphors,* p. 26.

30. *Ibid.,* p. 33.

31. *Ibid.,* p. 37.

32. *Ibid.,* pp. 60–97.

33. *Ibid.,* p. 50.

34. TeSelle, *Speaking in Parables,* p. 104.

35. *Ibid.,* p. 69.

36. Bellah, *The Broken Covenant,* p. 144.

37. Simon, *Story and Faith,* pp. 3–4.

38. Ricoeur, *The Symbolism of Evil,* pp. 10–13, describes symbols as cosmic, oneiric, and poetic. I have applied these categories to the narrative symbol.

39. Simon, *Story and Faith,* pp. 83–84.

40. *Ibid.,* p. 121.

41. Frye, *The Educated Imagination,* p. 43.

42. von Franz, *Interpretation of Fairy Tales,* pp. III, 1–7.

43. Robert McAfee Brown, "My Story and 'The Story' ", *Theology Today,* XXXII (1975), 167–171.

44. Hyemeyohsts Storm, *Seven Arrows* (New York: Harper & Row, 1972), p. 10.

NOTES TO CHAPTER 8

1. T. S. Eliot, *Selected Essays: 1917–1932* (New York: Harcourt, Brace, and Co., 1932), pp. 247–248.

2. Bellah, *The Broken Covenant,* pp. 74–75.

3. Dean M. Kelley, *Why Conservative Churches are Growing: A Study in Sociology of Religion* (New York: Harper & Row, 1972), p. 83.

4. Farley, *Ecclesial Man,* pp. 152–153.

5. Margaret Mead in a personal communication to the author.

6. Victor Turner, "Passages, Margins, and Poverty: Religious Symbols of Communitas—I," *Worship,* XLVI (1972), 390–392.

7. *E.g.* John G. Neihardt (ed.), *Black Elk Speaks: Being the Life Story of a Holy Man of the Ogala Sioux* (Lincoln: University of Nebraska Press, 1961), p. 279.

8. James M. Gustafson, *The Church as Moral Decision-Maker* (Philadelphia: Pilgrim Press, 1970), pp. 83–95.

9. Mircea Eliade, *Cosmos and History: The Myth of Eternal Return,* trans. Williard R. Trask, Harper Torchbooks (New York: Harper & Row, 1959), pp. 105–112.

10. Back, *Beyond Words,* pp. 3–4.

11. Myerhoff, *The Peyote Hunt,* p. 263.

12. Keen, *Apology for Wonder,* pp. 195–196. Keen calls the movement back and forth between the Apollonian and the Dionysian "the principle of oscillation." It is one more

NOTES

paradigm for the pilgrimage between the structure and the antistructure.

13. Charles Williams, *Descent into Hell* (London: Faber & Faber, 1937), pp. 94–107.
14. Charles Williams, *He Came Down from Heaven* (London: Faber & Faber, 1950), p. 85.
15. Moran, *The Present Revelation,* pp. 168–170.
16. Gibson Winter, *The Suburban Captivity of the Churches* (New York: The Macmillan Company, 1962), *passim.*
17. James E. Dittes, *The Church in the Way* (New York: Charles Scribner's Sons, 1967), *passim.*

NOTES TO CHAPTER 9

1. C. G. Jung, *Archetypes and the Collective Unconscious,* trans. by R. F. C. Hull, Bollingen Series XX (Princeton: Princeton University Press, 1968), pp. 81, 162.
2. Holmes, *The Future Shape of Ministry,* pp. 8–57.
3. C. G. Jung, *Two Essays on Analytical Psychology,* trans. R. F. C. Hull, Bollingen Series XX (New York: Pantheon Books, 1953), pp. 226–227.
4. Holmes, *The Future Shape of Ministry,* pp. 246–248.
5. Castaneda, *Tales of Power,* pp. 286–287.
6. Jung, *Archetypes and the Collective Unconscious,* p. 217.
7. Enid Wellsford, *The Fool: His Social and Literary History* (Gloucester, Mass.: Peter Smith, 1966), p. xii.
8. Storm, *Seven Arrows,* p. 7.
9. *Ibid.,* p. 7.
10. *Ibid.,* p. 16.
11. Castaneda, *Journey to Ixtlan,* pp. 294–298.
12. *Ibid.,* p. 289.
13. Richard Pearce, *Stages of the Clown: Perspectives on Modern Fiction from Dostoyevsky to Beckett* (Carbondale, Ill.: Southern Illinois University Press, 1970), p. 1.
14. *Ibid.,* p. 155.
15. *Ibid.,* p. 147.
16. *Ibid.,* p. 155.
17. *Ibid.,* pp. 102–104
18. I am indebted to the Rt. Rev. Girault M. Jones for these last three recollections of "Daddy" Hall.
19. Roth, *St. Luke's Journal of Theology,* XVIII, 243–249.
20. Harvey Cox, *The Feast of Fools* (New York: Harper & Row, 1969), pp. 139–142.
21. *Ibid.,* p. 157.
22. Leszek Kolakowski, *Toward a Marxist Humanism: Essays on the Left Today,* trans. Jane Z. Peel (New York: Grove Press, 1968), pp. 36–37.
23. Jung, *Archetypes and the Collective Unconscious,* pp. 173–177.
24. *Ibid.,* p. 179.
25. Campbell, *Myths to Live By,* p. 102.

NOTES

26. Nancy D. Munn, *Walbiri Iconography: Graphic Representation and Cultural Symbolism in a Central Australian Society* (Ithaca: Cornell University Press, 1973), p. 115.
27. Roth, *St. Luke's Journal of Theology,* XVIII, 234.
28. Henri J. M. Nouwen, *Reaching Out,* p. 97.
29. Cited by Merton, *The Asian Journal,* p. 59.
30. Loren B. Mead, *New Hope for Congregations* (New York: The Seabury Press, 1972), p. 105–106.
31. Urban T. Holmes, III, *Young Children and the Eucharist* (New York: The Seabury Press, 1972), pp. 101–105.

NOTES TO CHAPTER 10

1. *The Cloud of Unknowing,* p. 80.
2. Jürgen Moltmann, *The Crucified God: The Cross of Christ as the Foundation and Criticism of Christian Theology,* trans. R. A. Wilson and John Bowden (New York: Harper & Row, 1974), pp. 45–53.
3. Roth, *St. Luke's Journal of Theology,* XVIII, 239.
4. Ronald A. Knox, *Enthusiasm: A Chapter in the History of Religion* (Oxford: At the Clarendon Press, 1950), p. 583.
5. Cited by George Celestin, "A Christian Looks at Revolution," *New Theology No. 6,* eds. Martin E. Marty and Dean G. Peerman (New York: The Macmillan Company, 1969), p. 98.
6. As quoted by Richard Shaull, "Christian Faith as Scandal in a Technocratic World, *New Theology No. 6,* eds. Martin Marty and Dean G. Peerman (New York: The Macmillan Company, 1969), p. 126.
7. "To be truly free and yet social means to cultivate detachment." Philip Rieff, *The Triumph of the Therapeutic: Uses of Faith After Freud,* Harper Torchbooks (New York: Harper & Row, 1966), p. 60.
8. Knox, *Enthusiasm,* p. 259.
9. H. Richard Niebuhr, *Christ and Culture* (New York: Harper & Brothers, 1951), pp. 69–76.
10. *Ibid.,* p. 105.
11. Richard J. Neuhaus, *Time Toward Home* (New York: The Seabury Press, 1975), *passim.*
12. Leon Joseph Cardinal Suenens, *A New Pentecost?,* trans. Francis Martin (New York: The Seabury Press, 1974), p. 173.
13. Piet J. Schoonenberg, *Man and Sin: A Theological View,* trans. Joseph Donceel (Notre Dame, Ind.: University of Notre Dame Press, 1965), pp. 104–106.
14. Myerhoff, *The Peyote Hunt,* pp. 131–132.
15. Cited by Kenneth Slack, *Martin Luther King* (London: SCM Press, 1970), p. 101.
16. Celestin, "A Christian Looks at Revolution," p. 102.
17. Rollo May, *Power and Innocence: A Search for the Sources of Violence* (New York: W. W. Norton & Company, 1972), p. 141.

NOTES

18. *Ibid.,* pp. 111–112.
19. Karl Rahner, *Theological Investigations,* Vol. IV: *More Recent Writings,* trans
Kevin Smyth (Baltimore: Helicon Press, 1966), p. 399.
20. *Ibid.,* p. 400.
21. Castaneda, *Tales of Power,* p. 155.
22. Victor Turner, *Revelation and Divination in Ndembu Ritual* (Ithaca: Cornell University Press, 1975), p. 33.